**John Freely** was born in 1926 in Brooklyn. In 1944, at the age of 17, he enlisted in the US Navy and served for two years, including combat service in the Pacific and China–Burma–India theatres. In 1960 John and his family moved to Istanbul, where he taught physics and the history of science at Boğaziçi University. Aside from his travels across the world, he has lived there ever since. He is the author of over 60 acclaimed travel and history books, including *Strolling Through Istanbul, The Western Shores of Turkey, Strolling Through Venice, Inside the Seraglio, Children of Achilles, Light from the East, Celestial Revolutionary* and *The Grand Turk*.

'Imagine Zorba the Greek as a wandering Irishman from Brooklyn and you have the beginnings of John Freely. His odyssey has been a wild ride across continents, a microcosm of modern history. Freely is a born storyteller and an expert on everything from mysticism to physics to the back streets of Athens, Istanbul and Venice. The only danger of reading this book is envy for such a dazzling life.'
**Stephen Kinzer**

'Always, as he writes, "sailing against the wind", John Freely provides a wonderful portrait of Istanbul and Athens in their Bohemian heyday, before they turned into harassed business cities.'
**Philip Mansel, author of *Levant: Splendour and Catastrophe on the Mediterranean***

# THE ART OF EXILE

## A Vagabond Life

John Freely

I.B. TAURIS

LONDON · NEW YORK

Published in 2016 by
I.B.Tauris & Co. Ltd
London • New York
www.ibtauris.com

Copyright © 2016 John Freely

The support of Boğaziçi University in the publication of this book is
gratefully acknowledged.

The right of John Freely to be identified as the author of this work has
been asserted by the author in accordance with the Copyright, Designs
and Patents Act 1988.

ISBN: 978 1 78453 498 1
eISBN: 978 0 85772 987 3

A full CIP record for this book is available from the British Library
A full CIP record is available from the Library of Congress

Library of Congress Catalog Card Number: available

Typeset in Goudy Old Style by A. & D. Worthington, Newmarket
Printed and bound in Sweden by ScandBook AB

In Memory of My Beloved Toots
My Penelope
And for our Crew
Maureen, Eileen and Brendan


*Love Also is a Dream*
Eaven Boland

# CONTENTS

# ILLUSTRATIONS

# ACKNOWLEDGEMENTS

I would like to acknowledge the help of my editor Tatiana Wilde, who believed in this book and nursed it through to completion. I would also like to acknowledge the support of family and friends who kept me going through the most difficult time of my life: Gülen Aktaş, Selcuk Altun, Tony Baker, Hulya Baraz, Maureen Freely, Eileen Freely Baker, Brendan Freely, Tony Greenwood, Ömer Koê, Nina Köprülü, Emin Saatçi, Memo and Ann Marie Sağıroğlu, Ayşe Soysal and our nurse Ayşe.

# INTRODUCTION

I live alone in the House of Memory, in one or another of the suites know as Youth, War, Love, Age and Dreams, where I spend most of my time these days, moving along the interface between remembered Past and fleeting Present. The many rooms in my house are inhabited by the people whom I loved and who are no longer with me; the places where I've lived, worked, fought and visited; a voyage through tumultuous and uncharted seas; an odyssey which has taken me beyond the Pillars of Hercules in search of the Golden Apples of the Hesperides together with my Penelope, who now dwells in the Country of Dreams, waiting for me. This is the story of our journey.

# 1

# TWENTY YEARS

# AGROWING

My travels began even before I was born. According to my mother, I was conceived in Boston and arrived in New York by train three months before my birth, concealed in her womb, travelling without a ticket on the first of my life's journeys.

My mother was born in Ireland as Margaret Murphy, but everyone called her Peg. She never used her married name, Mrs John Freely, always identifying herself as Peg Murphy. This was not uncommon among the Irish women of her time, but it was mostly her fierce spirit of independence that made her keep her own name, for she was Peg Murphy and not Missus Somebody Else, she always said. We were led by her to believe that she had been born in 1904, but I eventually discovered that her true date of birth was 1897, though I never learned why she subtracted seven years from her age. Perhaps it was to be eternally young, for she often spoke of going off to Tír na nÓg, 'The Land of the Young', where in Celtic myth no one grows old. Years later I read of this land of eternal youth in the first lines from 'The Wooing of Etain':

> Fair woman, will you come with me
> to a wondrous land where there is music?
> Hair is like the blossoming primrose there;
> smooth bodies are the colour of snow

There, there is neither mine nor yours;
bright are teeth, dark are brows,
A delight to the eye the number of our hosts,
the colour of fox-glove every cheek.


Peg was one of 11 children, all but one of whom left Ireland and emigrated to the US. They were helped by relatives in Lawrence, Massachusetts, from an earlier family migration. Her paternal grandfather had 'died on the roads' when he and his family were evicted from their home during the Great Hunger, after which his widow and surviving children had emigrated to America and found refuge in Lawrence. But her eldest son, Peg's father Tomas Murphy, had not taken to life in America and returned to Ireland, though there was no one of his family left there.

Tomas was born in County Kerry on the Dingle Peninsula, the south-westernmost extension of Ireland. When Tomas returned from America he found work as a porter for the Irish Railways on the narrow-gauge line that operated between Tralee, capital of County Kerry, and Dingle, the main town on the peninsula. At the beginning of his first day at work, an English tourist, getting on at Tralee, pointed out his trunk on the platform and arrogantly ordered Tomas to put it up on the luggage rack. 'Put it up yourself,' said Tomas proudly, walking away to help an old Irishwoman board the train. The conductor, observing this, said, 'Murphy, you will not grow grey in the service of the Irish Railways.'

Tomas kept the job for about a year, but then he was dismissed for giving another English tourist a piece of his mind about Britain's treatment of Ireland. It was just as well that he did, for the following Whitsunday there was a terrible accident on the Tralee–Dingle railway. Locomotive Number One swerved off the tracks on the Curraduff Bridge and fell 30 feet into the river, killing the engineer, the conductor, the porter and 90 pigs, who were the only passengers that day. An old woman in Dingle remarked to Tomas that he had been spared by the hand of God, to which he responded, according to Peg, 'I'm sure the Almighty had more important matters to think about that day than the fate of three Irishmen and 90 pigs.'

Soon afterwards Tomas met and fell in love with a pretty young schoolteacher named Mary Ashe, whose father was the postmaster in Anascaul, the only town of any size between Tralee and Dingle. Tomas and Mary married and settled down in a tiny cottage by the sea four miles east of Inch, the enormous transverse sand cape on the south coast of the Dingle Peninsula. Tomas became a fisherman, making himself a small currach, a wickerwork boat covered with tarred canvas. He also built a little dock to moor his currach, in a cove below his cottage that is still called Murphy's Landing. On the hillside behind the cottage he cleared and walled in a small plot of land and planted it with potatoes, cabbage, wheat, corn and hay, building a small barn that sheltered a cow, a donkey and a score of chickens. He farmed his little plot and at intervals set his nets and lines for codfish and herring in Dingle Bay, searching the rocky strand at low tide for periwinkles and mussels. And with these resources Tomas and Mary raised 11 children, five of them boys and six girls, all of whom survived their childhood, something of a miracle in rural Ireland at the time.

The Murphy children learned reading, writing, arithmetic and not much more at the Kerry District school, a two-room schoolhouse three miles west along the coast from where they lived, making the journey barefoot in all seasons.

The Murphy children all left school in turn after four or five years and went to work, usually on their own or neighbouring farms. Peg found a place at Foley's Public House at Inch, where she looked after the publican's infant son, Jerry, and also helped out in the bar. She gave some of her wages to her parents and saved the rest in the hope that she would eventually have enough to go off to America, the dream of every young person in rural Ireland at the time, for their homeland had nothing to offer them.

Peg was the only one of the children who inherited her mother's love of reading. Mary Ashe had been sent to a convent school by her father, Thomas, who had been appointed postmaster of Anascaul after he returned from the Crimean War, in which he had served in the British Army. He had been badly wounded in the last battle of the war, the attack on the Redan, and had recuperated in Florence Nightingale's hospital on the Asian side of the

Bosphorus across from Constantinople. He was illiterate when he joined the 88th Regiment of Foot at the age of 17 years and nine months, but while he was in the Army he seems to have learned how to read and write and speak English, which qualified him to serve as postmaster in Anascaul when he returned to Ireland. Mary was a teacher for a few years before her marriage to Tomas, who was illiterate. I only discovered this many years later when I first saw Peg's birth certificate, where her father's signature appears as a scrawled X.

All but one of the children went off in turn to America. Peg was the sixth to leave, after her sisters Hannah, Bea, Annie, Mary and Nell, with her brothers Jerry, Tommy, Mauris and Gene following in turn soon afterwards. Her younger brother John was the only one who remained at home with Tomas and Mary, helping them to look after their farm. He too would have gone had he not been suffering from tuberculosis.

Peg had saved enough money from her wages at Foley's to pay for her passage to America in steerage, and she had set aside a bit to buy her first pair of shoes, but the friends who emigrated with her went barefoot. The same thing was happening all over Ireland, as the Irish once again left their native land, just as they had during and after the Great Hunger in the mid-nineteenth century, when tenants were evicted and either 'died on the roads' or emigrated, diminishing the population of Ireland from eight to four million in just a decade.

The story was much the same in the cottage where my father John was born, near the town of Ballyhaunis in County Mayo, in the north-west of Ireland. All the Freelys in the world come from in and around Ballyhaunis, the descendants of an O'Friel who had moved there from County Donegal in the north around 1600, the date of the thatched cottage in which my father was born. O'Friel was illiterate, and the English authorities in registering his name had written it down as Freely. Otherwise, like most Irish of the soil, the Freelys were a family without a history, just a succession of simple farmers, who at least owned their own plot of land, which is why they survived the Great Hunger.

John was uncertain about the date of his birth. He always

said that he had been born the 'year of the great wind', which
he thought was 1898, but eventually we learned that he too was
born in 1897. He was the second of nine children of Michael and
Ellen Freely, who had eight boys and one girl: Jim, John, Willie,
Tom, Pat, Mike, Charlie, Mary and Luke. All nine emigrated from
Ireland in turn, some to England but most to America, though
Jim, the eldest, eventually returned from the US with his wife
Agnes to run the family farm after the death of his parents.

John left home in the spring of 1916, along with his brother
Willie, hoping to find work in England. They had not tuppence
between them when they decided to leave, as John told me many
years later. The only cash in the house was their mother's 'egg
money', a few pennies which she had accumulated by selling eggs
now and then at the weekly market in Ballyhaunis. One morning, well before dawn, John awoke and dressed quietly, waking
Willie, and then went to the cupboard and took his mother's egg
money, vowing to replace it as soon as he found work in England.
Then they left the cottage and headed for Ballyhaunis, five miles
distant, to catch the weekly train that stopped there at six in the
morning. They cut across the fields to intercept the train a mile or
so before it reached the town, and when they saw it approaching
they stepped out on to the track to flag it down. The train duly
stopped for them and the conductor let them come aboard, for
he was from Ballyhaunis and knew the family. He didn't bother
to ask them for their tickets, for he knew they wouldn't have been
able to afford them.

The train had two cars, one for mail and the other for passengers. The seats were all taken, and so John and Willie sat down on
the floor at the back, covering their faces when the train stopped
at Ballyhaunis so that they wouldn't be recognized by anyone who
might get on there. But no one did, and after the mail was put
aboard, the train chugged off, just as the sun rose over the hills
of Roscommon, the next county to the east. Then Willie went
to sleep while John took one last look at Ballyhaunis, which he
would never see again. It was Easter Sunday, and he could hear the
church bell tolling for the first mass of the day. He blessed himself
and then he too fell asleep.

A while later the other passengers in the car began waking up, and some of them in the back seats began talking to John and Willie. It turned out that all of them were Irish sailors who had been aboard a British freighter that had been sunk by a German submarine off the north-west coast of Ireland. They had come ashore in lifeboats and were put on the first train leaving for Dublin. They had been given their full pay, and when they were all awake they began passing around a bottle of Irish whiskey, and it was then that John had his first taste of hard drink, which started him on the 'downward path to ruination', as Peg would later say.

When they arrived in Dublin John asked for directions to a 'Model Rooming-House', which he had been told about in Bally-haunis, and he and Willy spent the night there for a single penny, paying a ha'penny each. They and the other occupants did not sleep on beds nor even on the floor, but hung by their armpits on ropes suspended from the walls in parallel lines. The rooming-house and others like it was known as a 'Ha'penny Hanger', cater-ing to the hordes of young Irishmen who came to Dublin on their way to England in search of work.

When the ropes were let loose the next morning John and Willie went out to buy a loaf of bread for their breakfast. As they headed for the centre of Dublin they heard the sound of gunfire and cannonades, and soon they came within sight of the General Post Office, where the Irish Republican Army was being besieged by British forces. It was the beginning of the Irish Revolution, they learned, and a 'terrible beauty' was being born in Dublin, but John and Willie knew naught of that, as my father told me long afterwards, for on their isolated farm they had had little news of the outside world, with no radio or newspaper.

They quickly made themselves scarce, for the British forces were rounding up every young Irishman they came upon, shoot-ing some of them down. They walked all the way to the port at Dun Laoghaire, still barefoot and on empty stomachs. They were lucky enough to find a British freighter due to leave for Liverpool the following day, and they were hired as cargo handlers to pay for their passage across the Irish Sea.

They found work in Liverpool as longshoremen, for the port

was full of troopships and freighters carrying British soldiers and supplies to France. Willie wanted to enlist in the British Army, but John talked him out of it, for they had to save enough from their wages to pay for their passage to America and also to send money home, for the theft of his mother's egg money was weighing heavily on John's conscience.

Willie eventually married an Irish girl in Liverpool, where he lived for the rest of his life. John, however, was determined to get to America, and by 1921 he had finally saved enough to buy a one-way ticket to Boston on a Cunard liner, crossing the Atlantic in steerage, the lowest-class accommodation in the bowels of the ship in which immigrants always travelled. He soon found work as a ditch-digger in Boston, staying in a rooming-house that catered to young Irishmen recently arrived in the US, a big improvement on the 'Ha'penny Hangers' of Dublin and Liverpool.

The Irish immigrants in Boston held dances on Saturday evenings, and at one of these caleighs, as they were called, John met Peg Murphy, who was working as a maid for a wealthy family on Beacon Hill. They were married in September 1924 and moved into a furnished room in Roxbury, where I was conceived about a year later.

Peg was dismissed from her job on Beacon Hill the moment that her employers learned of her pregnancy. That same day she told John that they had to pack their bags and leave Boston without delay. She felt that there would be more freedom and opportunity in New York, particularly in Brooklyn, where John had an aunt who could help him find a better job than ditch-digging.

Early in the spring of 1926 they took the train to New York and moved in with John's aunt Helen Moran, whose husband Paddy was a supervisor for the BMT, the Brooklyn–Manhattan Transit Company. Paddy used his influence to have John hired as a conductor on the trolley-line that ran between Canarsie Bay and the Williamsburg Bridge, and Peg began looking for an apartment somewhere along the route. She finally found a ground-floor flat halfway along the route on Cooper Street at the corner of Wilson Avenue in the Bushwick section of Brooklyn, a predominately German neighbourhood. They moved in just before I, already an experienced traveller, was born, on 26 June 1926.

Peg told me that whenever John's trolley passed he would ring the trolley-bell and she would rush to the window and wave to him, and sometimes on a fine day we would ride with him to the Williamsburg Bridge and back.

Years later Peg told me that the main reason she decided to leave Boston was that there were too many Irish there, penned up in shantytowns and looked down upon by upper-class Yankees like the Brahmins she worked for on Beacon Hill. 'I did not leave Ireland to live among the Irish,' she said, usually when we moved from one apartment to another when the rent was overdue, to neighbourhoods with varying mixtures of Germans, Italians, Poles and Eastern European Jews, but never to one where the Irish predominated. Our successive apartments were all in what were once working-class neighbourhoods. When I first heard this term as a boy I asked my mother if we were working class, and she said, 'We would indeed be of the working class if your father could find steady work.'

But the Irish soon began moving into Bushwick, beginning with John's younger brothers Tom, Pat and Mike, and Peg's younger brother Mauris, all of whom married girls recently arrived from Ireland. Then all the girls began bringing out their younger brothers and sisters from the 'old country', and before long we had created what Peg called a 'Gaelic Ghetto' in German Brooklyn.

We were still living on Cooper Street when my sister Dorothy was born on 19 December 1927. John's brother Tom and his wife Chris were looking after me while Peg was in the hospital, where she had been taken by her sister Nell. Tom waited outside on the front steps of our apartment to tell John the news when his trolley passed. John then left the trolley, telling the passengers that he would be right back, while he and Tom went into a 'speakeasy' saloon on the corner run by Paul Hesse, who poured them each a schooner of beer on the house. One drink led to another and the party went on until the saloon was raided by the police, who had been called in because of the long line of trolleys that had stopped behind John's abandoned one. A reporter and photographer from the *Daily News* arrived together with the police, and a photo of the scene appeared on the front page of the newspaper the next day under the headline 'STORK SNARLS TRAFFIC'.

John returned to his trolley, but at the end of his run was fired by the supervisor in Canarsie. During the next two years he worked intermittently as a longshoreman on the Hudson River docks whenever a cargo ship arrived. But his pay was very irregular and eventually we were evicted from the Cooper Street apartment.

Peg felt that the situation was hopeless, so she decided that she would take me and Dorothy with her and go back to live with her parents in Ireland until John found steady work. Peg's sister Nell gave her the money for our one-way third-class tickets on a Cunard liner, which came to $80, $40 for Peg and half-fare for me and Dorothy. Nell gave Peg some extra money to buy new clothes for us all, for she didn't want their parents to know that the Irish in America were as poor as they were in Ireland.

I remember very little of that first round trip to Ireland, which Peg later told me began early in 1931. We were in Ireland only a few months when John wrote to say that he had found work and that he had saved and borrowed enough money to pay for our return tickets. He had found a cheap apartment on Chauncey Street, he said, a block away from where we had lived before, and we moved in there as soon as we returned.

John's job was with a gardening firm called Perpetual Care, which looked after burial plots in the Evergreens Cemetery, one of the largest burial grounds in the city, stretching for miles along Brooklyn's border with Queens. The work wasn't steady, peaking in summer, particularly on Memorial Day, tapering off in the autumn except for All Souls Day, and then leaving him virtually no work in the winter except shovelling snow for the city when blizzards struck New York.

Peg never had enough money to pay the rent, and she continually had to ask the landlord for an extension. Eventually we were evicted from our apartment and all our furniture was repossessed by the shop from which Peg had bought it. We then moved in with John's aunt Helen and her husband Paddy Moran, who had a big house in Flatbush, all four of us sleeping in the hall bedroom they usually rented out to bachelors. Peg once more felt that the

situation was hopeless, and after a few weeks there she decided
that she would return to Ireland with me and Dorothy until John
had found a proper job. Nell again bought tickets for us on one of
the Cunard liners, and gave Peg money for her expenses, for she
knew that their parents wouldn't have a penny to spare.

We left New York early in the spring of 1932, a few months
before my sixth birthday. Our departure is one of the most pain-
ful of my early childhood memories. I can still see John's receding
figure on the dock, waving up to us as the ship moved slowly away,
Peg beside me holding Dorothy in her arms, weeping as she waved
back to him. I can also remember passing the Statue of Liberty,
which most immigrants see when they first arrive in New York,
but we saw it when leaving, and for the second time, because of
what Peg called our 'contrary ways', always 'sailing against the tide'.

We landed in the Cobh of Cork, which Peg still called Queenstown, its name under British rule. We took a train to Tralee,
where we changed and boarded the narrow-gauge railway to
Anascaul, halfway out along the Dingle Peninsula. The sea was in
view on either side, Tralee Bay to the north and Dingle Bay to the
south.

Tomas was waiting for us at the station in Anascaul, and he
loaded the three of us and our trunk aboard what he called his
'trap', a cart pulled by a donkey whom he addressed in a language
Peg said was Irish. He spoke to Dorothy and me in English, and
as we drove off, heading eastward along the southern shore of
the peninsula, he gave us a lesson in local geography, myth and
history, tipping his trilby to those we passed along the way and
greeting them in Irish.

Off to the south, on the other side of Dingle Bay, we could
see the Iveragh Peninsula, and along its spine the Macgillycuddy
Reeks, the highest mountains in Ireland, nearly 3,500 feet above
sea level. The Slieve Mish Mountains, which formed the backbone
of the Dingle Peninsula, were almost as high. The tallest peak,
Mount Brandon, was some 3,000 feet high, rising from the tip of
the Dingle Peninsula, 10°30' west of Greenwich, the westernmost
point of Europe.

We came down to the sea at Inch, passing Foley's pub, where

Peg said she had worked when she was a girl. Just beyond Foley's we passed the church and the seaside graveyard where, Tomas said, some of my ancestors were buried. I counted four milestones before we came to the tiny hamlet of Lach, just three houses, two on the left side and one on the right.

The donkey, without being told, stopped at the first house on the left, a little stone cottage with a slate roof, set back a bit from the road, its door and two windows facing out to the sea. My grandmother Mary was waiting at the door to greet us, and she gathered the three of us into her arms, welcoming us in Irish and then switching to English. My uncle John was there too, looking frail and wan as he greeted us, trying to shield us from his tubercular cough.

A turf fire was burning in the hearth, which was the only source of heat in the house. There were small bedrooms on either side of the main room, which served as kitchen, dining room and living room. A stairway on the right led up to the attic, and a door on the left opened on to the barn, where the donkey, a cow and chickens were kept. Behind the house was the tiny farm, which was on the lower slope of the Slieve Mish Mountains, now shrouded in fog. And in front, out of sight behind the hedges that fringed the road, was the sea, which I could hear as its waves washed up on the rocky shore, leaving a salt tang in the wind that soughed in the trees behind the cottage.

After we finished supper we received a visit from Barry Callaghan and his daughter Peig, my mother's dearest friend, who lived in the next cottage along the road. My mother had wanted Peig to leave with her when she emigrated to America, but it wasn't possible, for her parents were old and she was the last of the children and was needed at home. Her mother had since died and Peig was living with her father Barry, who though he was in his 80s still had some red left in his full beard. The Sayers family from across the road then came to join us, and everyone sat around the fire talking, which made Peg happy, so she told me, for this was the Ireland she had missed so much in America.

The Murphy cottage had no electricity, running water, central heating, bathroom or toilet, inside or out. Oil lamps and candles provided light, and heat came from the turf fire in the hearth, where Mary cooked our meals and baked bread that we covered with the butter she made in her churn. Everything we ate was from their tiny farm except the fish that Tomas caught. Drinking water came from a barrel that captured rain running off the roof, or from the brook half a mile down the road where the local women did their laundry. Each of us took a bath once a week in a large wooden tub filled with rainwater that had been heated in a kettle over the turf fire. Bath time was early Saturday evening, in preparation for church the next day.

The attic in the Murphy cottage was full of books, mostly novels, poetry, history and travelogues, and Peg spent all of her free time there reading, as she had when she was a girl, so she told me.

I was very curious about the books in the attic, and so Mary began teaching me to read and write, starting with the primers she had used when she was a schoolteacher. When I had finished with those I began reading books that I found in the attic, the first one I can recall being *A Pictorial Journey Around the World*, a travelogue illustrated with engravings. Mary told me that her father Thomas Ashe, who had been badly wounded at the siege of Sebastopol and had convalesced in Florence Nightingale's hospital, had bought this book in Constantinople after he had been discharged. One of the chapters was entitled 'A Voyage on the Limpopo', and another was 'A Journey by Train Across the American West'. The chapter that fascinated me most was about Constantinople, particularly the engraving showing mosques and minarets rising from the seven hills of the ancient city at the confluence of the Golden Horn and the Bosphorus, the historic strait that divides Europe and Asia. Mary told me that her father had talked about Constantinople till his dying day, and it was this that started me thinking about the city, now known as Istanbul, where I was fated to spend a large part of my life.

I often went down to the cove with Tomas, watching him as he set his nets and lines, listening to him as he explained how the tides were influenced by both the moon and the sun and also by the wind. Occasionally he would catch a big codfish, which he would salt and hang outside the cottage door, from which at supper time he could cut off chunks to add to our meal.

Tomas told me that his own people came from a culture much older than that of those who tilled the soil, for they and others like them earned their livelihood on the margins of the land and sea, fishing in the deep and gathering cockles, mussels and periwinkles in the shallows, as well as the eggs of sea birds, and tending goats who could live on the sparse vegetation out on the end of the Dingle Peninsula and on the Blasket Isles off its westernmost promontory.

Around the time of my sixth birthday, 26 June 1932, Tomas took me in his donkey cart out to the end of the peninsula to Dunquin, the westernmost village in Ireland and all of Europe. There we stopped at the famous Kruger's pub, which Tomas told me was so called because the publican, Maurice 'Kruger' Cavanaugh, had supported the Afrikaners during the Boer War and took his nickname from their leader.

Peg had already told me that when the American aviator Charles Lindbergh made his solo flight across the Atlantic in 1927, his first sight of Europe was the tip of the Dingle Peninsula. Kruger told me that he had waved up at the plane and that Lindbergh dipped its wings in response. He pointed to an autographed photograph on the wall, showing Lindbergh standing in front of the *Spirit of St Louis*, which in my imagination I could see flying over the pub and dipping its wings.

Tomas and I stood out on the promontory behind the pub and looked down on the little cove that served as the harbour of Dunquin, as huge combers rolled in from the Atlantic and smashed against the cliff beneath us in showers of rainbowed spray. 'We're at the edge of the world, lad,' Tomas said. 'Here in Dunquin they say that the next parish is in America.'

Below us a long flight of stone steps led down to the cove, where the islanders beached their currachs when they rowed in from the Blasket Islands. There were just 150 or so still living on the archipelago, Tomas said, most of them on the Great Blasket, by far the largest of the half-dozen inhabited isles. Only years later did I learn that among the islanders living on the Great Blasket

at that time were three whose stories about life there would be
taken down and published: Maurice O'Sullivan, Tomas O'Crohan
and Peig Sayers. The first was O'Sullivan's *Twenty Years A-Growing*,
published in both Irish and English in 1933, while I was still living
on the peninsula. The title is from the old Dingle saying which I
first heard from Tomas: 'Did you ever hear how the life of man is
divided? Twenty years agrowing, twenty years in blossom, twenty
years a-stooping and twenty years declining. Such is the life of a
man.'

Late in the autumn Peg received a letter from John, saying that
he had found a job, and as soon as he had saved enough money
would send our return tickets. A few weeks later he wrote again to
say that he had bought us tickets on a Cunard liner, scheduled to
leave Queenstown on 1 February 1933. He asked Peg if she would
take me and Dorothy to see his parents in Ballyhaunis, enclosing
a money order to cover our expenses.

A few days before Christmas the postman delivered a pack-
age from John, with presents for Peg, me and Dorothy. My present was an American Indian chief's war bonnet, with a nimbus
of coloured feathers, which I put on and showed off to everyone
who visited the cottage on Christmas Day. Because of the headdress, the local boys invited me to join them the following day, the
feast of St Stephen, to celebrate the 'Hunting of the Wren', which
they pronounced as 'wran'. All of us, 'the Wren Boys', dressed up
in bizarre costumes, my Indian headdress making me an instant
celebrity.

We started the day by searching for a wren's nest in the thatched
roofs of the local cottages. The other boys had already made an
elaborate wickerwork cage, and when we found a wren we put it
inside the cage and paraded with it all the way to Inch, stopping
at every cottage along the way, singing the 'Song of the Wren',
begging for a 'trate', which was usually a sweet.

The Wran, the Wran, the king of all birds,
Saint Stephenses Day, he was caught in the furze.
Although he is little his honour is great.
So rise up kind sir, and give us a trate.

Early in the new year we took the train to Ballyhaunis, where my grandfather Michael Freely was waiting at the station. There was no mistaking him, for he looked just like John, with a little red left in his hair, though he was in his early 70s, Peg told us. He was driving a horse-drawn cart, and he put Peg and Dorothy in the back with our baggage, sitting me beside him for the five-mile ride out to the farm.

The Freely cottage was on the brow of a hill above the road, looking across a valley to a hillside covered with blackberry bushes. It was made of whitewashed field stones, with walls a yard thick, and it had a thatched roof. Peg said that the Freelys had been living here since Queen Elizabeth I's time, or so they believed.

My grandmother Ellen was waiting there with my uncles Charley and Luke, and each embraced us and welcomed us into the cottage. Peg had told me that Ellen was about 60, though she was very pretty and looked much younger than her years. Charley was 23 and Luke, the youngest of the family, was going on 17. My father and his brother Willie had never met Luke, for he was born a few weeks after they left home in 1916. We had tea around the great hearth, which was also the room in which all the children had slept, in a series of niches hollowed out of the walls on either side, each with a curtain that could be drawn at night. Ellen said that the niches were called 'hags', and she pointed out the ones that John and Willie had been sleeping in the night before they left home.

Though it was mid-winter the weather was beautiful, and we spent a few days wandering around the farm and the surrounding fields. During the long evenings we sat by the hearth talking, and Peg had such a good time that she was sorry we had to leave so soon.

A few days later Michael died. He had been working in the barn and fell down against the door, and I could hear Charley and Luke shouting as they forced their way in to help him. They finally managed to open the barn door and then carried him to his bed, and I could hear Charley saying that he was not breathing and had no pulse. Ellen sent Charley off with the horse and wagon to Ballyhaunis to bring back the doctor, who told us that Michael had died of a sudden heart attack.

Ellen took it very well and dispatched Charley to Ballyhaunis to arrange the funeral and burial. Then the rest of us left the room, for she said that she was going to wash Michael's body in preparation for his burial, and as we waited in the kitchen I could hear her weeping.

When I saw Michael again the next day he was dressed in his Sunday suit and laid out in a plain wooden casket, which had been placed on two chairs in front of the hearth, with tall candles at his head and feet. Throughout the day people came in from Ballyhaunis and the surrounding farms to pay their last respects, many of them Freelys, as I learned when they were introduced to us. Then the priest arrived and led the mourners in a rosary, blessing Michael and placing a crucifix against his forehead. Then they all went up in turn to kiss Michael and say a prayer for him, after which they offered their sympathy to Ellen, Charley and Luke.

The moment the priest left Charley opened a jug of poteen, home-brewed Irish whiskey, which he and Luke served to the men, while Ellen and Peg made tea for the women. Someone had brought along a fiddle and someone else an accordion, and when they began to play, all the younger people got up to do the jig and the stack-of-barley, dances that I remembered from our parties in Brooklyn.

This was the first time I had ever been to a wake, the traditional Irish farewell party for someone who had died in the fullness of their years, though I would go to many more when we returned to Brooklyn. I later learned that this was a pagan Irish custom, now banned by the Catholic Church, which eased the pain of death for those who had lost their beloved, as I could see from looking at Ellen, who was tapping her feet to the music, though I knew that she was grieving inside.

We left Ballyhaunis a few days after the funeral and took the train back to Anascaul, where Tomas was waiting for us in his trap. He was not his usual talkative self, and as we drove along in silence I realized that he was sad because we would soon be leaving, and that made me sad as well.

Peg was silent too on our ride back to the cottage and in the days afterwards. As the time of our departure approached she spent much of her time in conversation with Peig Callaghan, talking of the mixed feelings she had about returning to America. She hadn't been happy there, I heard her tell Peig, but there was no way we could remain in Ireland, for we were a burden on her parents and her ailing brother John, who could hardly look after themselves.

Our train would be leaving at noon from Tralee, and Tomas had arranged with a friend in Anascaul who had a motorcar to pick us up in the cottage at eight in the morning. A short while later the motorcar arrived and the driver loaded our trunk in the boot. When all was ready we said our tearful goodbyes and boarded the car, as Tomas sent us off with the traditional Irish farewell: 'May the road rise up to meet you and the wind always be at your back; may the sun be warm upon your brow and the rain fall softly on your fields; and until we meet again may God hold you in the hollow of his hand.'

The voyage from the Cobh of Cork to New York was my fourth trip across the Atlantic, which gave me a feeling of great pride, for though I was only six and a half I could already claim to be a world traveller. We were out on deck all day throughout the voyage, which was unusually calm for that time of year, as one of the crew told us. When we approached New York I stood out on the prow so that I could be the first passenger to spot the Statue of Liberty, which I was now passing for the fourth time, though I hardly remembered the first two trips.

John was waiting for us on the dock when we moored at Pier 92, and I recognized him at once, though Dorothy hardly remembered him. Peg was very happy to see him, and I could tell that she was more hopeful about the future than she had been in Ireland. He had written to tell her that he was now working as a gravedigger in the Evergreens Cemetery and that he had found an apartment not far from where we had lived before we left for Ireland.

Our apartment was on the top floor of a three-storey building on Macdonough Street, in the Bedford-Stuyvesant district of Brooklyn, which disappointed Peg, since she had been hoping for a ground-floor flat with a yard in front and a garden at the back. I

could see that she wasn't too pleased with the secondhand furniture that John had bought on credit, putting down $10 that he
had borrowed, the rest to be paid in weekly instalments for two
years, though he had already missed the first two payments.

A week or so after we moved in, there was a fire in the apartment downstairs and we were forced to flee from the building
down the fire escape and stand out in the freezing cold until the
firemen put out the blaze. After we were allowed back in the building Peg wept when she saw the condition of our apartment, for all
our belongings were soaked. We had to stay with my uncle Tom
Freely and his family until our bedding and furniture dried out a
bit, though everything was still damp and mildewed.

That was the first of seven apartments we lived in during the
next four years. During that time Dorothy and I were enrolled
successively in three schools, Our Lady of Lourdes Parochial
School, a public high school in Flatbush, and Fourteen Holy
Martyrs Parochial School, where we began on 19 January 1937.

Meanwhile, late in the autumn of 1934, John was laid off at the
Evergreens Cemetery, which had been forced to cut its workforce
drastically. He tried shaping up on the docks as a longshoreman,
as he had in the past, but there were many hundreds of unem-
ployed men doing the same, and so he was never hired, and came
home at the end of the day minus the ten cents he had spent on
the subway fare. Finally we were evicted from our apartment and
forced to move in with the Morans in Flatbush, where my sister
Nancy was born on 1 November 1935.

John finally managed to find a part-time job as a labourer with
the WPA, the Works Progress Administration, one of the new
agencies created by President Roosevelt. The pay wasn't much but
at least we were no longer paupers, as Peg said to me one evening.

Then the saints in heaven worked a miracle, as Peg told me
one day when I returned from school, for John had finally found
a full-time job. She said that Paddy Moran knew Mike Quill, head
of the Transport Workers Union, who used his influence with the
BMT to have John rehired as a trolley-car conductor. Paddy said
that to do this they first had to clear up John's file by removing the
record of what had happened on 19 December 1927, though those

who drank in Paul Hesse's saloon could still see on the wall the front page of the *Daily News* and the headline 'STORK SNARLS TRAFFIC'.

John was once again assigned to the trolley line that ran between Canarsie and the Williamsburg Bridge, beginning late in the autumn of 1936. Soon afterwards we left the Morans and moved back to our old neighbourhood in Bushwick, where my uncle Tom had found us a flat directly above his own on Central Avenue between Eldert and Covert Streets, directly across the street from the Fourteen Holy Martyrs Church and School, where he worked as the janitor. My brother Jimmy was born there on 11 June 1937.

As soon as we were settled Peg took Dorothy and me across the street to enrol in the Fourteen Holy Martyrs School, which was directly above the church. The teachers were all nuns of the Dominican Order, and their principal was the Mother Superior, who assigned me to the fourth grade and Dorothy to the third. She said that we were obliged to attend mass every morning at 8:15 before school, and she showed me and Dorothy the pews to which our classes had been assigned: boys to the right of the aisle, girls to the left, the lower grades in front.

The spring term began on 15 January 1937. Peg got us up early so that on the first day of school we crossed the street to the church at eight o'clock sharp. No one was there except our uncle Tom, who was sweeping up after the 6:30 mass, and we talked to him for a few minutes before going to our seats.

I took Dorothy to her pew and then went to find mine. I saw that a boy about my age had come in and was sitting in the first row of the fourth-grade pews, and he motioned for me to come and sit beside him. He said his name was Jimmy Anderson, and that the Mother Superior had told him that I would be joining the class and that he should look after me. Then the other boys in our class began filing in, and Jimmy whispered their names to me. The girls in our class were sitting across the aisle with our teacher, a ferocious-looking old nun whom he identified as Sister Saint Peter, and even though he had barely whispered her name she turned and silenced me with a look that I soon learned to fear.

After mass I followed Jimmy up to our classroom, where Sister Saint Peter read out our names, 31 girls on the left side of the room and 20 boys on the right. I was put by the window in the last row next to Jimmy Anderson, who told me that Sister Saint Peter seated her students according to their final grades, in which he had ranked last among the boys. 'And that means she thinks you're just as dumb as I am,' he whispered, and when we laughed Sister Saint Peter smacked each of us on the side of the head, making my ears ring.

But I found that Jimmy wasn't dumb, for he seemed to know a lot about the street life of Brooklyn, though he wasn't particularly interested in book-learning. I thought I would show Sister Saint Peter that I was as smart as Richard Holtzman, John Mione and Albert Kreyl, the three top boys, whose marks were higher than those of Mary McCabe, Muriel Rogers, Ruth O'Kane and Jean Caputo, the four smartest girls. But that would mean I would be moved up to the front of the room, where it would be more difficult to look out of the window and daydream. Besides, I wasn't interested in anything that Sister Saint Peter taught except geography, and when she pulled down the maps from above the blackboard I daydreamed of faraway places to which I would one day travel.

Jimmy's father was dead and his mother was an invalid. His elder sister, who was about 20, supported the family on her wages as a secretary, but one day she disappeared and was never seen again. Jimmy's mother had a small pension but it wasn't nearly enough to support them, and he made ends meet by delivering newspapers and other odd jobs.

One of his jobs was making the rounds on Saturday with a homemade wagon in which he collected old newspapers, discarded furniture, broken household appliances, worn-out radios, scrap metal and other assorted bric-a-brac, which at the end of the day he sold to a junk dealer. I became his helper, although he wasn't able to pay me anything other than buying me a Baby Ruth chocolate bar if it had been a good day. But the reward for me was getting to learn things about Brooklyn that I would otherwise not have known: the garbage dumps where he found most of his newspapers and other junk, the boarded-up houses where he helped himself to whatever could be carried away, the railway freight yard where he picked up scrap metal along the tracks, and the abandoned ice-house where he stripped the lead roofing and ripped the copper refrigeration pipes from the walls.

Later I made my own wagon and scavenged for junk independently of Jimmy Anderson, now that I had learned the ropes from him. We scoured the neighbourhood on separate blocks, meeting up at the end of the day in the junkyard, after which we would go to the abandoned ice-house. We had built a little ramshackle clubhouse there, where we counted our earnings and talked about our day's adventures until it was time to go home.

The only girl in my class I came to know well was Jean Caputo, whose father owned a barber shop on Cooper Street. He and his wife were both from northern Italy, and they had met and married in Brooklyn. I heard Italian opera for the first time in the Caputo's living room, listening to Enrico Caruso singing an aria from *Rigoletto*. I borrowed the record and played it for Peg that evening, and she said that Caruso sang like an angel.

Peg finally found a new apartment late in July 1937. It was about half a mile west of Fourteen Holy Martyrs at 225 Cornelia Street, near the corner of Wilson Avenue, which was on the route of the trolley-car that John drove. Our new apartment was what they called a 'parlour floor and basement' in a three-storey brownstone house owned by Harry and Josephine Simmons. Peg didn't know what nationality Mr Simmons was, although she thought he may have changed his name to hide his origins, but Mrs Simmons was Polish and proud of it.

Mr and Mrs Simmons lived on the top floor, while we had the ground floor and two rooms on the middle floor. The front room on the ground floor was the parlour, the middle room was a bedroom where John and Peg slept, with Jimmy's crib beside them, and the back room was our kitchen. Dorothy and Nancy had the front bedroom upstairs and I had the middle room, while the back room was rented out to bachelors.

There was a yard in front and another yard and garden at the rear, all of which we had to ourselves. There was also a basement, where John looked after the furnace and where he could hide his extra bottles of beer, for Peg allowed him only two a day. I bought the beer for him at the corner grocery, where I cashed in on the three-cent deposit on the empty bottles. The store was owned by a Jewish couple named the Hellmans, who kindly gave us credit when we were short of money, starting from the first week that we moved to Cornelia Street. Mrs Simmons was very kind and told us not to worry if we didn't have enough to pay the rent, starting from our first month in the apartment.

During what was left of that summer we settled into our new apartment, which was by far the nicest place we had ever lived in, and Peg seemed very happy. When John was on the day shift we would all sit out together on the front steps in the early evening together with Mr and Mrs Simmons. I'd fill a bucket with cold water so that John could cool his feet after a long day of standing at the controls of his trolley. Then I would 'rush the growler', Brooklyn slang for fetching a pitcher of draft beer for John from the local saloon, making sure that the bartender didn't give me too much foam, which I would lick off on the way home.

But our world suddenly changed when John was laid off by the BMT, which had decided to economize by cutting its workforce. Peg was heartbroken, because for the first time in her married life she had been able to raise her family in a nice apartment, and so when John told her the news she burst into tears and cried for hours. She finally stopped when Mrs Simmons came down to comfort her, telling her not to worry about the rent until John found another job.

John went back to shaping up on the Hudson River docks, but although he lined up every day for a week he wasn't once chosen for a work gang, for he didn't know any of the foremen. Finally our money ran out and he didn't have enough for the subway fare, until I found four empty beer bottles in the basement and returned them for the deposit of 12 cents, which was two cents more than we needed. But John found no work that day either, and when Peg sent me to the grocery store to get something for supper I had to ask Mr Hellman to put it on the bill. Peg had told me to get a bottle of milk but I ordered four, one of which we drank at supper, after which I emptied the other three into a big pot. Peg asked me what in God's name was I doing, and I explained to her that I would take the four empty bottles out to the grocery store first thing in the morning for the 12-cent deposit, which would be enough for John's subway fare, with two cents to spare.

But John didn't find work the next day either, and Peg had to borrow money from her brother Mauris. Mauris called on Paddy Burke, a friend of the family who had connections with the Long-shoremen's Union. Paddy lent John the money to join the union and introduced him around to the foremen.

It was my job to read the shipping news in the *Journal American* every evening, to find out when a cargo ship was arriving in New York harbour and note the pier at which it would be dock-ing. Usually it took three or four days to unload a ship, and John earned five or six dollars a day and sometimes a couple of dollars more if he worked overtime. That was enough for Peg to run the house and to begin paying off the back rent to Mrs Simmons and the grocery bill to Mr Hellman. But I knew that John wasn't giving of all his pay to Peg, for once again he began sending me out to buy bottles of beer that he hid in the basement.

I spent some of the money I earned going to the movies, usually to the Saturday matinée at the Colonial Theater, when there was a double feature along with a cartoon and an episode of a ten-part thriller. After one of these matinées at the Colonial I bought the late afternoon edition of the *Journal American* and saw the headline 'NAZIS INVADE POLAND'. The date was 1 September 1939, the beginning of World War II. That night we listened to Gabriel Heatter on the evening news, who said that the Germans had invaded Poland at several points and were advancing rapidly. Mrs Simmons was with us and was very upset, for most of her family was still living in Poland. Sixteen days later we learned on the evening news that the Russians had invaded Poland too, divid-ing up the country with the Germans.

About a month later I came home from school to find Peg in tears. She said that a policeman had just been to the house to tell her that John had been badly injured in an accident on the docks and was in Bellevue Hospital, and she told me to look after the other kids while she went to see him. When she came home she said that he was out of danger but that he had a broken leg and internal injuries that would keep him in hospital for several weeks. It seems that a crate of heavy machinery had fallen on him and another longshoreman, who had been killed instantly, and so John was lucky to be alive.

It was three weeks before John came home, and Peg was told that it would be at least six months before he could go back to work. Workmen's Compensation paid his hospital bills, but he received nothing to compensate him for his injury or to support him and his family while he was out of work.

And so we went on the dole, which in those days was known as Relief and is now called Welfare. But it shamed Peg to wait in line at a government office to get coupons that entitled us to some free food, although not enough to live on, and so our bill at Hellman's grocery store once again began to rise, as did the amount of rent that we owed Mrs Simmons. But Peg was determined not to despair, and one evening when she and I were talking she said that, as bad as things were, at least her children had never gone to bed hungry. I have never forgotten that.

I graduated from Fourteen Holy Martyrs in mid-January 1941, ranked first in the class. Jimmy Anderson was next to last, but at least he passed, while our friend Cliffy, who was 17 and a professional boxer, was left back once again. Neither Jimmy nor I were invited to the class party, so we went to a double feature of horror movies at the Halsey Theater, watching Boris Karloff as Frankenstein and Bela Lugosi as Dracula while we gorged ourselves on popcorn.

I started classes at Brooklyn Tech early in February 1941. The school was in the Fort Greene section of Brooklyn and it took nearly an hour to get there on the Halsey Street trolley. The school was enormous, an eight-storey, red-brick building that took up a whole block, with 4,000 students from all over New York City, all boys. I borrowed money from my aunt Nell to pay for my textbooks and the other things I needed for school, including a slide-rule and the materials for my mechanical drawing course. I earned only about $3 a week scavenging, and after I gave half of it to Peg and paid 50 cents on carfare to and from school I had only a dollar left for everything, including lunch, which I saved on by making my own sandwiches, although I sometimes splurged by buying a lemonade in the school cafeteria.

I knew I had to find an after-school job, and so I went to the school employment office. The lady in charge said that there was an opening at the Willis Paint Company, and when I said I was interested she phoned to make an appointment for me that after-noon after school. She showed me where it was on the map, just behind the Brooklyn Edison powerhouse on the East River under-neath the Brooklyn Bridge. I checked the scale on the map and saw that it was about a three-mile walk from school, which would take me about an hour.

I had no trouble finding the factory, for I just followed the approach to the Brooklyn Bridge, where I could see the huge powerhouse on the East River, its towering smokestack belching out a cloud of black smoke, and there behind it was a three-storey building with a large sign reading 'WILLIS PAINT'.

I rang the bell and the middle-aged man who answered it said, 'You must be the boy from Brooklyn Tech.' I said I was, identifying myself, and he said he was Herman Willis. He introduced me to his wife and said that she was his office staff, and then pointed to a man in paint-smeared overalls, identifying him as Saul Greenberg, his brother-in-law. 'We're the Willis Paint Company,' he said, 'just the three of us, and so if you join the firm you'll have to be a man of all work.'

I said that I was willing but that I had no experience. 'Never mind,' he said, 'you'll learn on the job.' He told me that my hours would be four to seven Monday through Friday and nine to six on Saturdays, with a half hour off for lunch. Then he asked me how old I was and I told him that I was fourteen and a half. 'But then you don't have working papers,' he said, 'because by law you have to be 16 before you can work.' I nodded, and he told me that he could only pay me 40 cents an hour, because if the authori-ties found out that he had hired an underage worker he would be fined and he would have to withhold part of my salary to cover himself. I had no choice but to agree, though a lightning calculation determined that my salary was only $9.60 a week, minus carfare, which would reduce it to just $9, half of which I would give to Peg.

It was nine when I got home, and by the time I finished supper, which Peg had left on the stove for me before going to work, it was nearly ten. By then John and the kids were asleep, and so I read the newspapers before starting my homework. But I was so tired I gave up after half an hour and went to bed.

During the summer I worked nine to six Monday through Saturday, earning $21.60 a week minus carfare, half of which went to Peg. On Sunday Jimmy Anderson and I went to the beach, either Coney Island or Rockaway. Our other friends would be there with their girlfriends, but Jimmy and I were still odd men out, for we didn't have any extra money to spend. I was saving up to buy a bicycle, but I never accumulated enough money to do so, for family financial crises always seemed to arise whenever I had almost enough money saved.

We were at home listening to the news in mid-afternoon on Sunday, 7 December, when the announcer interrupted the regular programme to say that Japanese planes had attacked the US Navy base at Pearl Harbor in Hawaii, and later we learned that they had destroyed half of America's Pacific Fleet.

On Monday we heard President Roosevelt's speech to Congress in which he called for a declaration of war against Japan, and on Friday evening Gabriel Heatter told us that Hitler had declared war on the US. Then on Saturday night I was listening to the Green Hornet mystery programme, where the hero Britt Reid was always assisted by his 'faithful Japanese companion Kato'. But now Kato had suddenly become Britt's 'faithful Filipino companion', and I knew that our world would never again be the same.

The Sunday after Pearl Harbor I went to Otto's ice cream parlour and met Jimmy Anderson, who told me that he had just enlisted in the Marine Corps. He was six months older than me and had recently turned 16, a year less than the minimum age at which you could enlist with parental consent, but he had altered his birth certificate to make it appear that he was a year older. He said that Phil Gould, one of our former classmates at Fourteen

Holy Martyrs, who was almost exactly my age, had done the same, and that both of them were awaiting orders to report for duty.

Jimmy and Phil received their orders early in February 1942, when they left for the Marine Corps training camp at Parris Island, South Carolina. Three months later they came home on a week's furlough before taking the train to San Pedro, California, where they were to board a troopship that would take them to some unknown destination in the Pacific. They figured that they were probably going with the First Marine Division to Hawaii, where the US was beginning to group its forces to mount a counter-attack against the Japanese, who in the meantime had taken the Philippines, Malaya and Burma. After I said goodbye to Jimmy and Phil I decided that I too would try to enlist, but Peg must have read my mind, for she put my birth certificate away in a locked box.

As soon as I turned 16, on 26 June 1942, I applied for working papers, because my experience with Mr Willis had taught me that I had to do this to get a decent job. I read through the want-ads in the *Daily News* and the *Journal American*, looking for an opening as a stock clerk or delivery boy, for those were the only jobs I could think of that I could do without experience. There were a number of openings, but by the time I appeared they were taken, and after a couple of weeks I began to get very discouraged.

But then my friend Ed Casey, who had graduated from Fourteen Holy Martyrs a year ahead of me, told me how I could get a head start on applying for a job. He worked as an apprentice pressman at the *Journal American* and said that if I came there one day he would give me a copy of the want-ad pages as soon as they came off the press. We made a date and I met him at the employees' entrance during his mid-morning break, when he handed me the freshly printed want-ad pages and wished me good luck. I went through the pages quickly and checked them against the previous day's edition to see which ads were appearing for the first time. I circled the first new ad I found, which was for a stock clerk at the Allied Art Company at 123 West 23rd Street.

I ran across town to Broadway and Fifth Avenue, where I turned onto West 23rd Street and found no. 123 on the south side of the street near Eighth Avenue. I looked at the directory in the lobby and saw that the Allied Art Company was on the sixth floor, and so with great trepidation I entered the elevator, the first one I had ever used, and pressed the button marked 6. The elevator was enclosed with an ironwork grille, and as we passed the successive floors I could see the names of the firms that did business there: an industrial printer on the second floor, a book supply firm on the third, children's clothing on the fourth and the Eagle Druggist Supply Company on the fifth.

I was surprised when the elevator came to a stop on the fifth floor, where a rather distinguished looking gentleman opened the elevator door as if he had been expecting me. He asked me if I was answering the ad for a stock clerk at the Allied Art Company, and when I said yes he invited me in.

He introduced himself as Mr Mendoza, president of the Eagle Druggist Supply Company, and said that he had an opening for a stock clerk. He explained that he had been about to put an ad in the *Journal American* when he learned that the Allied Art Company had already placed one in today's paper, and so he thought that he would save himself the trouble by intercepting the first applicant to appear, though he was surprised at how early I had arrived. I told him how I had beaten the gun and he smiled appreciatively, saying that he admired my initiative and that the job was mine if I wanted it.

I said that I would like to work full time for the rest of the summer and then part-time after school, beginning in the fall. He said that would be fine and that during the summer I would work from nine to six Monday through Saturday with half an hour off for lunch. My salary would be 50 cents an hour, minus a two per cent deduction for social security. I agreed and presented my brand new working papers, which he returned to me after his secretary recorded my name, address and social security number. He told me I could start right away and that he would introduce me to the people with whom I would be working.

He explained that the Eagle Druggist Supply Company packaged and distributed everything that you would find in a pharmacy except the actual medical drugs themselves, their main items being condoms, finger cots, nipple guards and plastic combs, as well as their own brands of septic powder and smelling salts, the manufacture of which would be right up my alley, since I was a chemistry student at Brooklyn Tech.

He took me out into the main production floor, where about 50 young women were working at a series of long wooden tables. There I was introduced to the forelady, Nan MacDowell, a little Scotswoman of about 40 with a mop of carrot-red hair, who told Mr Mendoza that she would take good care of me.

As soon as Mr Mendoza left, Nan told the girls to stop working so that she could introduce the new stock clerk. Then, when she had their full attention, she smiled and grabbed me by the testicles, so that I jumped and let out a yell. After the girls stopped laughing Nan patted me on the behind and said that she just wanted to break the ice and make me feel at home.

Nan then took me to the stock room to meet Harry Epstein, whom I would help whenever he needed me. Then she brought me to meet the chief shipping clerk, Nathan Cohen, and his assistant, Isaac Jefferson, a giant black man who put his arm around my shoulder and said I'd be working with him most of the time.

Nathan showed me how to make up a big cardboard carton, which Isaac and I packed with boxes of condoms. When the carton was filled Nathan showed me how to seal it, write the address with a black marker pen, weigh it and figure out the postage, after which Isaac and I stacked it in the rope-operated freight elevator. After we packed a few cartons Isaac showed me how to operate the ropes of the elevator to take us down to the ground floor. There we carried the cartons out to the back entrance of the building on 22nd Street and loaded them on to a big truck. When we were finished Isaac smiled and said that now we would take a little sweet-assed time on our own, which I thought was a great idea. When he offered me a cigarette I said I didn't smoke, but I enjoyed the heady aroma all the same, though I had the feeling that it was something other than tobacco.

Most days I worked with Nathan and Isaac in the shipping room, but if there wasn't enough for me to do there I reported to Harry in the stock room. Harry also showed me how to mix the materials for the septic powder and smelling salts, which I worked on in a little room that I called my laboratory, from where I could see a patch of sky through a tiny window near the ceiling. And as I worked there on hot summer afternoons, running with sweat, choking on septic powder, and half-blinded by ammonia fumes, I would occasionally see a cloud passing in the blue sky and longed to be on the beach at Rockaway, where most of the boys I knew were swimming and sunning themselves with their girlfriends.

Our family fortunes changed early in 1943 when John was hired as a gravedigger in the Evergreens Cemetery, replacing a young unmarried man who had been drafted into the Army. The Portal-to-Portal Pay Act had just been enacted, and now John was guaranteed a full week's pay even when the dead were not dying regularly. Peg was beside herself with joy because now we could begin paying off the money we still owed Mrs Simmons and the Hellmans.

As soon as I turned 17, on 26 June 1943, I asked Peg if she would give me permission to join the Navy. She refused and said that I should wait until I was drafted, which would be at least another year, by which time the war might be over, which is exactly what I was afraid of.

That fall I began to lose interest in my studies, for I longed to be in the Navy. The only subject that that interested me was humanities, where we were reading Homer's *Odyssey*. My report card of January 1944 showed that I had flunked all my courses except humanities, in which I received a perfect grade of 100. The REMARKS entry at the bottom of the card said that I was being expelled from school because of my unsatisfactory academic record, and I was required to report to my advisor along with at least one of my parents.

Peg was devastated when I showed her my report card, and when she went with me to see my advisor she said not a word but just signed the forms that he put in front of her. I hadn't seen my advisor since the day I entered school, and now as I left it he offered no advice nor did I need any, for I knew what I was going to do – join the Navy.

Peg reluctantly agreed to let me enlist, and so early in February

I went to the main US Navy recruitment headquarters in Manhattan and asked for the parental permission form. Peg and John signed the form and I returned it, and so began the process of enlistment, which involved a series of medical, dental and psychological examinations and the filling out of endless forms and questionnaires.

Two months later I received an official letter informing me that my application to join the US Navy had been accepted and that I should report to the recruitment centre to be sworn in. I did so, expecting to go into the Navy right away, but I was told that I would be informed by mail as to when and where I should report to be sent off to training camp.

The letter from the Navy finally arrived at the beginning of May. I was informed that on the 26th I should report to the officer on duty at Penn Station at 8pm sharp, when I would be mustered along with other recruits and be sent off on a troop train to Sampson Naval Training Center in upstate New York. Peg sighed when I told her and said that I would be going into the service at almost exactly the same age as her maternal grandfather Thomas Ashe had been when he went off to fight in the Crimean War. She said that he came back alive, though badly wounded, otherwise none of us would be here today, and that I should take good care of myself, for there were unborn generations depending on me.

The day before I left I said goodbye to all my relatives and friends. That evening I took one last stroll around the neighbourhood, and on the way home I passed the park on Wilson Avenue and Halsey Street where some of my pals went to go 'necking' with their girlfriends. When I passed the entrance to the park a girl whose voice I didn't recognize called out to me, but then she laughed and I just kept walking, figuring that one of my friends had put her up to it just to make fun of me. Then I remembered the episode in the *Odyssey* where Odysseus puts wax in his ears and has his men tie him to the mast of his ship so that he will be able to resist the call of the Sirens, and so, to buoy up my feelings, I thought of the Halsey Street Park as Siren Land.

I went to bed and set the alarm for 3am so that I could get up for one last nocturnal dialogue with Peg when she came home from work. But the alarm must have failed to go off, for I awoke to find Peg holding me in her arms and telling me that when she came home she heard me crying in my sleep. When she asked me what was wrong I couldn't tell her, for I didn't know, and she said not to worry, for all would be well, as the Irish say. She told me that she would take the next night off from work so that she and John could go with me to Penn Station, and then she kissed me goodnight and I went back to sleep.

The next evening I kissed Dorothy, Nancy and Jimmy goodbye and then Peg and I left for Penn Station, taking the subway at Wilson Avenue. When we arrived at the station I saw a sign directing US Navy recruits to Gate Number 8, where a chief petty officer was waiting along with two sailors wearing leather leggings and carrying billy clubs, identified by their arm bands as SP, Shore Patrol. I give my name to the chief, who ticked my name off a list and told me to stand by the entrance to Gate Number 8. Then other recruits began arriving, none of them accompanied by family, and I kissed John and Peg goodbye, watching them until they reached the entrance to the subway. They turned and waved goodbye to me, and I could see that they were trying not to cry. I did my best not to cry too, for I was in the Navy now.

The train took us to the US Naval Training Base at Camp Sampson, in upper New York State at the southern end of Lake Ithaca, which I thought was a fitting place from which to go off to war.

Training at boot camp, as they called it, was physically gruelling, but I enjoyed it anyway; however, my failure to pay attention in a knot-tying class earned me a minor court-martial known as a 'captain's mast'. My punishment was 100 hours of hard labour, which was to be served after the completion of my basic training. As a result I didn't ship out with my friend Charles Shelmerdine and others in my unit who were assigned to the USS *Dickerson*, an attack transport docked in San Pedro, California. Another good friend, Pete Hansen, was assigned to a destroyer in San Pedro, the main port on the West Coast for the Pacific Fleet.

When I completed my 100 hours of hard labour, repairing the roads in and around the camp, I was assigned to the Electrician's

Mate School at Camp Sampson. Since I had absolutely no interest in what was being taught I flunked the course and didn't receive the automatic promotion to fireman first class given to those who graduated from the school. (Enlisted men who worked mainly in the engine room of a ship were rated firemen, while all others were seamen.) So for the rest of my Navy career I remained a fireman second-class, and wherever I served I was given what in GI slang were known as 'shit details'.

The only friend I made at the school was Bernard Cooper-smith, a Jewish boy from Jersey City, who advised me to go to college after the war, but at the time that seemed an impossible dream.

I was transferred to the US Navy Amphibious Base at Little Creek in Norfolk, Virginia, the Navy's main base on the East Coast. There I was assigned to an LSMR (Landing Ship Medium Rocket), of which only a dozen had been launched so far, all of them now docked at Little Creek awaiting crews.

Shortly after New Year a notice was posted on the bulletin board in our barracks calling for volunteers for a top-secret commando unit, so I immediately signed up, for it seemed more exciting than serving as an apprentice electrician aboard an LSMR. Two days later I found my name on a list of those who had signed up for the commando unit, with orders to muster the following day outside the base headquarters. I informed the captain of my LSMR, and spent the day being examined and interviewed. The next day I found my name on a list of those who would report the following week for shipment to the Amphibious Training Base at Fort Pierce, Florida.

There I learned that our unit was part of a top-secret operation run by the US Naval Group China, a clandestine organization known as SACO, an acronym for the Sino-American Cooperative Organization. SACO had been founded in 1943 through an agreement between President Roosevelt and Generalissimo Chiang Kai-shek, in which the US would aid the Kuomintang Nationalist (KMT) government of China in the war against Japan.

The commander of the Naval Group China was Admiral Milton Miles, an Annapolis graduate who had been director of the Office of Strategic Services (OSS) in the Far East. Miles was also deputy director of SACO, whose director was General Tai Li, Chiang Kai-shek's right-hand man and spymaster. The activities of the Naval Group China included the collection of meteorological data for the US Air Force, gathering Japanese shipping information and other intelligence for the US Navy and Army, as well as training Tai Li's guerrilla force, the Loyal and Patriotic Army (LPA), which had been very effective fighting against the Japanese in China.

The Roger Amphibious unit was established later in 1943, when Miles decided that the US Navy should train its own commandos to go into action with the LPA, and as a result Roger One had been trained and sent to China in 1943, followed by Roger Two in 1944, and then our Roger Three, which was scheduled to be shipped out in the spring of 1945. All of this was very exciting, and as soon as I became fully aware of the great adventure involved I did everything I possibly could to survive the winnowing-out process that began on the first day of training.

Then on 12 April came the news that Franklin Roosevelt had died and that Harry Truman had succeeded him as president. Two weeks later we learned that Hitler was dead, and then on 8 May the news came that Germany had surrendered. The war in Europe was over but fighting continued unabated in the Pacific and the Far East. Scuttlebutt, Navy slang for rumour, said that our outfit would take part in the invasion of Japan along with General Tai Li's LPA, crossing over from China to attack one of the main Japanese islands.

Scuttlebutt also had it that our training would now be terminated so that we could be sent to China as soon as possible, and for once rumour turned out to be true, for a few days later we were informed that we would finish our programme in a week's time, after which we would have a week's home leave before being shipped out. My orders noted that after my leave I should report at Penn Station to be sent by train to the naval base at San Pedro, California, the main port for troop ships leaving for the Pacific and Far East.

At San Pedro we shipped out on the USS *General E. T. Collins*, a troopship carrying 3,000 soldiers. The *Collins* was shorthanded, and since our outfit included men who were qualified in virtually every deck and engine-room rating, we could fill in any vacancies in the regular ship's company, which normally had a crew of about 450. What is more, since all of us were also qualified in gunnery because of our training at Fort Pierce, we would also fill in on the gun crews of the *Collins*, which had four five-inch naval guns, two twin 40-millimetre anti-aircraft guns, and 15 20-millimetre machine guns.

I was assigned to a 20-millimetre machine gun on the starboard side of the flying bridge, the outward extension of the superstructure on either side of the ship's bridge. I took my place in the swivelled seat attached to the gun, which was mounted within a gun-tub on a platform at the outer end of the flying bridge, one of the most exposed positions on the ship. The Chief Gunner's Mate checked me out on the gun, which I had already learned to operate at Fort Pierce. I was to man the gun whenever GQ (General Quarters) was sounded over the PA system, which would be for drills early on our voyage, but when we reached the war zone it would be the real thing, either an air-raid or a submarine alert.

I asked the chief where we were going and how long it would take, and he told me that we were headed for Calcutta via Fremantle-Perth on the western coast of Australia and that it would take 37 days. I wondered why it would take so long, and he said that through most of the voyage, both in the south-west Pacific and in the Indian Ocean, we would be continually zigzagging during the day to avoid Japanese submarines. We would also be stopping for three days in Fremantle, where we would replenish our fuel and water supplies and would pick up an escort of two Australian corvettes to accompany us through the Indian Ocean, for we would be within range of Japanese air and naval bases, particularly when we passed between the Burmese coast and the Andaman and Nicobar Islands.

Then I heard my name on the PA system, ordering me to report to the engine room. I went back to the main deck, which was swarming with GIs making their way from the gangway to their compartments, and I forced my way through the crowd, trying

to make my way down to the engine room, whose hatch I finally
found on the aft deck. I descended by a series of almost vertical
metal ladders, hardly using my feet but sliding down the hand rails
to the engine room, where I reported to the officer in charge. He
checked my name on his list and turned me over to the chief electrician's mate, who told me that I would report to him every day
with the other electrician's mates, eight hours on and eight hours
off, which meant that every other day I would be on duty for 16 of
the 24 hours.

My main duty on watch would be to monitor the twin genera-
tors that powered the *Collins*, making sure that they remained in
balance so that neither of them drew too much power and tripped
the main circuit breaker, which would leave the ship dead in the
water. I would also be given other jobs, which I knew would be
'shit details', since as a fireman second-class I was the lowest-rank-
ing man in the engine room and not even ship's company at that.
I was dead right, for the chief said that my first job would be to
clean the bilges, the crawl space beneath the deck plates of the
engine room. And when I was finished with that I would be given
a pot of red lead to paint the interior of the ship's hull where
it enclosed the main boilers. He showed me the rope harness in
which I would be suspended from pulleys between the hull and
the boilers and said with sadistic pleasure that if the ship was hit
by a torpedo it was a toss-up as to whether I would be drowned or
scalded to death by high-pressure steam.

The only time I had off was Sunday morning, when I went to
mass in the chapel given by the Catholic chaplain, Father Ryan. I
stayed after mass to talk with him and our conversation turned to
books. He apologized for having none to lend me at the moment
as they were all checked out. He asked me what I had been reading
before I went into the Navy, and I told him that I had just finished
the *Odyssey*. He said that I should go on to read the *Iliad* and after
that continue with Herodotus and the other classics of Greek and
Roman literature.

I asked Father Ryan for advice on what I might read to educate
myself after I left the Navy, for there was little chance that I would
go back to school. He looked through his desk and handed me the

catalogue for the Great Books programme at St John's College in Annapolis, Maryland, which he had attended before going into the seminary. The curriculum began with Homer's *Iliad* and *Odyssey* and ended with James Joyce's *Ulysses*, and included not only the Great Books but also works about the authors themselves and the times in which they lived. I asked him if I could borrow the catalogue and he said I could keep it, for he had used it to the fullest in his own self-education and now it should be passed on to someone else who would benefit from it. I took the catalogue back to my compartment where I tucked it away in the bottom of my sea bag, with the thought that some time in the unforeseeable future I might have a chance to read the Great Books.

We stopped for three days in Fremantle, the port of Perth, to take on supplies and refill our fuel and water tanks. The PA announced that all the troops on the ship would be given a few hours' shore leave and that we should go to our muster stations and prepare to disembark. I was due to stand watch in the engine room but the engineering officer gave me permission to go ashore. We assembled on the dock, staggering from the unaccustomed feel of terra firma under our feet instead of a rolling deck after nearly a month at sea.

We then proceeded to march into town four abreast, with our outfit leading the way, since we were US Navy, with the Marine detachment from the *Collins* riding herd on us to make sure no one escaped. We marched along what appeared to be the main street leading in from the port, and everyone in town seemed to turn out to cheer us as we passed. The parade ended at the football stadium, where we were turned loose for a couple of hours to run around or walk or just talk with the locals as we pleased, with most of the GIs heading for the girls, who were all chaperoned. The townspeople had provided free sandwiches, cakes, candy and soft drinks, though the GIs would have preferred beer or booze. The town band played what for them and me were old favourites, including 'The Wild Colonial Boy', a song about a lad from the Dingle Peninsula who becomes a lawless Robin Hood in Australia.

The next day we continued to take on supplies and to top up

our fuel and water tanks. We then weighed anchor the following morning, with a crowd of townspeople waving farewell, along with a detachment of Australian veterans of World War I, while the town band played 'Waltzing Matilda'. I realized that Australians were much closer to the war than we Americans, particularly here in Fremantle, where ships like ours were constantly sailing off into the combat zone.

We were escorted by two Australian corvettes and a series of fighter planes, which flew out from air bases along the west coast of Australia. I had a good view of it all, since I had to man my anti-aircraft gun from before dawn until nightfall. We soon left behind our Australian air cover, and I was told the only air bases along our route would be those of the Japanese in Burma near the Andaman and Nicobar Islands, which extended northwards from Sumatra for some 700 miles into the Bay of Bengal.

The heightened alert lasted till we were well clear of the Andaman and Nicobar Islands, after which the two Australian corvettes split off from our convoy, presumably heading back to Fremantle. Nevertheless we manned our guns throughout the day, and our troopship continued to zigzag because there was still a danger from Japanese submarines.

A few days later I emerged on deck after morning mess and noticed that the colour of the sea had changed from clear blue to muddy brown, with clumps of vegetation and other flotsam forming a scum on the surface of the water. I asked one of the ship's company about this and he said that we were looking at effluents of the Hooghly River, the branch of the Ganges that flows through Calcutta into the Bay of Bengal. He said that we would soon be picking up a pilot who would take us up the Hooghly to Calcutta, where we would be docking before nightfall.

The pilot came aboard about an hour later, and with him were half a dozen barefoot 'natives', as the old travelogues I had read called them, all of them carrying beads and other trinkets which were quickly bought up by the GIs. I reported to my gun post but was soon informed over the intercom that I should secure my weapon and its ammunition. After I did that I remained on the flying bridge as the *Collins* made its way up the Hooghly.

It was dusk by the time we reached our dock on the east bank of the river, downstream from the centre of Calcutta. The Hooghly was teeming with traffic, including freighters, lighters, barges and junks, as well as marigold-covered rafts carrying what I was told were corpses cremated at the burning ghats along the river upstream from our dock.

Then an announcement came over the PA for all troops to go below and pack up their gear and prepare to disembark. I went below to my troop compartment, which was now packed with GIs getting ready to leave, and emptied my foot-locker and stowed my gear, making sure that the catalogue for the Great Books programme was safely tucked away in the bottom of my sea bag.

It took me the better part of an hour to make my way up on deck, for the passageways were jammed with GIs struggling under the weight of 40lb packs, which were at least strapped to their backs, whereas I had to balance my equally heavy sea bag on my left shoulder while I held my ditty bag in my right hand, which made it difficult to climb the almost vertical ladders that led up from the troop compartment.

The PA announced that the Naval Group China would muster on the quarterdeck, and so I headed that way and saw our commanding officer for the first time since we left San Pedro. After we were mustered he told us that we would be the first to disembark, but still it took another hour before we made our way down the gangway and lined up on the dock, where we were herded on to Indian Army trucks. No one told us where we were going, but from watching the road signs, which were in both English and Indian, I figured we were heading for an airport with the funny name of Dumdum. We finally stopped near Dumdum Airport at a base called Camp Knox, the Calcutta headquarters of the US Naval Group China.

Some of the men in our barracks were from Roger One and Roger Two, the two contingents of our outfit that had preceded us at Fort Pierce. They told us that they were waiting to be flown up to Kunming, the capital of Yunnan province in China, but that there were only a few seats available every day on the 'Gooney Birds', the C40 transport planes that flew over the 'Hump', the enormously high mountains of northern Burma, the south-eastern extension of the Himalayas.

The only other way of getting up to China was by the Ledo–Stillwell Road, which had been built by US Army engineers from the north-eastern tip of India down through northern Burma as the Japanese retreated, finally linking up with the old Burma Road early in 1945, so that convoys could go all the way to Kunming, from where there was a good road to SACO's headquarters at Chengdu. Scuttlebutt had it that our Amphibious Roger unit would be with the LPA in the final offensive of the war, attacking the Japanese in China, while the American and British forces launched an amphibious assault against the home islands of Japan. This made me all the more anxious to get up into China before it was too late, and I listened for word of the truck convoy that was supposedly being organized to take us to Kunming over the Ledo–Stillwell–Burma Road.

The following day a notice was posted on the bulletin board announcing that a convoy was being formed to carry ammunition and supplies to SACO headquarters in China, with a call for volunteers who could drive a truck. I signed up immediately, though I had never driven anything other than a rented bicycle.

Those who volunteered were ordered to meet in the drill hall with Commander John Boots, the officer who would command the convoy. He said that everyone who had volunteered, 18 officers and 170 enlisted men, would go with the convoy, which would leave in a couple of days. There would be two men in each truck, he said, one to drive and the other to 'ride shotgun', and we would be expected to spell one another. He told us to 'buddy up' and passed around a list so that we could sign up, two to a truck.

I signed up with my friend Ed Hill, who at least had driven his father's car a few times. We were told that the US Army Quartermaster Corps would send one of their men to the motor pool at Camp Knox that evening to give driving instructions to any who needed it. Ed and I were the only volunteers who signed up for the instruction, and after evening mess we went to the motor pool for our lesson. A black sergeant was there with one of the six-by-six trucks that would make up the convoy, and he spent an hour

showing us how to 'double clutch' and to use the low-low gear that
we would need for the worst stretches of the Burma Road, which
he himself had driven a few months earlier. Ed was a quick learner
but I was hopeless, the sergeant told me, shaking his head. And so
Ed and I decided that he would do all the driving, at least in the
beginning, while I would ride shotgun.

We were told that we would be informed about the convoy's
departure and that we should be prepared to leave at any moment.
Meanwhile each of us was issued a carbine rifle with bayonet and
a 45-calibre pistol, along with ammunition for both weapons, as
well as a bayonet, a combat knife, a helmet and helmet-liner, an
entrenching tool, a foul-weather jacket, a waterproof poncho, a
pup-tent, a mess-kit and canteen, and a supply of virtually inedible
K rations.

We learned that on the first stage of our journey our trucks
would be carried on flatcars of the Bengal–Assam Railway, which
would take us up to the head of rail in the North-East Frontier,
where India borders Tibet, China and Burma. There we would
drive to the frontier post at Ledo, the town that gave its name to
the Ledo–Stillwell Road, which led south from there through the
mountains of northern Burma to the point where it joined the old
Burma Road, north-east of Mandalay. There we would cross into
China and drive to Kunming, the capital of Yunnan province,
from where we would go on to Chengdu, a drive of more than
1,000 miles.

The convoy set out from Calcutta on 2 August 1945 and arrived
in Kunming on 31 August. En route we had come in contact with
the defeated Japanese Army in Mongyu, the last US Army base on
the Burma Road before the Chinese border. We were all assigned
watches on the defence perimeter around the camp at night, along
with the Kachin scouts who worked with the US Army, for Japanese stragglers had been caught as they attempted to sneak into
the base at night trying to find food. About halfway through my
watch I suddenly heard someone screaming in the darkness to
my left. It went on for a few seconds, ending in a gurgling sound
before it stopped abruptly. I was absolutely terrified and held my
pistol at the ready as I stared into the darkness, waiting for some-

one to emerge. But I saw nothing, and when my relief took over at four o'clock I returned to our truck. On reflection, I figured that a Kachin scout had cut a Jap's throat, in which case he had added another pair of severed ears to his collection, as was their custom.

The following day we crossed the border between Burma and China, and in the two days following crossed the Salween and Mekong Rivers on bridges recently built by US Army engineers. Two days after crossing the Mekong we were caught by the monsoon, which turned the mile-high road into a sea of mud, and we were benighted short of the US Army camp at Yongping where we were to spend the night. When our truck reached the approach road to the camp an ensign ordered me to stand at the roadside with a flashlight. I did as I was ordered and Ed drove off behind him into the camp, though after they left I could barely see where the side road led off from the Burma Road.

The trucks behind us came along every minute or so at first, and as they approached I waved my flashlight to direct them into the camp. Then the interval between trucks became longer and longer as I waited in mud up to my ankles, and although I was wearing my poncho I was as drenched as if I had been swimming in my clothes. One of the trucks got stuck in the mud as it turned into the side road, though the driver did manage to manoeuvre it so that it wasn't blocking the way. The driver and his buddy decided to abandon the truck there for the time being and walk on into the camp, locking the cab since they had stowed their weapons there.

I was already so drenched that it hardly mattered, but I thought I would take cover under the truck, where I would at least be out of the rain. So I crawled under the tailgate and wrapped myself up in my poncho, emerging whenever I heard the roar of an approaching truck so that I could wave my flashlight to direct the driver into the camp road. Finally, after a long interval during which no more stragglers arrived, I crawled back under the stalled truck and prepared to remain there till told otherwise.

I'm sure no other trucks arrived during the night, for although I dozed off I would have been awakened by the roar of their motors. When I did wake up I could see from under the truck that the sun was shining, though the road was a sea of wet mud. Then I became aware that someone standing behind the truck was nudging me with his boot, and I crawled out to find a tall black American soldier standing over me, his stripes and insignia identifying him as a top sergeant in the US Army Engineers. He had a big smile on his face as he looked down and helped me to my feet. 'Wake up, soldier,' he said, 'the fucking war's over!'

He told me that last night on the US Army news broadcast it was announced that the Japanese government had surrendered unconditionally earlier that day, 15 August 1945. On the way into the camp the sergeant told me that on 6 August the US had dropped a powerful new weapon called an atom bomb on the Japanese city of Hiroshima, obliterating its centre and killing a large part of its population. Three days later an even more powerful atom bomb had destroyed Nagasaki and incinerated everyone in the city centre. President Truman had demanded that the Japanese surrender unconditionally and they announced their submission yesterday, with the details of the formal end of hostilities to be worked out in the coming days. We had been out of touch with the rest of the world since we left Ledo, and so we knew nothing of the events that had led up to this apocalypse.

That day everyone in the Yongping camp got very drunk, including the pet monkey that had become the base mascot. We spent the rest of the day sleeping it off, and then after evening mess the party started again. But I hit the sack, as did everyone in our outfit, for we were all exhausted. We would have another very difficult stretch the next day, when we would drive 121 miles to Yunnanyi, crossing the Quingshuillang Mountains at an altitude of 9,200 feet.

We started out after morning mess and by noon were high in the mountains, snaking from one vertiginous ridge to another, with the edges of the road partially washed away in many places by the monsoon. We were making our way cautiously along the side of a steep canyon when the truck in front of us stopped so suddenly that we almost skidded into it. I jumped out to learn what had happened, and I saw that the second truck in front of us had skidded off the road and tumbled down into the canyon, where I could see it lying on its side among the trees and underbrush far below.

A group of us climbed down to the wreck and found the driver unconscious behind the wheel, while the other man in the truck, who had been thrown clear, was conscious but bleeding profusely from a gash in his forehead. I recognized the driver as Coxswain John Jacob Esau and the other man as Ensign Dawson. We were soon joined by the two pharmacist's mates, one of whom looked after Esau and the other Dawson. They strapped Esau in a stretcher tied to the cable of our emergency vehicle, which then winched it up to the road as we lifted it along the way. Dawson was brought up the same way, and then when they were laid out in the ambulance it set off for Yunnanyi where there was a small field hospital.

When we arrived in Yunnanyi we were told that Esau and Dawson had been sent off to Kunming in a regular ambulance with a doctor and a nurse in attendance. Dawson was stable but Esau had a fractured pelvis along with internal injuries and was in a critical condition.

The next day we drove over the pass at Tienatze Miao Po, the highest point on the Burma Road, 9,200 feet above sea level, from where I could see the snow-plumed summit of the Snow Dragon Mountain and beyond it the peaks of the Himalayas in easternmost Tibet. During the next four days we drove across the mile-high Yunnan Plateau, a cloud-rimmed saucer, where for the first time in a month we were clear of the jungle, the monsoon rains, the mosquitoes and the leeches.

At Xiaguan the Burma Road was joined by two other roads: the one from the north was the old caravan trail from Tibet, while the other from the south was a continuation of this route down to southern Yunnan and Burma. We were told that the Chinese divisions that had been fighting in southern Burma were now being evacuated along this route, turning onto the Burma Road and heading for Kunming, marching throughout the day without stopping.

When we set out the next morning on the last stage of our journey to Kunming, a distance of 120 miles, we found ourselves driving between two seemingly endless columns of Chinese soldiers, their rifles slung over their shoulders, hardly glancing at us as we passed. Most of them had no shoes, and their tattered uniforms hung like shrouds from their emaciated bodies as they staggered along, some of them barely able to walk. Every now and again we had to swerve to avoid dead Chinese soldiers lying face-up in the road, their bodies swollen and covered with flies, unnoticed by their comrades as they marched impassively by, heading for Kunming, so we were told, to march in a parade to celebrate Chiang Kai-shek's victory over the Japanese.

It was dark by the time we reached Kunming, where we were met by a US Army jeep that led our convoy to where we would camp for the night. Our campsite was on the edge of the airfield on the southern side of Kunming, where we set up our tents just beyond the end of the runway. I was so exhausted that I got into my sleeping bag soon after I finished my K rations, but it took me a long time to fall asleep because of the succession of aeroplanes coming in to land just over our tents. They were still landing when I awoke at dawn, most of them C46 transport planes that had been carrying troops and supplies over the Hump from India to China for the past three years.

When we mustered, Commander Boots said that he had just received word that the Japanese were going to sign a formal document of surrender aboard the battleship USS *Missouri* in Tokyo Bay on 2 September 1945, in two days' time. We would drive to Camp Hank Gribbins, a SACO base on the outskirts of Kunming, where we would receive orders for our individual assignments. Some of us would go on with the convoy to Chengdu in Sichuan province, where SACO had its main headquarters. Each truck would now only have one driver, for since hostilities had ended it was no longer necessary to have an armed guard. That meant that about half of us would be flown over the Hump to Calcutta to be shipped back to the US, but he said that the details were still uncertain.

He told us that most of our outfit would be put up at Camp Hank Gribbins, but due to lack of space a few of us would be temporarily housed in the main camp of the Chinese First Army

Group, where General Tai Li's LPA was based. An ensign read out the list and I found that I was one of five assigned to the Chinese Army base, to which we were taken by a Chinese lieutenant. He assigned each of us to a hut together with a Chinese soldier who would act as our interpreter. Mine was a private in the LPA who introduced himself in basic English as Ching Ging Too, which he wrote out for me in both English and Chinese.

Ching led me to our tent, whose only furnishings were two US Army-issue folding cots. He offered to take me to the mess hall, but said that the food was pretty bad, so I broke out two K rations and cans of fruit cocktail and grapefruit juice I had stashed away from our cargo. I had also smuggled in two bottles of rice wine that I had managed to buy in Kunming.

Ching said that there was going to be a military review at the base on 2 September to mark the official Japanese surrender, and he expected that all of Kunming would join in the celebration. He suspected that things might get out of hand in town, for there would be tens of thousands of armed Chinese soldiers on the loose and many of them would be drunk and disorderly.

The review was held early in the afternoon of 2 September on the huge drill field of the base. Ching identified the various contingents of the LPA and of the regular Chinese Nationalist Army as they passed in review, led by their generals and other officers. I was hoping to catch a glimpse of General Tai Li, the commander-in-chief of the LPA, but Ching said that he was probably still in Chongding along with SACO's American commander, Admiral Milton Miles. Towards the end of the review Ching pointed out the women's battalion of the LPA and said that most of them were from the Nakhi, Miao and Bai minorities in Yunnan and Sichuan provinces.

After the review, which lasted all afternoon, Ching and I went back to our tent and had supper: rancid spam, rock-hard cheese which I carved with my bayonet, and year-old fruit cocktail, washed down with grapefruit juice whose smell reminded me of hydrochloric acid in the chemistry lab at Brooklyn Tech. We then opened the two bottles of rice wine, pulling out the plugs of waxed paper that served as corks, and toasted the end of a war, which in China had lasted for ten years. As we drank our wine, Ching began to sing what he said was an old folksong of the Tibetan borderlands which I found quite beautiful though I didn't understand a word of it. When he finished he said that it was called 'Waves Washing the Sand', meaning that time passes like the waves of the sea lapping upon the shore, and memory is the faint pattern the ripples leave on the sand, soon to be washed away.

Our party was interrupted by a burst of fireworks, and we rushed out of the tent. I could see that there were two separate firework displays, one on the drill field of our camp and the other in the city below, in what Ching said was the main square of Kunming. The displays lasted for about 15 minutes, and when they ended we went back into our hut to continue our party.

Soon afterwards our party was interrupted again by what we thought at first was a resumption of the fireworks, which surprised us. When we went out to see what was going on we quickly realized that it was not fireworks we were hearing but gunfire, including bursts of machine-gun bullets and cannonades of artillery fire, sounding as if there was a battle being fought between the two sides of the camp. We went back inside the tent and took cover, for we could hear bullets whizzing over our heads. I crawled into my sleeping bag and lay down on the ground under my cot, for whatever protection that might furnish, having brought my rice wine with me. Ching did the same, and as we sipped our wine we chatted during intervals in the gunfire until we dozed off.

When I awoke the next morning Ching was already up and he showed me about a dozen bullet holes in the sides of our hut, some of them very close to where we had been. He said that what we had heard was a fixed battle between two armies in the camp, one commanded by General Lung Han, the Yunnan warlord, and another by General Tu Yu-ming, one of Chiang Kai-shek's right-hand men. It seems, from what Ching had heard, that Chiang Kai-shek had ordered Tu Yu-ming to take control of Kunming before the Americans pulled out, and though the battle was a standoff, Ching was sure that the two armies would resume fighting before long. He was right, and years later I learned that the brief battle was part of the prelude to the Chinese Civil War.

Later that morning a US Army truck came with orders to take the five of us from SACO down to Camp Hank Gribbens, for it was obviously too dangerous for us to remain in the Chinese Army base. So Ching Ging Too and I said goodbye, promising to try to get in touch with one another after we returned to our homes, though I knew that there was little likelihood that we would ever see each another again.

Camp Hank Gribbins was in the village of Hai-ling, ten miles south of Kunming, where five of us moved into a barracks with the rest of our outfit. Three days later we learned that John Jacob Esau had died of his injuries in the US Army hospital in Kunming. The following day we buried him on a hillside above Kunming, where a small military cemetery had been laid out for the American servicemen who had died in Yunnan during the war. A US Army chaplain conducted a brief service, then a bugler sounded 'Taps' while a guard of honour fired a volley as his coffin was lowered into the grave. Commander Boots took the American flag that had covered the grave and said that he would make sure that it was delivered to Esau's parents. I wondered how they would feel when they learned that their son had passed away four days after the official ending of hostilities, probably the last American fatality of World War II, buried half a world away from his home.

Two days later a notice was posted on the bulletin board informing us of our next assignment. I learned that I was one of a group of 30 who would be flown back to Calcutta on 15 September, while all the others in the convoy, including Ed Hill, would drive the trucks on to Chengdu, starting the following day. There would be only one driver in each truck, which was why I had been left off the list of those going on with the convoy, for Commander Boots knew I couldn't drive. Nevertheless, I was very disappointed, for scuttlebutt had it that at Chengdu the trucks would be put on barges that would take them and their drivers down the Yangtze to Shanghai, from where they would be shipped back to the US. The rumour turned out to be true, as I learned several months later when I received a postcard that my friend Ron Foster had sent me from Shanghai.

Around noon on 15 September I said goodbye to Ed and my

other friends who were going on with the convoy to Chengdu. The 30 of us who were leaving were taken in trucks to the airfield. There we boarded a C46 cargo plane, one of the aircraft that had carried troops and supplies from India to China throughout the war. Hundreds of them had crashed or been shot down while flying over the Hump during the past three years, but at least now we wouldn't have to worry about encountering Japanese fighter planes or anti-aircraft fire. But I was still very nervous when I boarded the C46, for I had never flown before.

We sat on canvas bucket-seats facing one another across the central aisle. The sergeant who was flight engineer told us that the flight might be very rough, which was why they called flying the Hump 'Operation Vomit'. He said that we should put on our foul-weather jackets since we would be flying at 28,000 feet and it would be quite cold, for the cabin was not pressurized, which also meant that we might have trouble breathing.

The sergeant said that we would be taking off as soon as the last passengers arrived, which puzzled me, since there were no seats left. Soon a black corporal in the US Army Transportation Corps came up the ramp leading a line of half a dozen mules, which he tethered to a rope along the aisle of the aircraft. The corporal laughed when he saw the expressions on our faces and said that the US Army was abandoning trucks and jeeps as it pulled out of China but not its mules, which had carried supplies and weapons all through the war and were being brought back to the US to spend their remaining days in honourable retirement.

As soon as the mules were tethered we took off, and after a few minutes of sheer terror I relaxed and tried to enjoy the scenery, craning my neck to look out of the window behind me, since the view through the window across the aisle was blocked by the hind-quarters of the mule tethered in front of me.

The flight from Kunming to Calcutta took about four hours, whereas our journey overland had taken more than a month. After we landed at Dumdum Airport we had to wait for the mules to be led off before we disembarked ourselves.

I was immediately struck by a wave of moist heat, which was all the more uncomfortable since I was wearing my foul-weather jacket, surrounded by the seething mass of humanity that is Calcutta, so profoundly different from the cool and sparsely inhabited high-lands of Yunnan that we had left only a few hours before. We had come down from the roof of the world to the inferno at its core.

We were put on trucks which took us back to Camp Knox, where we were all assigned bunks in one of the SACO barracks, which seemed like a luxury hotel after the primitive accommo-dation we had endured, and we showered for the first time in a month.

On the morning after our return to Calcutta we turned in our weapons and ammunition and then mustered with the other personnel of SACO at Camp Knox. We were told that soon we would all be shipped back to the US and that in a day or two lists would be posted with our new assignments.

Those of us who had just returned from China were marched off to the infirmary for a physical examination, which was more thorough than usual, for we had been exposed to bush typhus and dengue fever, which were endemic in the China–India–Burma theatre, not to mention malaria. We were all given a clean bill of health, though every one of us had lost a lot of weight and was suffering from sores caused by leeches and insect bites, not to mention the fungus known as jungle rot whose marks I still bear on my right ankle. We were infested with lice, so that all our hair was shaved off and our heads, armpits and crotches were painted with purple ointment. Our skin had turned yellow from the atabrine tablets we had been taking to ward off malaria, so we were indeed a sorry sight.

Six days later a notice was pinned on the bulletin board saying that all the personnel of Amphibious Roger at Camp Knox would be shipped out on 28 September, when we would embark on the troopship USS *General W. F. Hase*, which would take us to New York via the Indian Ocean, the Suez Canal, the Mediterranean and the Atlantic.

Since we were US Navy personnel, we were the first to board the *Hase* on the morning of 28 September. The *Hase* was a sister ship of the *Collins*, the troopship that had taken us from San Pedro to Calcutta, and so the two were identical. I was relieved to find that I was not assigned to work in the engine room, as I had been aboard the *Collins*, and since the war was over there was no need to man the anti-aircraft guns. I could just relax and enjoy the voyage.

I kept track of our overall progress through the ship's daily four-page newspaper, *Westward Ho*, which on its masthead each day gave the distances to New York and Calcutta. I still have a crumbling copy of *Westward Ho* dated 5 October 1945, with the distances given as 'Miles to New York 7,959' and 'Miles to Calcutta 2,056', along with an apology from the staff for having given the mileages incorrectly for the two previous days.

The last issue of *Westward Ho* came out on 26 October 1945. The headline informed us that we would be arriving in New York the following day. Nine other troopships would be arriving with us, four of them having been diverted from the Pacific via the Panama Canal. There would be a gala reception for us in New York harbour and the welcoming committee would be headed by President Truman.

It was about noon when we finally entered the harbour, where a fireboat was making an aquatic display and a launch carried a brass band of WACs, the Women's Army Corps, playing patriotic songs, while all the ships in the port repeatedly sounded their horns. A launch came beside the *Hase* and put aboard a number of civilians, including women, and from their notebooks and cameras I figured they were journalists.

We followed the other troopships in turn as they passed the reviewing stand at Battery Park, where another army band was playing. I borrowed a pair of binoculars from one of the crew on the bridge, and as we passed Battery Park I scanned the reviewing stand, where I could see President Truman waving to us along with a crowd of dignitaries.

I realized that our welcome home had been stage-managed for the publicity it gave the president, for the moment we were past the reviewing stand we were no longer the centre of attention, just ten troopships crammed with thousands of war-weary GIs anxious to get home and resume their lives. But it didn't bother me in the least because for a short while I had been part of a truly historic occasion, which in my imagination I compared to the return of the victorious British Fleet after the Battle of Trafalgar. And as our ship pulled into the dock at Pier 88 I could take pride in the fact that I had just completed a journey around the world.

As soon as we were all on the dock we mustered and Commander Boots told us that we would be taken to the US Armed Guard Center near the Brooklyn Navy Yard, where we would be processed for discharge or further assignment. He explained the points system used to determine the order in which we would be discharged, with a point for each year of our age, another point for every year that we had been in the Navy, and extra points for time spent in combat as well as for any decorations we had received, all of which seemed to put me at the bottom of the list, so I figured it would be a while before I got out.

We then boarded trucks which had neither windows nor seats in the back, more suitable for cattle than humans, which led me to moo like a cow. Soon I had everyone mooing and laughing at the same time, while we tried to keep our footing as the truck lurched through the streets of Manhattan on its way to Brooklyn. When I stopped mooing and laughing I felt a deep sense of resentment, wondering if President Truman knew that some of the servicemen he had just welcomed home from the war were now being trans- ported like cattle on their way to a barn.

We were in fact going to a barn of sorts, for the Armed Guard Center turned out to be an old trolley-barn, converted into a barracks for the US Navy personnel who manned the guns on American freighters in the Atlantic during World War II. We were given bunks and told to check the bulletin board to learn our next assignment, but in the meanwhile we were confined to base.

There were no facilities for making telephone calls, for the Armed Guard Center was just a temporary facility for transfer- ring naval personnel from one ship or shore station to another, with no conveniences or frills of any kind. In any event, no one in my extended family had a telephone, nor did anyone I knew, and besides that I was probably going to be shipped out again right way, so there was nothing I could do.

The following day I checked the bulletin board and found my name on the roster assigned to troopship AP 145, the USS

*General Harry Taylor*, a sister ship of the *Hase* and the *Collins* that had entered New York harbour the day before in our flotilla. The notice said that those assigned to the *Taylor* should report to the duty officer at 10am the next day with all their gear ready to ship out.

Next morning I reported to the duty officer, along with about a dozen other men, all of them about my age and none of them looking very happy. After he checked off our names we were herded aboard the same kind of truck that had brought me to the Armed Guard Center, but this time I didn't moo like a cow, for I no longer saw anything funny in my situation.

The truck brought us to Pier 90, where we boarded the *Taylor*. I reported to the chief electrician's mate, a Puerto Rican named Gonzalez, who led me to my quarters. After I stowed away my gear Chief Gonzalez brought me to the mustering place of the electrician's mates, a compartment at the stern of the ship, below the fantail deck and just forward of the twin screws, the two propellers. There he introduced me to the other electrician's mates, two petty officers and two firemen first-class. The chief was regular Navy, and from his three hash marks I could tell that he had been in for at least 12 years and that he would serve until his retirement, usually after 20 years. The other electrician's mates were, like me, USNR, US Navy Reserves, and we would serve until we had enough points. They were all somewhat older than me and had been in the Navy longer, and they expected to be discharged in the next few months.

Chief Gonzalez told me that on our coming voyage, which would begin the following day, we would go first to Le Havre in France, from where we would take German prisoners of war to Bremerhaven in Germany. Then we would bring GIs from Bremerhaven back to New York. He told me that my duties would include checking all the electric motors on the ship as well as the tilt-indicator, the degaussing apparatus for protection against magnetic mines, the remotely controlled auxiliary steering gear and the searchlight on the foremast. I told him frankly that I was totally incompetent in matters electrical, since I had failed my course in the Electrician's Mate School, and all I knew was how to operate an anti-aircraft gun and blow things up. The chief was very patient and said he would teach me everything I needed to know. He gave me circuit diagrams for all the electric motors on the ship, as well as instruction manuals for the tilt-indicator, degaussing apparatus, remotely controlled steering gear and searchlight.

On our first voyage we brought 5,000 German prisoners from Le Havre to Bremerhaven, and then took aboard 3,000 GIs. The next day, as we headed through the North Sea towards the English Channel, we ran into the worst storm I had ever experienced, and all the GIs were ordered to stay below. Those of the crew who had to go out on deck had to be attached to safety lines and wear life jackets, for the decks were as often as not awash when the ship hit a big wave.

The storm grew even worse that night, and when I finished my eight-to-midnight watch in the engine room I was almost washed overboard making my way back to my bunk. I was so exhausted that I fell asleep almost immediately, despite the violent pitching and rolling of the ship which set everything movable sliding across the decks. But then I was awakened by a tremendous crash and almost thrown out of my bunk, and my first thought was that we had struck a mine, for we had been warned that many of them had broken loose from mine fields in the North Sea and the English Channel.

A General Quarters sounded over the PA and I dressed quickly to go on deck. When I went out on deck I could see that the bow of our ship had been damaged, though I couldn't tell if it had been caused by an explosion or by the sea. Chief Gonzales said that we would be part of a damage-control unit to examine the bow and make whatever emergency repairs we could. We found that the damage had been caused by the sea, which had ripped open a large hole on the starboard side of the hull near the bow. The officer in charge of the damage-control unit said that we were in no immediate danger of sinking, since the internal bulkheads were watertight and confined any intake of sea water to the small forward compartment, which was being pumped out. He went on to say that we would be changing course to head up along the east coast of England where we would be shielded from the full force of the storm.

The machinist's mates rigged up a metal plate over the hole in the bow and sealed the leak, after which Chief Gonzalez put our unit to work checking the electrical apparatus and repairing any damage. While this was going on I was relieved to see that the storm was abating, with the wind diminishing in intensity and the waves no longer as high and powerful.

By the time the repairs were finished it was beginning to grow light, and since the storm was now virtually over I decided to remain out on deck by the prow to see where we were. Soon after sunrise I spotted land to the north-west, and as it took form I could see that we were heading into the calm waters of a large bay, where a number of fishing boats were heading towards us. One of the boats came beside us just as we dropped anchor, and an older man in oilskins waved up to me. I waved back to him and asked, 'Where the hell are we?' He smiled and said, 'You're in the Humber, lad!'

When the repairs were finished the captain of the *Taylor* and the chief engineering officer came to inspect the hull. They decided that the ship was seaworthy, and since the weather forecast was favourable we set out again in a couple of hours, resuming our voyage across the Atlantic to New York.

After we docked in New York and disembarked the GIs, we were informed that we would remain in port until our bow was fully repaired. All of us with engineering ratings would be needed for this work and would not be granted liberty, particularly since many of the crew were now eligible for discharge and their departure would leave the *Taylor* short-handed. And so once again I was back in New York and unable to go home and see my family.

We finally left New York in mid-January, once again scheduled to pick up German prisoners at Le Havre and bring them to Bremerhaven, from where we would take GIs back to New York. That voyage passed uneventfully, as did the two that followed, though on all of them we ran into Atlantic storms.

After each voyage we docked in New York only long enough to unload the troops we were carrying, and so I never received leave to see my family. When we began what would be my fourth round-trip across the Atlantic on the *Taylor* we were told that this would be our last, since by then, mid-April 1946, most of the GIs in Germany who were eligible for discharge had been brought home and we would be bringing the last lot of German prisoners back from Le Havre to Bremerhaven.

When we docked at Le Havre on our last voyage the PA announced that all the ship's company except a skeleton crew would be given three days' liberty to see Paris. My name was on the list and so I got to spend a weekend in Paris, travelling there and back by troop train from Le Havre.

Waiters in the sidewalk cafés on the Champs Élysées, Montparnasse and Saint-Germain told us that we had brought with us the first spring days since the end of the war, whose effects I could see in the bullet-marks on the facades of buildings, in the scarcity of food, wine and other things to buy, in the threadbare and out-of-fashion clothes the women wore, and in the almost total absence of men of military age. But the city was coming to life again and regaining its old gaiety, or so it seemed to me on Saturday night in Pigalle, when some of us made the rounds in the company of Senegalese troops in the French Army who were also seeing Paris for the first time.

We sailed from Le Havre after the German prisoners were brought aboard, the last to leave France by sea. At Bremerhaven we took aboard both GIs and German war brides and some war babies as well, probably the first time that an American troopship had ever carried children. I was allowed a day's liberty in Bremerhaven, which was as sombre as Paris was gay, the city still in ruins and its inhabitants showing the bitterness of humiliating defeat.

When we arrived in New York I was informed that I now had enough points to be discharged and that I would be taken to the US Naval Separation Center on Lido Beach, Long Island, where I spent less than 48 hours.

While I was there I spotted Pete Hansen, one of my friends from boot camp at Sampson Naval Training Center. We embraced one another and swapped stories about what we'd been doing since we left Sampson. Pete told me that he had been on a destroyer in the Pacific and that he had been in action in the landings on Okinawa. I told him that I had originally been assigned to an

LSMR, one of a dozen that were slated to go to Okinawa, and I asked him if he had seen any. He said that he had seen the wreckage of six of the 12 LSMRs on the beach at Okinawa, all of them destroyed by Japanese artillery.

I asked Pete if he had any news of Charles Shelmerdine and our other friends in boot camp who'd shipped out on the USS *Dickerson*. He was silent for a moment before handing me a copy of *Our Navy* magazine, telling me that I could read all about it there. Then he said goodbye, for his train was about to leave, and that's the last I ever saw of him.

The lead article in the magazine was about the *Dickerson* and her role in the amphibious landings on Okinawa, which began on 1 April 1945. According to the article, on the second day of the landings a Japanese kamikaze made a long, low glide and sheared off the tops of the *Dickerson's* two smokestacks before crashing into the base of her bridge, toppling her mast and starting intense gasoline fires. Almost simultaneously, another Japanese plane dropped a 500lb bomb on the five-inch gun in the forecastle, killing all the gun crew and tearing a hole in the deck almost the whole length of the ship. The article gave the names of the gun crew, and among them I saw that of Seaman Second-Class Charles Shelmerdine, aged 18.

I was so shocked that it took a while before I could continue reading the article, which went on to say that 54 of the *Dickerson's* crew of 113 had been killed, including her commanding officer, and that the ship was scuttled two days later with most of her dead crewmen and captain still aboard. Those in the gun crew besides Charles included two other friends from boot camp, Ed Grant and a Greek-American named Spiro, both 18.

I was still somewhat shaken when I was interrogated by the yeoman's mate who processed my records. While he was clacking away with one finger on his typewriter I did a rapid calculation in my head, as I had when I was interviewed for my job at the Willis Paint Company. I figured that I had been in the combat zone for 96 days, been overseas for 344 days, and in 352 days had been though nine seasons, while the yeoman's mate had been through only four. My monthly salary as a fireman second-class was $54,

with 20 per cent extra for duty in the combat zone, which came to
$64.80, about what it had been in the Willis Paint Company.

I still have the single-page document he handed me, where he
recorded that I served for exactly two years; that I was awarded
the Victory Medal, the American Theater Medal, the European
Theater Medal, the Asiatic and Pacific Theater Medal with one
battle star, and the Presidential Citation Ribbon for service with
the US Naval Group China, though I did not receive the Good
Conduct Medal because of my court-martial. I later learned that as
a member of SACO I also received two service ribbons from the
Chinese Nationalist Government.

The yeoman was surprised that my rank was only fireman
second-class, and so, being a nice guy, he arbitrarily changed it
to fireman first-class, a rank I held for approximately one hour,
my last in the Navy. The document also records that I received
a mustering-out allowance of $100 plus a final salary payment of
$39.13, which included a transportation allowance of $1.15, the
latter paying for a $1.10 ticket on the Long Island Railroad and a
nickel for the subway. At the bottom of the document is my signature, the imprint of my right index finger and the date 26 May
1946, a Saturday, exactly one month before my 20th birthday.

## 2

# BLOOD PACT

I boarded the Long Island Railway, which took me to Broadway Junction, where I changed to the Eighth Avenue subway line, attracting some attention because of the two souvenirs I was carrying in addition to my sea bag and ditty bag – a Ghurkha *kukri* from Calcutta and a German rifle from Bremerhaven.

I got off at Wilson Avenue and looked out over the Evergreens Cemetery, where John was still working as a gravedigger. But it was nearly six o'clock and he would now have left work and gone home. So I left the station to start walking down Wilson Avenue, and when I passed Paul Hesse's Bar he came out to welcome me back, saying that my father had been stopping there every afternoon on his way home from the Evergreens Cemetery, hoping that he would see me emerge from the Wilson Avenue Station, and now here I was.

I continued down Wilson Avenue, passing the park that I remembered as Siren Land. Then I turned left on the far side of Cornelia Street where Mr Hellman waved to me from his grocery store and came out to welcome me home, saying that my family had been anxiously awaiting my return.

When I rang the bell my brother Jimmy answered the door, and when he saw me he let out such a yell that it brought the rest of the family into the hallway, first my sisters Dorothy and Nancy and then John and Peg. They hugged and kissed me and welcomed me home, and then we all sat around the kitchen table and talked while Peg prepared supper.

I told them where I had been and what I had done since I last saw them, showing them my Ghurkha *kukri* and my German rifle. Then Peg gave me all the family news, telling me that everyone was fine, and when I asked her about Jimmy Anderson, she said that he had dropped by and was waiting to hear from me.

After supper that evening we all sat out on the front steps, together with Mr and Mrs Simmons. When the Good Humor truck came by I bought ice cream for everyone, and when we finished my sister Dorothy went off on a date while Nancy and Jimmy went to play ringelevio and hide-and-go-seek with their friends on the street. I took a pitcher from the kitchen and had it filled with beer at the Decatur Street Bar and Grille, which I poured into a mug for John, but I didn't have any myself because I didn't want to drink in front of Peg.

On Sunday evening we went to a welcome-home party for me at my uncle Tom's flat on Central Avenue. This was the first family gathering I had been to in two years and everyone in our extended clan was there, including my uncle Mike, who had been badly wounded in Normandy, and my aunt Mary Freely and her French-Canadian husband Phil Pelletier, who had served two years in the Army even though he only had one eye. Peg's friend Mauris Guiheen had brought along his accordion, which he played while he and others sang, alternately in Irish and English. One of the songs was my uncle Tom's favourite, 'Down by the Tanyard Side', which he sang whenever he was drunk, never missing a word:

I am a rambling hero, and by love I am betrayed.
Near to the town of Baltinglass, there dwells a lovely maid.
She's fairer than Hypatia bright, and she's free from earthly
     pride.
She's a darlin' maid, and her dwellin' place is down by the
     tanyard side.

Before he passed out Tom told me that he had met Jimmy Anderson, who said he'd be waiting for me at two on Monday afternoon in John's Bar and Grille on Central Avenue and Hancock Street.

When I arrived at John's on the dot of two I found Jimmy waiting for me at the front end of the bar, the only one there besides the bartender. We embraced and stood back to look at one another, for we hadn't met in more than four years. I hardly recognized Jimmy at first, for he looked tough and hard, but after we exchanged a few old jokes and stories, particularly about our days scavenging together, I recognized the shy smile that I had seen when we first met in Fourteen Holy Martyrs Church the day I started school there.

Jimmy and I decided that we would drink our way through the cocktail list posted on the wall, which started with a Tom Collins and ended with a Pousse Café, whatever that was. We each put a $100 bill on the bar, our mustering-out allowance, for 90 per cent of our service pay had been sent home to our mothers. The money on the bar was far more than all that we had earned between us in our years of scavenging and other odd jobs, and as we drank our Tom Collins we reminisced about our clubhouse in the abandoned ice-house and other adventures together.

Jimmy told me that he had fought all through the Guadalcanal campaign and in the landings at Okinawa, but although his outfit had suffered heavy casualties he had come through without a scratch. He said that Phil Gould had also fought at Guadalcanal and Okinawa and that he too had got through unharmed, though both of them had gone down with malaria.

Jimmy also told me that he was engaged to a girl who was serving in the women's branch of the Marine Corps and that they would be married as soon as she received her discharge in the coming weeks. He asked me to be his best man and I said I certainly would but that I hoped the wedding would be informal, as I didn't have a suit to wear. He said not to worry for neither did he.

We didn't make it through the whole of the cocktail list before we called it quits for the day, hardly making a dent in our mustering-out allowances. Jimmy was going off the next day to see his fiancée at the Marine Corps base in Quantico, Virginia, and said he would look me up when he returned.

That evening I went to see Jean Caputo, who was working as a secretary at the *New York Times*. She had seen the photograph of the returning troopships that had appeared on the front page of the *Times* on 28 October 1945, and she had saved it, thinking that I might have been aboard one of the ships. She gave me a copy of the front page, which had a close-up photo of a young woman reporter coming aboard the USS *Hase*, and I remembered seeing her as I looked down from the flying bridge of the troopship.

Jean told me that she was engaged to marry Bob Batchelder, a very nice guy, and I wished her well. She asked me what I was going to do and I said that I had no idea, but for the time being I was going to collect unemployment relief for a year and read through the Great Books programme of St John's College in Annapolis. Jean suggested that I might go to college on the GI Bill. I said that I would think about it in the fall, but first I wanted to enjoy the summer, because for the last six years I had been either working or in the Navy, and for the next two months I just wanted to read and swim and lie on the beach at Rockaway. Jean smiled and asked simply, 'Alone?', to which I could only reply, 'Time will tell'. Then she put on a recording of *Cavalleria Rusticana* and we listened together in silence, just as we did before I went off to war.

The next day I went to the New York State Unemployment Bureau to enquire about the benefits for war veterans. I produced my Navy discharge papers and filled out a form, listing my job skill as 'demolition'. The clerk who processed my forms said that I should report again the following Monday, and if there were no jobs available in my speciality I would receive a cheque for $20. She said that unemployment benefit would last for 52 weeks, provided that when I reported each week there was no work available in my speciality. So I was now a member of what veterans called the 'Fifty-Two-Twenty Club'.

During the 52 weeks that followed I read through the entire curriculum of the Great Books programme, starting with Homer, in Chapman's translation of 1595, and ending with James Joyce's *Ulysses*.

Each week when I received my unemployment relief cheque,

I gave $10 to Peg and kept the rest for myself. The subway was a nickel and beer was ten cents a glass in most bars, and so, when I wasn't reading, I explored New York's libraries, museums and bars, my favourite drinking-place being the San Remo in Greenwich Village, which later became a hang-out for writers of the Beat Generation.

My unemployment relief ran out at the beginning of June 1947, and so I took a summer job cutting grass in the Evergreens Cemetery, where John was still working as a gravedigger. The pay was 50 cents an hour, and I worked eight hours a day, Monday through Saturday, so that my weekly pay, after deducting social security and union dues, was just over $20, half of which I gave to Peg. The job ended on 1 September, leaving me high and dry, with no idea of what I was going to do with myself. I had already tried to find work as a merchant seaman, but there were no jobs available, for there were thousands of Navy veterans who wanted to go back to sea and there were no berths left.

The only one of my SACO comrades who lived in New York was an Irish-American named Bill Glennon, whom I had seen quite often during the year after the war. Bill had graduated from high school before going into the Navy, and the previous September had used the GI Bill to enrol at Iona College in New Rochelle, New York, a Catholic school run by the Irish Christian Brothers. On the first weekend in September I went out drinking with him in his neighbourhood in the Bronx. His brother was the registrar at Iona, and Bill persuaded me to come with him to New Rochelle on Monday. I passed a High School Equivalency Test and started college that same day, majoring in physics, commuting all the way from Brooklyn. This involved taking the subway from Brooklyn to the last stop in the Bronx and then hitchhiking to New Rochelle.

The next week I met and fell in love with a very beautiful girl named Dolores, known to her family as Tootsie, which I shortened to Toots, for the jukebox in the tavern where I met her along with her family was playing 'Toot Toot Tootsie Goodbye'.

Toots had just graduated from high school and, like me, dreamed of being a world traveller. A month after we met we signed a pact in blood on a parchment scroll, swearing that we would spend our lives travelling together around the world on a sailboat. She had just started work as a secretary at the Matson Steamship Lines in Rockefeller Center, where she served in the Hawaii Visitors' Center, thinking that this would lead to a life of travel.

Toots lived just a few blocks from me, in the Bedford-Stuyvesant district, where her father, Harry Stanley, ran a radio and television repair business. His shop was next door to Joe Proscha's Bar, where Harry used to play the piano for Jackie Gleason when he was beginning his career as a singer and comedian. Later, in Gleason's *Honeymooners* television sit-com, he often mentioned a character named 'Radio Harry', referring to Toots' father.

When I met Toots she was headed for a career as a singer and dancer, for she had a superb voice, particularly singing the blues, and she had been trained in dance ranging from ballet to tap. She was also a talented painter and had attended art school in the evening, but she gave up thoughts of a career when she signed her blood pact with me.

The Stanley family moved from Brooklyn to Red Bank, New Jersey, in 1950, and from then on Toots had to commute to her job in Manhattan, an hour each way on the train. I took the train out to see her at weekends, and we spent our time taking long walks in the countryside, trying to think of how we would ever begin our travels, which seemed an impossible dream.

The GI Bill paid for my tuition at Iona and I also received $70 a month for expenses, $60 of which I gave to Peg for my room and board. That didn't leave enough money for carfare and entertainment expenses, so once again I had to get a part-time job. I finally found one as a postal clerk in the Church Street branch of the New York Post Office, working from six to ten in the evening, Monday through Friday. That came to $10 a week, which was enough to pay for my carfare and expenses, usually leaving me with about $5 to spare, which I spent taking Toots out on late evening dates and at weekends. During the summers I also worked six days a week in the Evergreens Cemetery, cutting grass at a rate of 50 cents an hour.

I did most of my studying on the subway, which wasn't nearly enough time, for I was majoring in physics, with minors in philosophy and mathematics, and since I had never taken a course in any of these subjects it was extremely difficult at first, but eventually I began to get the hang of things.

The physics department was run by Brother Thomas Bullen (at the time, the only member of the department), who had received his doctorate at Cambridge under the aegis of P.M.S. Blackett, winner of the Nobel Prize for physics in 1948. Blackett in turn had been a student of Lord Rutherford, one of the pioneers of nuclear physics, who won the Nobel Prize for chemistry in 1908, and Rutherford had been a student of William Clerk Maxwell, the founder of electromagnetic theory. Thus through Brother Bullen I could trace my scientific lineage back to Isaac Newton, Galileo and Copernicus.

With the help of Brother Bullen and his colleagues at Iona, I graduated with a BS in Physics in June 1951. My friend Bill Quinn beat me to the physics prize, but I won the prize in literature for the essays I had contributed to the *Iona Quarterly*. Toots, Peg, John and all my uncles and aunts came up from Brooklyn to attend my graduation, for I was the first in our extended family to graduate from any kind of school. And I wasn't the only one in the class with that distinction, for several other Irish-American veterans had the same background, including my pal Jim Trainor, who had been a machine-gunner in the US Army during the European campaign. All in all, it was a great day for the Irish.

During my last semester at Iona I passed a Civil Service exam and was appointed research physicist at the US Army Signal Corps Laboratory in Fort Monmouth, New Jersey, where I began work on 16 July 1951, five days before Toots and I were to be married in Red Bank.

The laboratory was in an army base called Camp Evans, about five miles inland from Belmar, a seaside town south of Red Bank. On my first day of work I started out at dawn from the Stanley house and took the bus from Red Bank to Belmar, from where I boarded another bus out to Camp Evans, which took me around the shore of the Shark River inlet to the laboratory. About halfway there I noticed a huge old ramshackle mansion beside the inlet, and when I asked the driver about it he told me that it was called the 'Diamond of the Marshes'. He said that it was originally a three-masted schooner that in the early nineteenth century had been driven into the inlet during a hurricane and gone aground. The locals stripped its superstructure and one of them had built the house on the keel and ribs of the ship. He said that the present owners rented out the top floor during the summer months, but at the moment it was vacant.

When I arrived at Camp Evans I went to the reception centre, where I was photographed and given an ID card. A guard then escorted me to the lab building where I would be working and presented me to Dr Harold Jacobs, who would be my boss. Dr Jacobs, who asked me to call him Harold, then introduced me to Dr Dietrich Dobischek, who in turn asked me to call him Dietrich. Harold explained that Dietrich was one of the many German scientists at the lab who had been captured by the Americans and brought here to work after the war. I wondered if Dietrich had been among the thousands of German prisoners we had herded aboard the *Collins* during my last eight months in the Navy, but I said nothing.

Harold said that the three of us would be working together and explained what we would be doing. He then introduced me to the other scientists and technicians in our section, after which he brought me to his office to talk with his secretary, Esther Cohen, so that she could fill out forms for my social security and US Army Security clearance, for some of our research would be top secret. When Esther asked me whether I was married, I told her I wasn't but that I would be getting married on Saturday. Harold laughed and said that I could have next Monday off so that I could take my bride on a brief honeymoon.

Harold told me that the lab had a policy of giving its research staff two afternoons a week off so that they could take evening graduate courses at New York University, and he advised me to take advantage of this. I said that I certainly would do so and that I'd apply for admission in the fall semester.

I told all of this to Toots that evening and suggested that we try to rent the apartment in the Diamond of the Marshes. She thought it was a great idea and so the next day after work I stopped off at the house and asked to look round the apartment. It turned out to have just two sparsely furnished rooms in the attic: a kitchen and bedroom, as well as a tiny enclosure with a toilet and shower. There was no central heating, for the owner and his family had a huge fireplace downstairs, and anyone who rented the apartment had to rely on whatever warmth seeped up through the floor-boards. The rent was $40 a month, to be paid in advance. I said I'd take the place but didn't have the money on me now and would have to pay him when we moved in the following week. The owner agreed and we shook hands.

On the way back to Red Bank I wondered how I would come up with the money, since I had just enough to pay for my carfare until the first payday two weeks hence. I knew that Toots didn't have a penny either, since she had to give most of her salary to her mother. But I didn't worry about it, for at least I had a job and had survived my first day as a physicist, which seemed unbelievable.

My extended family came out from Brooklyn to Red Bank for the wedding, and at the party afterwards at the Stanley house John and my uncles (I had 13 of them, including those who had married my aunts) stuffed money into my pockets. When it was time for us to leave, Harry Stanley drove us to the station at Red Bank, where we boarded a train to New York. Then I went through my pockets and found I had been given nearly $200, which was enough for us to pay our first month's rent and support us until payday, with enough left over for our two-day honeymoon.

On the way to New York we talked about where we might go, and when we reached Penn Station we went to the information booth and checked the prices of trains and hotels. We decided that we had just enough money for a two-day honeymoon in Montreal, and so off we went. Our travels together had finally begun, and now we would wait with some hope for the next stage in our journey.

On the day after our return from Montreal, Harry drove us to the Diamond of the Marshes. After we took our things up to the apartment I went on to the lab, a two-mile walk, and arrived there more than an hour late, for which I received a note of reprimand from the laboratory director.

I walked back from the lab after work and found that Toots had set up our little apartment as best she could, with a bouquet of flowers in an empty wine bottle on the kitchen table, the wine decanted into a bowl. She said that Harry had brought the flowers and the wine for our first supper together, a can of baked beans and two apples for dessert. After supper we took what was left of the wine and went out onto the little jetty across the road, where we sat and watched the changing colours of the inlet through sunset and twilight. Then, when Venus appeared in the western sky, we finished the last of the wine and returned to the house and went to bed, ending our first day of life together in the Diamond of the Marshes.

Toots had left her job at Matson Lines the day before our wedding. But she soon found another job in Belmar, at the office of the US Internal Revenue Department. From then on, after work I took the bus from the lab into Belmar, where we would go shopping and then sit on the boardwalk for a while before walking back along the inlet in the last glow of twilight.

But as the days shortened we had to take the bus back to the house, which was cold, damp, gloomy and swarming with cock-roaches. As it got colder rats moved into the house from the marsh and we could hear them scurrying around in the walls. Then one evening a rat jumped onto the table while we were having supper and we decided that we would have to move.

I gave the owner a month's notice and we began looking for another apartment. One of the technicians at the lab told me of a nice apartment for rent that he knew of in Asbury Park, a resort town about five miles north of Belmar, and so the next Saturday we went to look at it. It was at 301½ Third Avenue, in an alleyway between a large wooden house and a funeral parlour. The apart-ment had been added to the back of the house just recently, the landlord said, and the furniture was brand new. There were just two rooms – a living room and a kitchenette – with a small toilet and shower. The living room converted into a bedroom at night by pulling out two Murphy beds, as they were called, from the wall. He said the rent was $40 a month and we agreed to take it, saying that we would pay him when we moved in the following Saturday.

Harry hired a pickup truck to move us, for we had bought a few things during the time we had lived in the Diamond of the Marshes, including a secondhand radio. Harry again bought us a bottle of wine so that we could celebrate moving into our new home, which although tiny was clean and comfortable, a great improvement on the romantic dump we had just abandoned.

When we sat down for supper I took the seat facing the window that looked out across the alleyway to what turned out to be the main salon of the funeral parlour, where a corpse lay in an open casket as a succession of mourners came in to pay their last respects. I quickly drew the curtains and turned on the radio, tuning in to WQXR so that we could listen to some classical music. It took a minute or so for the vacuum tubes to warm up, but as soon as they did a big cockroach emerged from the set. Before I could stamp on the creature it crawled under the door separating our kitchenette from the landlord's dining room, where a woman I presumed to be his wife let out a scream. Then I heard stamping and someone swearing in Yiddish. It was the landlord's father, as I learned the next day when he called on us, and I assured him that we would get rid of the old radio and buy a new one.

In mid-September I enrolled in the graduate school at New York University, which had an evening programme designed for working men and women. The main campus at NYU was in Greenwich Village, but the physics department was still partly on the old campus at the northern tip of Manhattan. Both the physics courses were on the old campus, so that in addition to the hour-long train ride from the lab to Penn Station, I also spent the better part of another hour making my way uptown by a combination of subway and elevated line, plus a long walk that ended near Spuyten Duyvil, the creek that forms the upper end of Manhattan Island.

The evening classes were two hours long, with a short break in the middle, which meant that two days a week I would leave the lab at two in the afternoon and not get home until nine in the evening at the earliest. But I didn't mind because I studied on the train and I knew that Toots would have a great supper waiting for me when I got home, and the thought of that and of spending the rest of the evening with her carried me through the long day.

Then early in December Toots learned that she was pregnant, which meant that now there would be at least three of us on our voyage and we would need a larger sailboat. Maureen was born on 30 July 1952, 53 weeks after our wedding. All my extended family came down from Brooklyn for the christening, which was held in the same church in Red Bank where we had been married. By that time we had moved to Red Bank, for our fractional flat in Belmar, as I called it, was now much too small. We rented a place in a development called Molly Pitcher Village, named after a local heroine of the Revolutionary War. We had far more space there, but it was unfurnished except for a few things we had brought with us, and until we bought some furniture there were sepul-chral echoes when we listened to WQXR on our new radio in the evenings.

I was owed a week's vacation at the beginning of August, and I spent the time helping Toots set up the apartment and taking care of Maureen, for we knew absolutely nothing about childcare and had to learn on the job. At the end of the week, after I had a couple of shots from a bottle of rye whiskey my uncle Tom had given me at the christening, I allowed myself a moment of satisfac-tion, for we had started a family and I had survived a year of work-ing as a physicist by day and doing graduate studies in the evening.

During my first year at NYU I had taken a course in atomic phys-ics with Serge Korff, an émigré Russian, who had just published a book called *The Primeval Atom*, a translation from the French of Georges Lemaître's Big Bang theory of the expanding universe. That same year I also took a course in statistical thermodynamics with Fritz Reich, an émigré German who had studied with Max Planck, founder of the original quantum theory and winner of the Nobel Prize for physics in 1918. The following year I took a course in advanced calculus with Richard Courant, another émigré German, whose book *Mathematical Methods of Theoretical Physics*, written in collaboration with David Hilbert, had laid the founda-tions of modern quantum theory. Courant, who had taught at the University of Göttingen before coming to the US, was considered to be the most influential modern teacher of mathematics, his students including Werner Heisenberg, who won the Nobel Prize for physics in 1932, and Robert Oppenheimer, who during World War II had directed the Manhattan Project that created the atom bomb. So, with that as well as the lineage I had inherited from Brother Bullen at Iona College, I felt that I was part of the scientific revolution that had created the atomic age, which was pretty good for a high school dropout.

Despite my total lack of experience, during my first year at the Signal Corps Lab I had made, quite by accident, an interesting discovery in electron physics, which I wrote up together with Harold and Dietrich. It was published in the November 1952 issue of *Physical Review*, the most prestigious physics journal in the US.

During the peer review of our paper I corresponded with the famous émigré Dutch physicist Samuel Goudsmit, co-discoverer with George Uhlenbeck of electron spin, who at the time was editor-in-chief of *Physical Review*. He had no criticism to make concerning the physics in our paper but he did offer some suggestions about the paragraphing of our article.

Harold presented our paper at the January 1953 meeting of the American Physics Society at Columbia University, where I caught a glimpse of Niels Bohr, Enrico Fermi and several other Nobel laureates. Our paper was well received, and years later I received a letter from a Japanese physicist who said he had made the same discovery in 1945 but that his work was lost when his laboratory was destroyed in an American air raid, 'just as the cherry trees were blossoming'.

That spring I wrote up the work I had done at the lab and presented it as my master's dissertation at New York University, which awarded me an MS in physics in June 1953, after which I qualified to enter the doctoral programme.

That fall our lab was thrown into turmoil when Senator Joseph McCarthy gave a speech in which he said that he had acquired information indicating that there were at least a hundred communist agents working at Camp Evans. On 10 October we were informed that Senator McCarthy would be inspecting the lab that day and under no circumstances were we to leave whatever building we were working in.

I was scheduled to leave the lab that day at two in the afternoon, for I had an evening class in nuclear physics at NYU. As the hour approached I asked Harold for permission to leave, for we were having an exam that evening and I simply couldn't miss it. He advised me to see the laboratory director, and he wrote me a pass so that the security guards would allow me to leave our building and go to the administration centre. When I got there I barged into the director's office without knocking, for time was running short and I didn't want to be delayed.

The director was being grilled by Senator McCarthy and his acolytes Roy Cohn and David Schein, whom I recognized from their newspaper photos. They looked at me with annoyance, but I ignored them and told the director that I needed his permission to leave the lab to attend an evening class at NYU. He seemed at his wits' end, but he scrawled a note for me and I left immediately. I just made the bus that would take me to Belmar to catch my train for Penn Station, passing through the crowd of reporters and camera crews who were covering the McCarthy investigation, which was now dominating the newspapers and television news programmes.

During the following weeks 98 of my colleagues at the lab were suspended without pay on trumped-up charges of being communist sympathizers. They were all eventually reinstated, except for two who committed suicide. The last one to be reinstated, five years later, was my friend Ed Brophy, a physicist, who in the interim had been working at a fast-food restaurant in Asbury Park. The *New York Times* reported his reinstatement on its front page so that readers would know that the McCarthy fiasco was finally over.

Despite the disruption, during the next two years Harold, Dietrich and I published two more papers in *Physical Review*, as a result of which I received a telephone call offering me a possible job as a research physicist at Princeton University in their Forrestal Research Center, which was a couple of miles east of Princeton, just off highway US 1.

On 1 March 1955 I went to Princeton for the job interview

and was taken to see Professor Lyman Spitzer, the chairman of the astronomy department. He greeted me very warmly and said that he was director of Project Matterhorn, a research programme that was being carried out at the Forrestal Research Center. He said that I would be interviewed there by Dr Melvin Gottleib, the assistant director, and he arranged for a driver to take me to the lab.

Dr Gottleib told me that Project Matterhorn was top secret and so couldn't tell me what they were doing. He said that the scientific staff was divided into two sections, experimental and theoretical, each with half a dozen members. The job for which I was applying was in the experimental section, and so he called in half a dozen of his colleagues to interview me. The interview went very well and Dr Gottleib, who asked me to call him Mel, enquired whether I could start right away. I said that my wife was expecting a baby any time now, and so we agreed that I would start at the beginning of June. I was to have two afternoons off every week so that I could continue my graduate studies at NYU.

After the interview I had about an hour to spare before my train was due, and so took the opportunity to walk along Mercer Street in the hope that I might catch a glimpse of Einstein, for I knew that he lived there at No. 126, a short walk from the Institute for Advanced Studies, where he had been working since 1930. When I passed No. 126 the door opened and out stepped Kurt Gödel, the great mathematician, a close friend of Einstein and his colleague at the institute for many years. I continued down Mercer Street and walked to the institute, where I saw the director, Robert Oppenheimer, mowing his lawn.

Toots began having labour pains the following evening, 2 March. I called a taxi and dropped off Maureen at the Stanleys before taking Toots to the Red Bank hospital. After she was taken into the maternity ward I sat down in the waiting room, ready to spend the night there if necessary.

The only other person there was an equally worried guy a bit older than me, and when we got talking we found that we had both been in the Navy during the war. I asked him what ship he had been on, and he said he been executive officer on the USS

*Dickerson.* I caught my breath, for it was ten years to the day since the *Dickerson* had been sunk off Okinawa, with the loss of nearly half her crew, including my dear friend Charles Shelmerdine and two other boys from my boot company at Camp Sampson. When I told him this he said that he had known Charles and my other friends and that the same bomb that had killed them had blown him from the bridge into the sea, where someone had dragged him ashore unconscious under Japanese machine-gun fire.

At that moment a nurse came to tell me that my wife had just given birth to a baby girl and that I could go in to see them now. I went in and saw Toots and Eileen, for that's the name we had chosen if the baby was a girl. I stayed as long as I was allowed and then went back to the waiting room to say goodbye to my new friend. He spoke to the nurse and learned that his wife was not expected to give birth soon, so he suggested that we have a few drinks in a nearby bar. I thought that was a great idea and we drank together for half an hour or so before we went our separate ways, saying that we'd probably meet the following evening at the hospital. But I never saw him again, and the last thing I remember him saying was that he was digging an underground bunker in his garden, for he was sure that there would soon be a nuclear war, as many others thought at the time.

On 19 March Toots and I were watching the evening news on television and learned that Einstein had died earlier that day at the Princeton Hospital, where he had been taken after suffering a heart attack at the Institute for Advanced Studies. After the news there was an hour-long programme presented by Martin Agronsky from Einstein's office at the institute, where the blackboard was still covered with the equations he had been working on that day. Years later I learned that during Einstein's last hours at the hospital, his step-daughter Margot read to him Plato's *Phaedo*, the dialogue that describes the last hours of Socrates at the state prison in Athens, before he drank the fatal hemlock at dawn.

We moved to Princeton late in May, and on 1 June I went to work at the Forrestal Research Center. For the first few weeks I worked in a Quonset hut outside the main laboratory building and was told that I would remain there until I received Q Clearance, the highest level of government security, which had been instituted during the Manhattan Project. When I finally received clearance I learned that Project Matterhorn was a programme to create controlled thermonuclear fusion; that is, to harness the power that was the source of the sun's energy and which had been used destructively in the hydrogen bomb.

The work in Project Matterhorn was very exciting but extremely demanding, particularly since I was also doing graduate work at NYU. But Toots loved it at Princeton, for she had joined a book club formed by wives of young faculty members at Princeton who were struggling for tenure. But she had to give up the book club for a while after Brendan was born, on 1 June 1959.

I was so busy that I had no time to enjoy the cultural activities at Princeton. But in December 1957 I learned that Robert Frost would be giving a reading in Alexander Hall, and I walked there with Maureen through a howling snow storm. All the seats were taken by the time we arrived, so I stood at the back of the auditorium, putting Maureen on my shoulders so that she could see.

When Robert Frost walked up to the lectern the audience cheered him as if he were a football star, and then I listened enraptured as he recited poems that I had known since my youth. When he finished his last poem the crowd applauded for several minutes and then began chanting in unison, 'One more, one more!' Then when they grew quiet he began reciting 'Stopping by woods on a snowy evening', and when he finished the crowd applauded him continuously as he bowed and left the lectern to walk down the main aisle towards the exit. When he reached the door he saw Maureen perched on my shoulders and he paused to chuck her under the chin before walking out into the snowy evening.

Early in January 1960 we were told that in two weeks' time a delegation from the Atomic Energy Commission would be paying us a visit. It would include a four-star general and several members of Congress and would be headed by Professor Edward Teller, the Hungarian émigré physicist who was famous as the Father of the Hydrogen Bomb, which made him the prototype of Doctor Strangelove. We had to give talks on our research, and when the schedule was posted I found that I was due to speak first. I was terrified, particularly when I saw Teller sitting in the front row centre, but once I started to speak I was OK. I thought that Teller had dozed off during my talk, but when I finished he looked at me and nodded his head as if in approval.

Six months later my doctoral dissertation was accepted, and in June 1960 I was awarded a PhD in physics at NYU. I was then offered a permanent research position at Princeton, but after conferring with Toots I asked for time to think about it, for we were still determined to spend our life travelling.

A few days after receiving my doctorate, when I was admiring a flowering cherry tree on the Princeton campus, my colleague Ed Meservy said, 'John, they're nothing compared to the Judas trees on the Bosphorus.' Ed told me that after the war he had taught for two years in Istanbul at Robert College, an American school that had been founded in 1863 on the European shore of the Bosphorus. I was very interested to hear more and so he introduced me to David Garwood, head of the humanities department at Robert College, who was on a sabbatical at Princeton, together with his wife Minnie. David told me that the dean of the faculty at RC, Howard Hall, was coming to New York in a week or so to recruit new faculty, particularly in science and maths. David arranged for me to meet Dean Hall at the New York office of the Near East Colleges Association. Hall, who asked me to call him Bob, said that they didn't have an opening in physics at the moment but they did in maths. When I told him that I had minored in maths at NYU he offered me a job and I accepted immediately, for I had already consulted Toots. He said that I would be acting chairman of the maths department and that I would teach four sections of calculus and an elective course for students in business and economics called Physics for Poets. My salary would be $2,400 a year plus 2,000 Turkish lira a month, which at the current rate of exchange was worth $222.22. The cost of living in Turkey was much lower than in the US, he said, and we would have free housing, so that we should have no trouble getting by. My contract was for three years, and if both parties agreed to renew it, we would be given free home leave. He said that the college had booked a charter flight to bring out new faculty and those returning from home leave. The flight would depart from LaGuardia Airport at 2pm on 15 September and we should be there at least an hour beforehand. We shook hands at that and he said that he'd see me in Istanbul.

I gave notice to Don Grove, my boss at Project Matterhorn, and then arranged to put our furniture in storage, though I hoped that we would never come back to live permanently in the US. On 12 September my friend Art Lind drove us to Red Bank so that we could say goodbye to Toots' family. Then the following day he drove us to Brooklyn, where we were going to stay with my parents until we left to board the charter flight.

Dorothy, Nancy and Jimmy had by then married and left Brooklyn, and so my parents had moved from Cornelia Street to a smaller apartment on Cooper Street, close to the Evergreens Cemetery, where John still worked as a gravedigger. The rest of my extended family had by then left Brooklyn too, as had all my friends, and so we spent that evening and the next day by ourselves, giving John and Peg a chance to get to know Maureen, Eileen and Brendan, whom they had seen only occasionally on family visits.

We got up early on the day of our departure, and when everyone was ready I called a taxi. When it came we said our tearful farewells, and Peg recited the same parting blessing that Tom of the Winds had given us when we left the Murphy cottage 27 years before: 'May the road rise up to meet you and the wind always be at your back; may the sun be warm upon your brow and the rain fall softly on your fields; and until we meet again may God hold you in the hollow of his hand.'

# 3

# THE ODYSSEY BEGINS

When we arrived at LaGuardia Airport I saw a sign directing us to the departure lounge for the Robert College charter flight. Some of those waiting there were talking to one another cheerfully, and I gathered that these were old hands returning to Istanbul after home leave, while those who were silent and somewhat apprehensive were new faculty, or so I figured.

The only ones we knew were David Garwood and his wife Minnie, who were there with their three children, John, Anne and Vicky. They introduced us to Keith and Joanne Greenwood and their children Tony, Debby and Brian, who were returning from home leave, and as we chatted with them I began to feel less like a total stranger.

David then introduced me to some of the new faculty: Donald Hoffman, who would teach music; the new professor of chemistry, Donald Rogers, who asked me to call him Buck; and Buck's wife Kay, who would be teaching at the Robert College Community School. Then another couple arrived, whom David introduced to us as Floyd and Ann Couch. Floyd said that he would be teaching literature at Robert Academy, the high-school division of Robert College, and Anne said that she would be working as Dean Hall's secretary. She and Toots hit it off immediately and began chatting away and laughing together while I began to exchange bad jokes with Buck and Floyd.

We walked out on to the tarmac and boarded a KLM plane, which, we were told, would be stopping in Copenhagen to refuel. We were the last to board, and since all the other seats were full we were taken up to a separate compartment in the nose of the plane near the cockpit. While we waited on the runway, I remembered that it was 15 years to the day since I had flown from Kunming to Calcutta, when I had sworn that I would never board an aeroplane again. Then the PA told us to prepare for takeoff, and as we rolled down the runway Toots turned to me and smiled, for we were finally starting our odyssey together, though in a plane with our three children rather than the two of us alone in a sailboat. But it didn't matter because we were at last on our way.

The flight to Istanbul took 24 hours, including the stopover at Copenhagen. When we landed I could see a flock of sheep grazing beyond the end of the runway, and as we taxied to the small terminal I saw that we were the only plane at the airport other than some military aircraft.

We boarded a bus that had been rented to take us to Robert College. We were all totally exhausted but I forced myself to stay awake, for we were approaching the imperial city that I had first learned of during my childhood from a book that my great-grandfather had bought here more than a century before. We were sitting in the front row of seats, with the Garwoods directly behind us and as we drove along David gave me a quick rundown of the long history of the city: founded around 660 BC as the Greek city of Byzantium; re-founded in AD 330 as Constantinople, capital of the Byzantine Empire; conquered by the Turks under Sultan Mehmet II in 1453 and renamed Istanbul, capital of the Ottoman Empire till the founding of the Turkish Republic in 1923. I already knew all of this because I had been reading about the city for years, though I didn't tell David.

After passing through miles of sparsely inhabited countryside we came within sight of the historic Theodosian walls built 15 centuries ago to protect Constantinople from invaders, its long line of towers and curtain walls stretching for four miles between the Sea of Marmara and the Golden Horn. We crossed the Golden

Horn and then drove up the European shore of the Bosphorus to the village of Rumeli Hisarı, named after the huge fortress built by Sultan Mehmet II in 1452.

The campus of Robert College was a third of the way up the European shore of the Bosphorus, which for 30 kilometres separates Europe and Asia in north-western Turkey, flowing from the Black Sea to the Sea of Marmara. At its southern end the Bosphorus is joined by the Golden Horn, a scimitar-shaped estuary that joins the Bosphorus just before it flows into the Golden Horn. This was the setting that I had first seen in an engraving in *A Pictorial Journey Around the World*, the book that Thomas Ashe had brought back after the Crimean War, implanting the vision that had now brought me to Istanbul.

When we reached the outskirts of Rumeli Hisarı we turned left on a cobbled road that led uphill past an old graveyard that David identified as the Aşiyan cemetery. At the top of the hill, crowned by one of the towers of Rumeli Hisarı, we turned left into the grounds of Robert College, which looked like a New England educational establishment, with neo-classical buildings arrayed around a quadrangle.

A welcoming committee led the new arrivals to their faculty housing, most of which were old American-style wooden buildings close to the campus. We were told that we would be housed in an off-campus apartment, but it wouldn't be ready for a couple of days, and in the interim we would be staying with Bob Hall and his family, who lived just down the road from the campus. Bob introduced us to his wife Ellen and their four daughters, Stephanie, Charlotte, Lindsey and Gretchen, who were about the same age as our own children. We had supper early that evening and went straight to bed, sleeping till past noon the following day.

After a mid-day breakfast Ellen said to me, 'Come on John, let's go buy a fish.' We walked down the Aşiyan road to the shore road, where we took a bus up the Bosphorus to the fish market at Emirgan, the next village. After Ellen bought the fish we stopped at a teahouse in Emirgan before taking a bus back to the Aşiyan road. As we passed the Aşiyan cemetery I noticed that the tombstones were different from those in the Evergreens. The older ones were topped with turbans and inscribed in Old Turkish, written in Arabic script, and a more recent one had the date of birth of the deceased recorded as 1319 and his death as 1955. Ellen explained that the reforms instituted by the new Turkish Republic that arose from the ashes of the Ottoman Empire in 1923 included changes from Oriental to Western clothing, from Arabic to Latin script, and from the Islamic to the Gregorian calendar. Then I spotted a gravedigger at work, and thought of John still digging away at the Evergreens.

After supper that evening we received a visit from the business manager, Ömer Yoldaş, who took me to visit the apartment that we would be moving into the next day, for it was now ready for occupancy. It was on the second floor of a chalet-like house on Arifi Pasha Korusu, a cobbled road that led uphill from the Bosphorus on the shore road between Rumeli Hisarı and Bebek, the next village to the south along the Bosphorus. The kitchen was small, as was the adjacent bedroom for the maid, but the other rooms – living room, three bedrooms and a bathroom – were huge, as was the balcony overlooking the Bosphorus. Ömer took me out onto the balcony, from where I could see the lights of the villages on both the European and Asian shore glittering like galaxies. Then he said, 'Is the apartment suitable, Professor Freely?', and I had to laugh, thinking of the Diamond of the Marshes and our fractional address in Asbury Park, and I knew that when Toots saw it she would swoon.

We moved in the following afternoon, and while Toots emptied our suitcases I walked down to Bebek to go shopping, which I did by pointing at what I wanted and holding up fingers to indicate the quantity. On the way back I passed an outdoor restaurant-café called Nazmi's, where I saw Buck and Kay Rogers drinking beer. They invited me to join them and so I did, pointing at the beer and indicating to the waiter, whose name was Fevzi, that I wanted one myself. Fevzi then brought us a menu, from which I learned that the Turkish word for beer is *bira*. We had been given an advance on our Turkish lira salary, and so after a few more beers we paid our bill, which was just a trifle, and left, walking along the shore of the Bosphorus together as far as Arifi Pasha Korusu. We parted company there and I walked up to our chalet.

After supper we all sat out on the balcony for a while, looking out across the Bosphorus as the sun set behind us, its golden light reflected in the windows of the seaside houses on the Asian shore. When it began to grow dark Toots put the children to bed, and then she and I sat out on the balcony finishing the wine I had bought that afternoon. It was pretty bad, but it didn't matter, particularly when the nearly full moon rose up out of the hills of Asia, silvering its path across the midnight-blue Bosphorus. We lifted our glasses to one another at that, recalling the blood pact we had signed 13 years before.

The following morning our upstairs neighbour came down and introduced himself as Bob McMickle, who said that he taught in the physics department. He invited us to come up to have breakfast with him and his family on their balcony, introducing us to his wife Gwen, who taught at the Robert College Community School, and their children Doug, Allen, Kitty, Barry and Margaret, who were about the same age as our own kids. That afternoon Bob took me up to Washburn Hall at the college to meet Robert Hardy, the dean of the School of Science and Languages, who showed me the maths department office and the room in which I would be lecturing.

Meanwhile Toots enrolled Maureen and Eileen in the Community School, where the majority of the students were children of faculty members. Maureen was placed in third grade and Eileen, although she was only five and a half, was put in first grade. I walked the two of them to school in the morning, since the school building was just outside the Robert College campus, and Toots walked them home in the afternoon, leaving Brendan with Ayşe, the janitor's wife, who helped out with the housework.

The fall term began two weeks later, and in the interim I hardly slept, for I was terrified at the thought of teaching. But I managed to get through it, and by the end of the first week of classes I was actually beginning to enjoy myself. The students, most of them Turks, with a few Greeks, Armenians and Jews, all of them Turkish citizens, were very bright, and their proficiency in English was in most cases excellent, though some of them complained to Dean

Hardy that I spoke too fast. So I tried to slow down a bit and the students eventually got used to my rapid-fire New York English.

Girls had been admitted to the college just two years before and there were a few of them in my class. One of them, Gulsun Kutay, spoke to me one day after class and offered to be a babysitter for us if she could have a room in our apartment. I introduced her to Toots and the children, who liked her very much, and so at the end of the week she joined us in our apartment, sleeping in the maid's bedroom. That left Toots and me free to go out in the evening, either to Nazmi's or to parties at the college, which were far more fun than any of those we had attended during our nine years in New Jersey.

Early in the autumn of 1960, Toots and I had begun going into Istanbul with the children virtually every Saturday, taking the ferry from either Rumeli Hisarı or Bebek at eight in the morning and returning on the express boat that left the Galata Bridge at five in the afternoon. Our first walk took us up the Golden Horn, through the ancient market district and the old Greek, Armenian and Jewish quarters out to the Theodosian walls, visiting ancient mosques, churches, synagogues, tombs, graveyards and holy wells, stopping for lunch at a little hole-in-the-wall eating place frequented by workmen. Subsequent walks took us to Byzantine and Ottoman monuments on all seven of the historic peninsula's hills.

We usually ended our walks along the Marmara shore of the old city outside the only remaining portal in the sea walls, Ahır Kapı, the Stable Gate, where we ate at a little seaside restaurant called Karışmasen, meaning 'Mind Your Own Business'. This became our base for later explorations in that district, the oldest in the city, where we walked along cobbled lanes with names like the Street of the Bushy Beard, the Street of the White Moustache and the Street of Ibrahim of Black Hell.

I also explored the area north of the Golden Horn, the late medieval Latin port quarter of Galata, as well as the heights above known to the Levantines as Pera and the Turks as Beyoğlu. The main avenue of Beyoğlu, the old Grand Rue de Pera, was now called Istiklal Caddesi, or Independence Avenue, its focal point being the crossroads at Galatasaray.

I was immediately drawn to the colourful Galatasaray fish market and the L-shaped alleyway known as Çiçek Pasajı, the Passage of Flowers, which connected it with Istiklal Caddesi. The name came from the flower market that was once located there, but that had long since vanished and been replaced by taverns known as *meyhanes*, which were famous for their draft beer, served in giant glasses called Argentines. The customers, all men, sat on high stools at long tables inside the *meyhanes*, as well as outside in the alleyway itself, where slabs of marble were set on top of beer barrels.

One of the *meyhanes* had a tiny outside bar where one or two customers could drink standing up, and so I stopped there and had an Argentine. The bartender introduced himself to me as Abdurrahman, and though my Turkish was primitive we chatted away, finding out about one another's lives, the first of many such conversations I would have with other Turks I met during my strolls through Istanbul, many of them in the Çiçek Pasajı.

I also met other foreigners in the Pasajı, for the American and British consulates and English High School were close by. The British tended to go to a *meyhane* directly across the alley from the one where I hung out. They called it the Church, for on Sunday mornings the men drank there while their wives and children attended services at the Anglican chapel in the old British Embassy. I called my *meyhane* the Senate because of the vociferous political discussions that were always going on there, particularly during our first months, for the government of Prime Minister Adnan Menderes had been overthrown in a military coup the previous May, and after a contentious trial he and two of his ministers were hanged later in the autumn.

One of the foreigners I met here early on was the American poet Jim Lovett, who at the time was teaching at the secondary school of the Daruşşafaka Orphanage in the old city. He was with a young Turk whom he introduced as Emin Saatçi, who would become my lifelong friend.

I also met the Turkish poet Cevat Çapan, who was a regular at the Church. Cevat had graduated from Robert College and gone on to get a doctorate in Irish literature at Cambridge, where he founded the Irish-Turkish Poetry Society. I sometimes joined Cevat and his friends at the Church, where they met regularly at mid-day on Friday, having their first raki at the time of the noon prayer, a ritual that goes on to the present day.

On Saturdays when we were not exploring the old city, Toots went shopping in the Galatasaray fish market, and we met for lunch in Rejans, an old restaurant run by White Russians, famous for its homemade lemon vodka. On Saturday evenings we often went to a Greek taverna in Beyoğlu called Boem, where the star entertainer was the old troubadour Todori Negroponti, accompanied on the piano by Madame Tashkin, a Russian baroness, along with several Greek and Russian musicians, all of them getting on in years. The customers were mostly Greek, and after Todori sang a few solos, he led the band in a round of songs from the Aegean islands and everyone got up to join in a round of *syrtos*, the beautiful encircling dances said to be patterned on Ariadne's leading of Theseus and his companions out of the Cretan labyrinth with her spool of thread, for which the dancers in Boem substituted handkerchiefs.

Early in the fall we accompanied the Garwoods to a big party given by Aliye Berger-Boronai, the famous painter, who lived in the old Russian Embassy at the south-west end of Istiklal, a building that had long since been converted to commercial use except for her apartment, where she had been living since the last days of the Ottoman Empire. Aliye's apartment was the social centre of bohemian Beyoğlu, a gathering place for eccentric and alcoholic artists, writers and composers, many of whom I met that evening, beginning friendships that lasted for many years, usually ending when one or another of them drank himself to death. Aliye herself became a close friend of ours, and she drew us into the bohemian world that swirled around her until the day she died.

One of the older teachers I came to know early on was Hilary Sumner-Boyd, who had dual US-British citizenship and had degrees from both Columbia and Oxford. Hilary joined the faculty at Robert College as professor of humanities in 1943, and from then on he applied his formidable scholarship to a study of the antiquities of Istanbul called *The Seven Hills of Constantinople*, which he passed on to me at cocktail time in his study at least once a week. As time passed I too began writing about Istanbul, in a book that I tentatively called *The Broken-Down Paradise*, which was very different from Hilary's work, since it was about the street life of the city past and present, the kind of lore I had picked up as a boy scavenging in Brooklyn and working in the condom factory in Manhattan.

Hilary and I were sometimes joined at cocktail time by his companion Michael Austin, who had just completed his doctorate at Oxford and had joined the faculty at Robert College, teaching in the humanities department. Michael was handsome, brilliant and wickedly funny, and we quickly became very good friends. He would usually leave us after the first drink and head off into town, where I would occasionally run into him in some of the more disreputable drinking places north of the Golden Horn, speaking fluent street Turkish to the somewhat scary young men with whom he would then disappear into the night.

Another older teacher whom I befriended was Godfrey Goodwin, who was professor of art history even though he had never attended university. Godfrey had joined the British Army in September 1939, when he had just turned 18, despite the fact that he was blind in one eye. He served in the North African and Italian campaigns and was finally discharged in the summer of 1945. After the end of the war he was honourably discharged from the British Army, having served five and a half years. He returned to England only long enough to train as a teacher, after which he found a position at Victoria College in Alexandria. He remained there until 1956, when the Suez crisis led the Egyptian government to dismiss all the British teachers from the school. The following year Godfrey was hired at the English High School in Istanbul, and then the following year he accepted a position at Robert College.

By the time we arrived in 1960 Godfrey was leading groups of friends from the college on Saturday tours of Istanbul, showing them the Ottoman monuments of the city. Toots and I and the children joined these tours, in addition to strolling through Istan-

bul on our own, and I learned much about Ottoman architecture
from Godfrey. As in the case of our own strolls through the city,
Godfrey's tours usually ended at a *meyhane* or Greek taverna or at
Rejans, continuing on into the evening.

When we first came to Istanbul we thought that we might
stay for only three years and so took every opportunity to travel,
particularly to places we might never be able to see again if we
returned to the US. So early in November, when a conjunction
of Muslim holy days and civil holidays gave us an unexpected ten-
day break, Toots and I left the children with Gulsun and booked
tickets aboard a ship of the Turkish Maritime Lines, the *Samsun*,
which took us along the Black Sea coast of Turkey as far as Trabzon, Greek Trebizond, capital of the medieval Byzantine Empire
ruled by the Comneni dynasty.

We spent a day in Trabzon before the return voyage and
explored the towering ruins of the castle where the Comneni ruled
for nearly two centuries until they finally surrendered to Sultan
Mehmet II in 1461, eight years after his conquest of Constantinople, bringing the long history of Byzantium to an end.

As we stood in the citadel, looking down on the ruins of what
in its time was known as the Golden Castle, I recalled the elegiac
lines with which Rose Macaulay ends her novel, *The Towers of Trebizond*:

> Still the towers of Trebizond, the fabled city, shimmer on
> a far horizon, gated and walled and held in a luminous
> enchantment. It seems for me, and however much I stand
> outside them, this must forever be. But at the city's heart lies
> the pattern and the hard core, and this I can never make my
> own: they are too far outside my range.

There were very few passengers on the outward journey, but
on the return voyage the ship was packed. A few of the passengers
had booked cabins, but all the rest were in deck class, sleeping
out on sacks of hazel nuts piled up in the cargo hold, surrounded
by all their worldly possessions. The great exodus had begun, as
the poor peasants of eastern Anatolia left their villages, hoping to

find a better life in Istanbul or as guest workers in Germany and elsewhere in Europe.

Those who came to Istanbul settled in ramshackle villages called *gecekondu*, meaning 'built by night', one of the largest of which was on the hilltop above the college, which grew into a village called Hisarüstü. Some of the men found jobs at the college, while the women worked as housekeepers in Rumeli Hisarı and Bebek.

A couple of weeks after we returned, one of the workmen at the college told me that all the people of Hisarüstü would be attending a concert that evening, and he invited me to join him. It was held in the auditorium at Albert Long Hall, and the performer was Aşık Veysel, the blind minstrel from central Anatolia, one of the wandering troubadours who since time immemorial have been the bards of rural Turkey.

Aşık Veysel, who was about 70, dressed in the shalvars and blouse still worn by Turkish peasants at that time, was on stage sitting on a wicker chair cradling his *saz*, the traditional stringed instruments of Anatolia. When the audience fell silent he began to sing, his cracked and wavering voice rising above the discordant twang of his *saz*, telling of how his mother gave birth to him in the wheat field where she was working, and of how his father taught him to play the *saz* when he was a boy, before he lost his sight. All his songs were about the joys and sorrows of Anatolian life – listening to the first nightingale in spring, unrequited love for a girl you could touch but never see, the injustice of landlords who owned you and the land you worked on, the heartbreak of burying your mother in the same field in which she bore you. Then he paused before beginning his last song, 'Kara Toprak', the 'Black Earth':

My sweetheart is the black earth,
Though I've wounded her with my hoe and shovel,
She smiled and gave me roses.
My sweetheart is the black earth.

Then as he went on the audience sang the refrain between verses, and I felt that I was listening to a choir singing a hymn to the black earth of Anatolia that had nourished them and which they had now abandoned, along with the graves of their ancestors. Then I thought of my own people in Ireland and of the songs of the Irish diaspora I'd heard in Brooklyn, where my father was still digging in the not-so-black earth of the Evergreens Cemetery.

The mid-term break was more than three weeks long, and since my finals were scheduled early, I would be free for nearly the whole month of January. We decided to go to Antalya on the Mediterranean coast of Turkey, which the Tourism Ministry was hyping as the Turkish Riviera. We booked passage on a ship of the Turkish Maritime Lines, the *Akdeniz*, which would take three days to reach Antalya, with stopovers in Izmir, Turkey's most important port on the Aegean, and Marmaris, on the Mediterranean coast.

The first stage of our voyage took us across the Sea of Marmara and through the Dardanelles, the Greek Hellespont, out to the Aegean. I was hoping to catch a glimpse of ancient Troy, whose site is on the European side of the strait near its Aegean end, but night had fallen by the time we reached the Dardanelles. All I could see were the lights of Gelibolu, Greek Gallipoli, on the European shore, then Çanakkale on the Asian side and the lighthouses on either side of the strait as we entered the Aegean and turned south.

I knew from my reading that there had been beacons on these promontories since antiquity. Aeschylus, in his *Agamemnon*, writes that Clytemnestra received news of the fall of Troy through the series of fire signals flashed all the way from the Hellespont to Mycenae.

At around noon the next day we reached Izmir, Greek Smyrna, where we would remain until late evening. We spent the day exploring the town, particularly the old market quarter and the ancient fortress of Kadifekale, the Velvet Castle, known to the Greeks as Mount Pagus, which loomed above the port on the summit of the acropolis hill.

Like most of the other ancient Graeco-Roman cities along the Aegean and Mediterranean coasts, Smyrna was founded by the Greeks early in the first millennium BC. Ancient Smyrna reached its peak under the Romans in the second century AD, when its population exceeded 100,000, only to decline in the medieval era when successive waves of invaders swept across Anatolia – Persians, Arabs, Mongols, Crusaders and Turks, who called it Izmir – until it revived in the late Ottoman era, its population once again exceeding 100,000, two-thirds of whom were Greek. But then in mid-September 1922, at the conclusion of the Graeco-Turkish war that followed World War I, the Greek quarter of the city was burned to the ground by the victorious Turkish Nationalist army. The surviving Greek population fled by sea, and the following year, after the founding of the Turkish Republic, the remaining Greeks in Anatolia, some 1,500,000, were deported in a population exchange that brought 400,000 Turks from Greece to Turkey, the irony being that most of the Greeks spoke only Turkish, while many of the Turks were Greek speakers. Greeks still refer to this as the Catastrophe, a cataclysm that ended the Greek presence in Anatolia after more than 3,000 years.

Around noon the next day we docked in Marmaris, which at the time had still not recovered from the powerful earthquake that had destroyed the old town in 1957. The *Akdeniz* remained in port only for a couple of hours, just long enough for us to walk around the old town, which clustered around the ruins of a fortress built in 1522 by Sultan Suleiman the Magnificent, who used Marmaris as the base for his conquest of Rhodes, whose northernmost promontory we could see on the southern horizon, just 15 nautical miles away. This brought to mind a line from one of the odes of Pindar: 'Sea-girt Rhodes, child of Aphrodite and Helios ... nigh to a promontory of spacious Asia.'

We got up at first light the day after we left Marmaris, for I knew that we would be passing under the seaward ramparts of the Taurus Mountains as we approached the Gulf of Antalya. When we went out on deck we found that we were in the teeth of a howling blizzard, so that we could hardly see the mountains. The force of the wind abated somewhat once we entered the harbour of Antalya, where we were in the lee of the cliff on which the upper town is perched. Antalya did not yet have modern harbour facilities, so we had to come ashore in small boats to the medieval port, where there were horse-drawn carriages waiting to take us to the upper town. Without being told, the driver dropped us at the Park Hotel, the only hotel in Antalya at the time.

I had sent a telegram to the hotel booking accommodation for the five of us, and when we arrived the manager greeted us in English. He said that we would be staying in the American Suite, which turned out to be a big room whose only furnishings were five single beds which looked as though they had been made for a school dormitory. In the middle of the room there was a toilet *à la Turca*, just a hole in the concrete floor straddled by two corrugated marble footprints. But since the manager knew that we were Americans he handed me the two halves of a wooden toilet seat so that at least we could sit down. He then left, wishing us a pleasant stay.

The blizzard lasted for two days, and during that time we never left the hotel, taking our meals in the dining room along with the other guests, who included a famous Turkish magician named Doctor Abracadabra, with whom I shared a bottle of raki during the first day of our stay.

The following day I was approached by three Turks about my own age who spoke perfect English. They worked in Istanbul and had also been led to believe that this was the Turkish Riviera. We got talking and decided that when the blizzard ended we would spend a few days together exploring the ancient Graeco-Roman sites in the area before returning overland to Istanbul. When the snow finally stopped the following morning we went to a one-man travel agency, run by a young man calling himself Munir Bey, who said that for a modest fee he would take us in his minibus to see all the ancient sites around Antalya during the next three days. So we had the hotel make us a picnic lunch and drove off in the minibus with Munir Bey, who told us that not much snow had accumulated and that the main roads were already being cleared.

Over the next three days we visited the Graeco-Roman sites of Termessos, Perge, Aspendos and Side. All four cities had been founded at the beginning of the first millennium BC and had reached their peak early in the Christian era. During the Middle Ages they were destroyed by earthquakes and invasions and then abandoned, except for Side, which early in the twentieth century was resettled by Greek-speaking Muslim refugees from Crete. Their descendants were still living there amidst the ruins of the ancient city, whose theatre and other monuments were half buried in the sand dunes around the silted up remains of the ancient port.

During those three days we encountered camel caravans of Turkish nomads known as the Yürük, who had come down from their summer encampments in the highland meadows of the Taurus Mountains to set up their black goat-hair tents in the olive groves and banana plantations of the Pamphylian plain. The Yürük were the descendants of the Turcoman tribespeople who had overrun Anatolia late in the eleventh century. They had not yet integrated into urban Turkish society, but their immemorial way of life was coming to an end, as we would see on subsequent trips through Anatolia.

At the end of our stay in Antalya we and our three Turkish friends boarded a bus that took us across the snow-bound Taurus Mountains, the first stage in a journey that brought us across the heart of Anatolia and back to Istanbul, having used up only half of our winter vacation.

The following morning I went up to the campus to check my mail, figuring that all our friends were still away on vacation. But I ran into my friend Cal Atwood, who had just returned with his wife Cary and their three children from a skiing holiday on Ulu Dağ, known to the Greeks as Mount Olympus of Bithynia, the highest peak in western Anatolia. Cal was one of the very few American faculty members who had a car, and he and his wife Cary were planning to spend the rest of the vacation driving through Greece, leaving their children with a babysitter. He invited me and Toots to join him, and so we left the children with Gulsun and drove off early the following morning, heading for the Greek border crossing at Edirne, ancient Adrianople, capital of the Ottoman Empire prior to the Turkish conquest of Constantinople.

The highway to Edirne followed the course of the ancient Via Egnatia, the highroad that the Romans had constructed across the southern Balkans to Byzantium. The road took us across the downs of Eastern Thrace, the only part of the Ottoman Empire's former possessions in Europe that was retained by the Turkish Republic. The only notable features on the monotonous landscape were the conical tumuli that I could see now and then in the distance, all of them funerary monuments of the Thracian chieftains who had ruled the southern Balkans in antiquity.

It was dark by the time we reached Edirne, whose magnificent Ottoman mosques towered all around us, but there was hardly anyone to be seen in the streets, nor could we find anywhere to eat or have a drink. So we drove on towards the border, crossing the Evros River on a medieval bridge, which was almost inundated by flood waters surging down from the Balkan mountains. This was the river known to the Greeks as the Hebros, the subject of a poem written in the mid-sixth century BC by Alcaeus of Lesbos, a contemporary of Sappho:

> Hebros, loveliest of Rivers, you issue
> hard by Ainos into the dark blue waters
> of the sea where, passing by Thrace, you end your turbulent
>     passage;
> there where young girls come in their crowds and, bathing
> with light hands their ravishing thighs, enjoy you
> all as if some magical salve were in your wonderful waters.

The military police manning the immigration and customs control stations on both sides of the border seemed surprised to see us, and I gathered that there was very little traffic between Greece and Turkey, particularly foreigners travelling in the dead of winter, but in any event they were very polite and wished us a pleasant journey.

We drove on to Orestiada, which in Ottoman times had been a twin city of Edirne. We thought that it too would be closed down for the night, but we were delighted to find the streets thronged with families taking their evening promenade, the restaurants and cafés full, Greek music blaring from several tavernas.

We checked in at the only hotel in town, where we seemed to be the only guests, and then we went to one of the tavernas, where we soon found ourselves swept up in a *syrtos*, one of the circle dances we knew from the Taverna Boem, and we didn't get to bed until what the Greeks call *i ores mikres*, 'the small hours'.

Nevertheless we started off early the next morning, for we had a long way to go and we had been told that the roads were very bad, particularly in north-eastern Greece, which was just beginning to recover from the destruction it had suffered during World War II and the civil war that followed. The road was barely wide enough for two vehicles to pass one another, and the water-filled potholes were so deep I occasionally had to throw a rock into one of them to see if we could drive over it without breaking an axle. All the bridges had been destroyed during the war years, replaced only recently by the metal Bailey bridges of the type I had seen along the Burma Road. The approaches to the bridges were flanked by concrete bunkers pockmarked with bullet holes, again reminding me of the Burma Road, while for Cal, who had served with the US Marines in the Pacific, it brought back memories of Iwo Jima, from which he still had part of a Japanese bullet lodged in his knee. But we kept going and the road gradually improved as we went on, so that we were able to reach Athens in three days.

We checked into a small hotel near Syntagma Square, and the next morning we had breakfast in an outdoor café before going up to the Acropolis. There we found only a handful of other visitors and an old photographer who had on display photos of the Parthenon he had taken in the decades between the two world wars, images of what now seemed like a lost world. He took a photograph of Toots which I still have in an album, showing her standing on the top step of the Parthenon all by herself, more beautiful than the caryatids in their porch nearby.

That evening we whooped it up in an old tavern in the Plaka, where I asked the musicians to play some of the songs I had heard Todori Negroponti sing at the Taverna Boem. Some of the musicians were from Istanbul, known to them as *stin poli*, the City, which they spoke of with what the Greeks call *nostalgia*, for that's where they had left their hearts, as one of them said to me.

The next day we drove on to Nafplion in the Peloponnese, which we used as our base for a two-day tour of the Argolid, where

we visited Argos, Epidavros, Tiryns and Mycenae, all of them
deserted except for a single watchman at the entrance to each site.

It was pelting with rain when we arrived at Mycenae, and the
watchman didn't even emerge from his booth as we entered. We
took cover from the rain in the tholos tomb known as the Treasury of Atreus, once thought to be the burial-place of Agamemnon. As we talked about the blood-drenched history of the House
of Atreus, I recalled a verse from Book 11 of the *Odyssey*, where
Odysseus speaks to the shade of Agamemnon in the Underworld:

> Shame it is, how most terrible Zeus of the wide brows
> from the beginning has been hateful to the seed of Atreus
> through the schemes of women. Many of us died for the sake
>     of Helen,
> and when you were far, Clytemnestra plotted treason against
> you.

We then returned to Athens for one last night before starting our return journey. This time we went to a taverna in Piraeus
frequented mostly by Greek refugees from Turkey, where the music
we heard originated in Smyrna during the last years of the Ottoman era, the haunting *rebetika*, or Greek blues, sung to the accompaniment of the bouzouki. The refrain of one song in particular
always comes to mind when I recall that evening in Piraeus, in
whose slums the Smyrna refugees began a new life after their
banishment from Asia Minor:

> Cheer up, my refugee girl, forget your misfortune
> And one day we'll return to our familiar haunt.
> We'll build our nest in our lovely Smyrna
> And you'll enjoy my sweet love and embraces

Our return journey was pleasantly uneventful, for the weather,
which had been dismal, suddenly changed and we enjoyed what
the Greeks called *halkiyonides meres*, or halcyon days, spring in the
depths of winter, when wild flowers and fruit trees suddenly burst
into bloom throughout the Greek countryside, lifting our spirits,

and we returned to Istanbul with light hearts, ready to get back to work after our long vacation.

The rest of the winter passed quickly, as we resumed our routine of school, parties and exploring Istanbul. We were scheduled to have a two-week spring break in April and so decided to visit the site of ancient Troy, which I had been thinking about since I first read the *Odyssey* at Brooklyn Tech. One of my students, a Greek named Andreas Dimitriadis, agreed to come with us, for he too had always dreamed of visiting Troy.

We booked passage once again on the *Akdeniz*, which brought us to Çanakkale, the largest port on the Asian shore of the Helle-spont, better known in English as the Dardanelles, where we checked in at a small hotel on the waterfront.

The next morning we boarded a bus that dropped us off near the site of Troy. Tourism had not yet begun in Turkey, and so we had the site all to ourselves except for a Turkish gendarme who was guarding the ruins. I had re-read the *Iliad* and *Odyssey* in preparation for our visit, as well as the works of Heinrich Schlie-mann, who in 1870 began excavating a mound called Hisarlık at the inner end of the Trojan plain, convinced that one of the layers of the stratified ruins he unearthed was that of the Homeric city.

It was a beautiful spring day, and after we explored the ruins we had a picnic under a valonia oak on the peak of the Hisarlık mound, which was still deeply scarred by Schliemann's excavation trenches. The mound commanded a sweeping view to the north-west, the noonday sun glinting on what Homer called the 'lovely waters' of the Scamander River as it meandered through the 'blos-soming meadow' of the Trojan plain, on its way to join the 'swift flowing' Hellespont just above Kum Kale, where the strait flows into the Aegean.

A short way to the south of Kum Kale we could see two conical mounds standing close by one another near the Aegean shore. I knew from my reading that the one to the south was the tumu-lus that Schliemann had identified as the tomb of Achilles and Patroclus. Andreas and I decided that we would hike out across the plain to Kum Kale to have a close look at the tumuli, while Toots watched the children as they played among the ruins on the mound. I estimated from my map that Kum Kale was about six kilometres distant, which shouldn't take us much more than an hour. But it took at least twice as long because our way was blocked by the Scamander, which we finally managed to cross near Kum Kale on a primitive Tarzan-like bridge made from two cables, one to tightrope walk on and the other to grasp hand over hand.

We found the tumuli about a kilometre south of Kum Kale, and we stopped to rest at the one that Schliemann had identified as the Tomb of Achilles and Patroclus, which was surrounded by the turbaned tombstones of an old Turkish graveyard. While we sat there I took out my copy of the *Odyssey*, reading the passage in Book 24 where the shades of the fallen heroes meet in the Under-world and Agamemnon tells Achilles of the funerary monument that the Achaeans had erected in memory of him and Patroclus, whose cremated remains they buried together on the Trojan plain, covering it with a great mound 'so that it can be seen afar out on the water / by men now alive and those to be born in the future'.

The next morning all three of the children woke up with high temperatures, and when we took them to the hospital we learned that they had come down with scarlet fever. The hospital direc-tor took it upon himself to look after us and gave us a private room with four beds, one of them for Toots so that she could stay with the children. After a few days the director said that they were well enough to leave, and so we returned to Istanbul aboard the *Akdeniz*, on which we were given our own stateroom to quarantine us from the other passengers.

Our summer holiday was to begin in mid-June, and we decided to travel by train to Spain, which would take us around most of the European coast of the Mediterranean. And so on the day after classes ended we boarded the train at Sirkeci Station on the Golden Horn.

The first stage of our journey took us from Turkish Thrace through Bulgaria, Yugoslavia and north-eastern Italy to Venice, where we stopped off for three days, vowing to return for a much longer stay as soon as we could. We then continued on through northern Italy, the south of France and along the Spanish coast as far as Valencia, where we took a bus to Benidorm.

Benidorm had already been inundated by the first wave of mass tourism, and we decided that we would try to find a less developed place further along the coast where we might spend a few weeks. So I rented a bicycle and set off early the next morning, passing the last of the seaside hotels and then heading on into open countryside. After cycling for half an hour or so, I saw a hand-lettered sign on the left side of the highway advertising a seaside pension at a place called La Cala de Finestrat, a couple of hundred metres down a dirt road. It turned out to be a small hotel with half a dozen rooms and a little outdoor restaurant on the balcony, looking out on a beautiful crescent beach about 200 metres long between two rocky promontories, with only a handful of bathers, who seemed to be locals. There were two adjacent rooms vacant, both of them with balconies overlooking the sea, and I booked both of them for a week with full board, which for all five of us came to less than $5 a day. The owner took me back to Benidorm in his jeep to pick up Toots and the kids, and that afternoon we enjoyed a siesta in our rooms, having had our first swim of the summer.

We stayed in the hotel for three weeks, and never once did we see another foreigner. There was a *guardia civil* post on the hillside above the hotel, and I got to know the sergeant in charge, who introduced himself as Juan. Juan spoke a bit of English and would sometimes join me for a few drinks when he was off duty. It was Juan who told me with sadness that Ernest Hemingway had committed suicide on 2 July 1961.

We loved La Cala de Finestrat but decided that we should move on to see more of Spain while we had the opportunity. So we left and went on to visit Granada, Cordoba, Seville and Madrid, where, after an evening watching flamenco dancers at a somewhat expensive restaurant, I counted my money and realized that I didn't have enough to get us home by the same route that we had travelled to Spain. So I booked train tickets to Barcelona, thinking that we might be able to return on a ship of the Turkish Maritime Lines, travelling deck class. But I learned that the next ship wouldn't leave for a week, so I booked train tickets to Rome, figuring that we could fly back to Istanbul from there on THY, the Turkish national airline.

When we arrived in Rome we checked in at a cheap hotel at the train station and then made our way to the office of THY, where I booked tickets on a flight to Istanbul for the following day. We didn't have nearly enough money to pay the fare, but the manager agreed to take a personal cheque, though I knew that our bank balance was close to zero.

When we landed in Istanbul the next day we took the airport bus into town and then a taxi to our apartment. The fare was ten Turkish liras, or slightly more than $1, and when I went through my pockets I found that all I had left was a $5 bill, so I handed it to the driver and he gave me the change in Turkish currency, which I used to buy groceries for our supper and breakfast.

The next day I went to the finance office at the college, where I got an advance on my dollar salary to cover the cheque that Toots had written at the THY office in Rome, as well as enough Turkish liras to get us through to the next pay day. Such was the end of our first year at Robert College, the beginning of our odyssey.

# 4

# AROUND THE EASTERN
# MEDITERRANEAN

On the Saturday night before school began the Green-woods gave a party to welcome the new faculty. It was the best party we'd yet been to, and we met people who would become lifelong friends, including Peter and Rosemary Shiras, Bob and Jonatha Ceeley, Lee and Carol Fonger, Roddy and Olga O'Connor, Magali Gaster and the young American writer Geoffrey Wolff. When the party ended I took Toots home and then joined Michael Austin and Geoffrey for a midnight swim in the Bosphorus, a dip that ended abruptly when I saw a huge freighter bearing down on us. Years later I read an account of this escapade in Geoffrey's autobiography, where the chapter on his two years in Istanbul is mostly a blur because he was seldom sober.

That fall I began teaching in the physics department, along with Bob McMickle and Hans Weltin, the chairman. Bob had told me that Weltin, a German émigré with a doctorate from Berkeley, was a cantankerous old tyrant who had made his life miserable for the past two years. But Weltin, who had a wry sense of humour, seemed to take a liking to me, though I could see that I would have to watch my step with him. When he questioned me about my experience I told him that I had never taught physics before but that I had worked for nine years as an experimental physicist. That pleased him, and he said that I would teach a course in freshman physics with him and help him set up the lecture demonstrations and the laboratory classes, while Bob would be in charge of the second-year course. We would all teach upper-level courses as well, since we were trying to develop a physics major programme, so I volunteered to offer a course in atomic physics, for that was the field in which I had done my research.

All went well for the first few weeks, as Weltin taught me how to teach elementary physics the old-fashioned way, with meticulously planned lectures accompanied by experimental demonstrations that he had designed and which I set up before class. But then we had a falling out when he accused me of having lost a student's test paper, which, as it turned out, he had himself misplaced. A few weeks later he had a serious argument with Bob Hall, after which he resigned and flew back to the US with his family. Bob McMickle was then appointed chairman and the two of us took over Weltin's courses, beginning a collaboration that would last for 15 years and develop a physics major programme that continues to the present day.

The college had just instituted a two-year humanities course required of all students, and I volunteered to lecture on the history of science, which I had been studying on my own since I first began working as a physicist. I also began teaching a course in astronomy, an interest that had begun when I learned about the discovery of Pluto when I was in elementary school.

During the autumn vacation Toots and I left the children with Gulsun and took a bus to Izmir, where we stayed in a small hotel near the waterfront. We then went on to visit the ruins of Pergamum and Ephesus, both of which we had entirely to ourselves. I still have a photo of Toots sitting on an ancient column capital in Ephesus, looking like the goddess Artemis surveying the ruins of her abandoned city. Whenever I look at that picture I think of the words written by the antiquarian Richard Chandler after his visit to Ephesus in 1765, when he searched for the famous Temple of Artemis: 'she who must be adored', but 'to as little purpose as the travellers who had preceded us ... We now seek in vain for the temple: the city is prostrate: and the goddess gone.'

Toots and I decided that we would travel through the Middle East during the mid-year break, for we might never have the chance to see that part of the world again. I went to a travel agent named Numan Bey, and with his help worked out an itinerary that would take us to Alexandria on a Russian ship; then, after ten days in Egypt, we would take an Italian ship to Beirut, from where we would make our way back to Istanbul overland through Syria and Anatolia. Numan Bey seemed a little dubious at first when I told him that we would be taking our children along, but then he smiled and said that he admired our spirit of adventure.

Early in January 1962 we boarded the *Felix Dzerzhinsky,* a Russian cruise ship whose home port was Odessa. Most of the passengers were Armenian refugees from Romania, all of whom disembarked in Piraeus. The remaining passengers going on to Alexandria all seemed to be Egyptians, including half a dozen army officers who sat at the table next to ours in the dining room, where a band played dance music after supper.

After supper on the first evening one of the officers came over and in perfect English asked my permission to dance with Eileen. I said that it would be fine, and he lifted Eileen up so that she could stand on his shoes as he led her around the dance floor in a slow foxtrot. After the dance I invited him to join us for a while, and he said that he and his companions were returning from Russia, where for two years they had been training as fighter pilots. He said that they had been under constant surveillance the entire time and now were happy to be going home. When he got up to leave, thanking us for our company, he handed me his card, which identified him as Major Hosni Mubarak. The name stuck in my memory, and in 1981, when he became president of Egypt, I reminded Eileen that she had once been his dancing partner.

After we landed in Alexandria we took a bus to Cairo and checked in at a hotel that Numan Bey had recommended. That fall I had gotten to know Peter Badeau, a young American who was studying at Robert College for a year. His father, John S. Badeau, was the US ambassador to Egypt and had previously been head of the American University in Cairo. Peter had grown up in Cairo and spoke fluent Arabic, and when I told him that we were going to Egypt he said that I should call him when we arrived and he would give us a tour of the pyramids.

I called Peter, who arrived at the hotel to pick us up with a car and driver from the US Embassy. We went first to see the pyramids at Giza and the Sphinx, and then to Saqqarah where we visited the Step Pyramid of Zozer, after which we went on to see the royal necropolis at Dahshur, particularly the Bent Pyramid. At Dahsur Peter took me up into the inner chamber of the Bent Pyramid, high on its west face, where we climbed a rickety ladder 50 feet long, joining a group of Bedouin squatting there in utter darkness. While Peter chatted with the Bedouin, I looked down towards the little rectangle of light at the entrance far below, thinking of myself and Jimmy Anderson hanging upside down from the pipes on the ceiling of our abandoned ice-house in Brooklyn.

We spent the next two days exploring Cairo before travelling up the Nile by train as far as Luxor. After seeing the Temple of Amun at Luxor and the Valley of the Kings, we hired a car to take us up to Edfu before returning by train to Cairo. The ancient Egyptian monuments were extraordinary, as I knew they would be, for I had first seen them in *A Pictorial Journey Around the World*. It was the Nile itself and the people living along it 'between the desert and the sown' that left the deepest impression, for this was one of the places where civilization began back in time immemorial.

As soon as we arrived in Cairo we got on a crowded bus that was leaving for Alexandria, where we were due to board the Italian ship later that day. Halfway there the bus stopped at a roadside restaurant where we had a quick lunch. We were separated getting back on the bus, and when I got on with Brendan, just as we started off, I saw Toots sitting in the back with Maureen. But there was no sign of Eileen, and I realized that we had left her behind in the restaurant. I was right behind the driver and I shouted at him in English to stop, but he didn't know what I was saying until one of the other passengers who understood what had happened spoke to him. As we headed back to the restaurant we saw two waiters running towards us with Eileen, who was screaming her head off, and even after we were reunited on the bus she sobbed all the way to Alexandria.

When we arrived we found that the port had been temporarily

shut down because of the arrival of President Tito of Yugoslavia, who was making a state visit to President Nasser of Egypt. We were caught up in the crowds trying to catch a glimpse of the two leaders, and Toots held on to Maureen and Eileen while I carried Brendan on my shoulders. I was standing alongside the railway line from the Maritime Station when I heard a tremendous cheer as an engine came along slowly, pulling two coaches and a flatcar on which Tito and Nasser were seated with their wives on two facing thrones, and they did a double take when they saw me and Brendan amid a sea of Arabs.

After they passed, the port reopened and we were able to get aboard the Italian ship we had booked to Beirut, where we arrived the following day. We then took a bus to Aleppo, where we checked into a hotel close to the bus station. The manager spoke English, so I asked him for advice on the best way for us to cross the border from Syria into Turkey. He pointed to a subterranean garage next to the hotel and said that I would be able to find a taxi there that would take us to Antakya, the first big town inside the Turkish border.

I went down into the garage, adjusting my eyes to the darkness, when I heard a voice call out, 'What are you doing here, Professor Freely?' It was Avram Hagopian, an Armenian student of mine at Robert College, who came running over to greet me. Avram's father owned the garage, and they arranged for a driver to pick us up at the hotel the following morning. They said that it would be better to go on to Adana rather than stop at Antakya, since from there we could take a bus directly to Istanbul, and I agreed.

When we arrived in Adana we checked into a hotel near the bus station. But on the way to the station the following morning I was approached by a taxi driver, who offered to drive us to Istanbul for 500 liras, a little over $50. I checked my pockets and found that I had $60 left, so I agreed. Our route took us right across the heart of Anatolia, and, since there was little traffic, we were home before midnight, just a day before the spring semester began.

As the spring vacation approached, Toots and I decided that we would fly to Beirut, and from there make our way to Israel and Jordan, but without the kids, since I was hoping to explore

places off the beaten track where it might be difficult to take children. Gulsun said she would be happy to babysit for us, and so we
booked a Turkish Airlines flight to Beirut, scheduled to depart on
the first day of our vacation. Godfrey Goodwin had invited all of
us for brunch at his apartment that day, so we spent half an hour
there with our friends before leaving for the airport.

After we arrived in Beirut we went to a very cheap hotel that
had been recommended by Numan Bey, who said that it was 'a
*little* native'. When the taxi dropped us off at the hotel, which
was on the seaside in a very rundown neighbourhood, we found
a drunk urinating on its front door. Our room was very small,
and we had to share the bathroom with a transvestite who sang in
Arabic while showering. But there was a balcony overlooking the
Mediterranean, and before we went out that evening we sat there
for a while to watch the sunset.

We went to a French restaurant called Lucullus, which we had
been told was the best in Beirut, and because of the favourable
exchange rate we could easily afford it. There were only a few other
guests, most of them older people, some of them speaking French,
and the atmosphere was very subdued. But then there was a racket
on the street outside and I could hear several people shouting in
English and laughing loudly as they made their way up the stairway to Lucullus, literally bursting into the restaurant. We were
flabbergasted, for they were the friends we had seen at Godfrey's
brunch just a few hours before: Keith and Joanne Greenwood, Lee
and Carol Fonger, Hilary Sumner-Boyd and Michael Austin. The
waiters set up two more tables so that they could join us, and after
they ordered drinks they explained that they had all decided to fly
to Beirut while at Godfrey's party.

So what began as a quiet supper for two became a continuation of Godfrey's party. Michael had taught for a year at the Arab
university in Beirut and knew the town well, particularly its lower
depths, or so I suspected, and after supper he took us to a bar
called 'Joe's Place', where an old-fashioned jukebox was playing
American songs that I hadn't heard in years, but which Keith and
Toots knew by heart and sang together. The party was still going
strong when Toots and I left the bar around midnight, for we were

leaving early the next morning for Jerusalem.

At Jerusalem we checked in at an old hotel that looked as if it dated back to the days of the Grand Tour, particularly the lobby, and I could picture Mark Twain sitting there during his tour of the Holy Land in 1867, when he wrote that Jerusalem was 'a dream world ... sacred to poetry and tradition'. More pious pilgrims would have recalled Psalm 46: 'God is in its midst; it will not be toppled.'

One of my students at Robert College, a Christian Arab named Emile Khoury, had asked me to call on his family while we were in Jerusalem. His father was a priest in a Greek Orthodox church near the Church of the Holy Sepulchre, and Emile had marked up a map of the city with a red line so that we could find it. Emile said that his ancestors had been priests in that church since its founding in the thirteenth century, and that he, as the only son, was expected to succeed his father. But he was engaged to marry a Turkish girl, and when he informed his parents they disowned him. Emile was hoping that our visit would be the first step towards a reconciliation, and he had written to his family to say that we would be calling on them.

We entered the Old City through the Jaffa Gate and turned left on the main street of the Christian quarter, passing the Church of the Holy Sepulchre, following the red line that Emile had drawn on the map until we found his family home, which adjoined his father's church. We were welcomed in by a young woman who in perfect English said that she was Emile's sister and introduced us to her father and mother and then served us tea. We passed an extremely pleasant hour or so with them, though when I mentioned Emile's name his father responded only by bringing out the family Bible, where on the front page were writ- ten the names of all his ancestors who had served as priests in the church for the past 700 years, after which he closed the book with a sigh.

We then visited the Church of the Holy Sepulchre as well as the rest of the Christian quarter, after which we spent the remain- der of that day and all of the following exploring the Armenian, Jewish and Muslim quarters and the Dome of the Rock, and then ascended the Mount of Olives to watch the sun setting over the Holy City.

There were very few guests in our hotel, which had seen better days, and that evening the only others in the dining room were a young couple with a baby who were seated at the next table. They introduced themselves as the Powells, and said that they were teaching at the American school in Üsküdar, on the Asian side of Istanbul. They had driven from Istanbul and were hoping to continue on through Jordan to Petra and Aqaba. After we got to know one another they invited us to join them, and so the following morning we set off.

Our route took us across the Jordan to Amman, and then past the Dead Sea south through the desert as far as the turnoff for Petra. It was almost sunset by the time we arrived at what is now the Visitors Centre, but which was then a Jordanian Army outpost. The officer in charge, seeing the Powell's baby, graciously invited us to spend the night in their guest room.

We started off early the next morning, passing through the Siq, a narrow passage through the gorge that leads to Al-Khazneh, the so-called 'Pharaoh's Treasury', a colossal temple facade deeply carved into the face of the sandstone cliff that towers above it. This is the iconic image of Petra, the 'rose-red city half as old as time', another place I had first learned of in reading A *Pictorial Journey Around the World*. We spent the whole day exploring the site and stayed overnight in the army outpost. Next morning we thanked the commander for his hospitality and headed south across the desert towards Aqaba.

Aqaba, Jordan's only port, is just a ten-kilometre strip of sand at the head of the Red Sea between Israel and Saudi Arabia. It is now Jordan's fastest growing city and industrial centre, with a population of over 100,000, but in 1962 Aqaba was just a seaside hamlet with a small and simple hotel and restaurant on the beach, along with a score of tents that had been set up for the filming of *Lawrence of Arabia*, directed by David Lean and starring Peter O'Toole. After we checked in at the hotel I spoke to one of the film crew, who told me that the cast were off in the Wadi Rum filming a desert scene and wouldn't return for a couple of days.

We started back early the next morning for Amman, where we planned to spend the night. Midway there we stopped at a petrol station, where we got out to stretch our legs. While we were there a black limousine pulled up behind us, its antenna flying the ensign of a four-star general of the Jordanian Army. Their radio was turned up to full volume, and I was thrilled to hear what I presumed was a Jordanian Army piper band playing songs that I recognized from St Patrick's Day parades in New York such as 'The Barren Rocks of Aden' and the 'Burial of Sir John Moore'. Then I realized that it was 17 March, St Patrick's Day, and as the skirling of the bagpipes resounded across the desert I gave a thumbs-up to the general, who was stretching his legs too, and he smiled broadly as he gave me a thumbs-up in return.

We parted company with the Powells in Damascus, since they were driving on to Aleppo and then to Istanbul. We spent that day and the following one exploring Damascus, visiting the Umayyad Mosque, shopping in the souk, and following in the footsteps of St Paul along the 'street called straight', the Roman Via Recta, which took us into the heart of the medieval Arab city.

Time and money were running short, so we spent only one full day in Aleppo, where we saw the Citadel, the Great Mosque, the Souk az-Zirb and the Khan al-Shouneh, and explored the old quarters in the Jdeydeh district.

Avram Hagopian was expecting us, so when we appeared in his family garage he immediately arranged for a taxi to take us across the border into Turkey. But this time we spent the better part of a day in Antakya, exploring the remains of the ancient city of Antioch before going on to Adana, where we took a bus back to Istanbul. We arrived home two days before the end of the vacation, spending the weekend telling the children of our adventures.

That same spring a group of us at the college founded a literary magazine called the *Golden Horn*, which came out annually for the next decade, with works by American, Turkish, British and Irish writers, playwrights, artists and photographers, including a short story by Yaşar Kemal, who had been nominated for the Nobel Prize, poems by Philip Booth and Richard Eberhart, both of whom had won Bollingen Prizes, as well as works by several of our faculty who went on to become well-known writers, most notably Geoffrey Wolff, Asa Baber and Godfrey Goodwin. Short stories and essays of mine were published in almost every issue, along with poems by Jim Lovett, for which I took a lot of heat from the 'Hill Crowd', the sophisticates who lived in the old college houses above the campus, who looked down upon us as a bunch of amateurs who could only get published in our own magazine. But it didn't bother me in the least and I just went on writing.

The rest of the spring passed quickly and we began planning our summer vacation, which we thought we would spend on the Greek islands. I had done a great deal of reading about the islands and decided that we would go to Naxos, the largest and most historic of the Cyclades, a spiral marine galaxy encircling the sacred centre at Delos, mythical birthplace of Apollo. Herodotus described it as 'the richest island in the Aegean'. Naxos had been at the centre of events in the Aegean throughout antiquity, and then early in the thirteenth century, after it was conquered by the Venetians under Marco Sanudo, it became capital of the Latin Duchy of the Archipelago, which lasted until the Aegean isles fell to the Turks in the mid-sixteenth century. This is the archipelago of which Keats wrote in his *Hyperion*: 'I dream of thee and of the Cyclades'.

We booked tickets on the *San Marco*, an Italian ship that stopped in Piraeus en route to Italy, an overnight journey that cost us just $40, travelling deck class without food, which we brought ourselves. After we landed in Piraeus the following morning, we walked around the port to the quay from which the island ferries docked. I looked at the schedule and saw that there was a ferry, the *Despina*, departing for Naxos, stopping at Syros and Paros. The fare for deck class was 40 drachmas a person, half-fare for children, which at 30 drachmas to the dollar came to $4.67 for the five of us. We walked along the quay until we found the *Despina*, which had just let down its gangway, so we went straight aboard, sitting on wooden benches on the open upper deck at the rear of the ship, beginning a voyage that took us out of the Saronic Gulf and through the heart of the Cyclades to Naxos.

It was past midnight when the *Despina* finally made her way into the port of Chora, the main town of Naxos, dropping anchor a couple of hundred metres from shore since her draft was too deep to tie up at the little mole that had been built by Marco Sanudo in 1207. Half a dozen rowboats came out to take us ashore, and our fellow passengers were all crowded around the approach to the gangway. I knew it would be a while before we disembarked, so I stood at the rail to survey the scene, identifying the places that I had been reading about.

The north side of the harbour was enclosed by a breakwater and causeway, which extended out to a rock-bound islet crowned by the colossal marble portal of an archaic temple dedicated to Apollo. The town itself extended from the inner end of the causeway to the rocky promontory that enclosed the southern side of the harbour, a tiered labyrinth of white houses dominated by the Castro, the seven-towered Venetian citadel surmounting the acropolis hill.

We were the last to be taken ashore, and as we stood there on the quay I could see some of our fellow passengers boarding a bus and others making their way into the town, which seemed to have closed down for the night, leaving us all by ourselves. Just then a middle-aged gentleman approached us and in perfect English said, 'Good evening, welcome to Naxos.' He introduced himself as Mihali Zevgolis and said that he had a small hotel, the Dionysos, where he would put us up during our stay on Naxos. I agreed without even asking the price, for I was beginning to worry about where we would spend the night.

I asked him if there was anywhere we could have supper first, and he led us across the road to the *plateia*, the arcaded Venetian square just off the quay. The only place that seemed to be open was a little restaurant with its tables set up in the square, though there was no one there except for a waiter who was sound asleep on a chair. The lights were still on in the kitchen, which was literally a hole in the wall under an archway of the arcade. A little old lady was sitting inside, and as soon as Mihali shouted 'Vangela!' she rushed out to greet us, kissing the children as she sat us down, shouting 'Yorgo!' to wake up the waiter. Yorgo, whose last name was Spiridakis, brought us a basket of bread, a jug of water, a flagon of retsina straight from the barrel, and some mezedes, after which he served us plates of souvlaki and a Greek salad. As soon as we were settled Mihali left to take our luggage to the hotel, saying he'd come back to fetch us after we'd finished supper.

I had picked up a bit of Greek in Istanbul and on our trip to Athens, so when Vangela and Yorgo sat down at the next table I was able to carry on a primitive conversation with them. Vangela said that she and her husband had opened the restaurant about ten years ago, and after he died she had run it with the help of two of her daughters, with Yorgo occasionally filling in. She laughed when she referred to him as Koukarakia, the Little Crow, since he was small and dark, shuffling his feet and flapping his bent arm when he walked, like a crippled raven.

When Mihali returned we said goodnight to Vangela and Yorgo and went off with him to the Dionysos, which turned out to be a thirteenth-century Venetian tower directly under the walls of the Castro. There were only two rooms, one above the other, each with a big four-poster bed. The children wanted to be with Toots, and so they took the lower room and I went to the upper one, where I took off my shoes and plopped into bed without undressing.

When I woke up in the morning I found someone curled up at the foot of my bed, cradling a violin in his arms. Then he woke up too, growling 'Kalimera' (Good Morning), as he put on his shoes and left with his violin in hand. I later learned that my bed-mate was the famous fiddler Mihali Karavoulas, who had been playing at a village festival and hadn't returned to town until three in the morning. Mihali Zevgolis had put him up in my room, telling him to leave before I awoke.

I didn't bother saying anything about this when I went down to the lobby and asked our host for the bill, which was much more than what we had paid at hotels during our trip to Greece with the Atwoods. I simply paid the bill, chalking it up to experience, and when Toots and the kids appeared we left the Dionysos with our luggage and walked back down to the *plateia*.

We had breakfast at a café on the waterfront, and while we were sitting there Yorgo appeared, selling lottery tickets. He laughed hilariously when I told him what had happened at the Dionysos, for it seems that Mihali Zevgolis was well known as a *kleftis*, a thief, as was everyone else in Apeiranthos, the Naxian mountain village of Cretan refugees where he had been born.

I asked Yorgo if he knew a place where we might stay, and when he said he did we followed him through the Borgo, the poorer part of the lower town, where we were greeted by a succession of little old ladies in black sitting outside their doorways, knitting and chatting with their neighbours. We finally stopped at the doorway of a two-storeyed house, where Yorgo shouted 'Maria!' and a very pleasant middle-aged lady welcomed us into the courtyard, kissing each of the children. She showed us a very nice two-bedroom apartment on the upper floor, and when she said that the rent was 40 drachmas a night, the equivalent of $1.33, we immediately agreed to take it.

As soon as we were settled in we went out to the *paralia*, the waterfront promenade that extended around the northern side of the harbour to the causeway that led out to the rocky islet I had seen the night before, crowned with the colossal marble portal of Apollo's temple. We decided that we would have a picnic out on the islet, known to the locals as Palatia.

We had our picnic sitting under the temple doorway, looking out across the strait towards the mountains of Paros. The strait between Naxos and Paros is the narrowest stretch of the maritime highway between Attica and Crete, and Hellenic mariners had been sailing through it since the time of Homer, who mentions Naxos in the *Odyssey*. Theseus and his companions passed this way on their voyage to Crete, and again on their return voyage after Ariadne had led them out of the labyrinth. But Theseus abandoned Ariadne on Naxos, sailing away in the night while she slept on the islet. She was found the next morning by Dionysus, who had himself been left on Naxos by the pirates who had captured him in his youth. They were wed in a *hierogammos*, a sacred wedding, after which Dionysus set Ariadne's bridal wreath among the stars, where it still illuminates the night sky as the constellation Corona Borealis. During the Middle Ages, when the ancient gods were no longer officially worshiped on Naxos but by no means forgotten, the islanders believed that the ruined temple on the islet had been Ariadne's *palatia*, or palace, the name by which it is still known today.

The townspeople always took a mid-day dip at the little beach at the northern end of the harbour, below the Palatia, and so we swam there after our picnic. We spent the next few days exploring the town, and then on Sunday, when everyone else in the Borgo was in the Greek Orthodox cathedral, we went to mass in the thirteenth-century Roman Catholic cathedral in the Castro. The priest, Father Marangoz, spoke perfect English and introduced us to several other members of the congregation, most of whom were descendants of the Venetians who had conquered Naxos in 1207 and who still lived in one or other of the seven towers of the Castro. One of them, Domina Sommaripa, invited us to have tea on the balcony of her tower-house, looking down on the Borgo and across the strait to Paros. Domina said that if we came back to Naxos she would find us a place to stay in the Castro, which we did the following year.

The next morning we boarded a bus for Apollon, a tiny port on the northern tip of the island. Our route took us through the heart of Naxos, stopping at or passing within sight of nearly all of the island's 54 villages, some of them embowered in vast olive groves, others perched on the flanks of tawny mountains, while our driver blessed himself repeatedly as our bus veered around perilous hairpin turns that reminded me of the Burma Road.

During our stay on Naxos we went to a *paniyeri*, or religious festival, in the village of Tripodes, which is mentioned in the *Odyssey*. The festival was celebrated in the village square, the dancers doing one *syrtos* after another while the musicians played *nisiotika tragoudia*, songs of the Aegean isles. The fiddler turned out to be Mihali Karavoulis, my bed-mate at the Dionysos, and the bouzouki player was Manoli Barbarakis, whom we had met at Vangela's restaurant. Manoli was also the vocalist, and one of the songs he sang that evening always carries me back to Naxos when I recall it:

The lute and the violin
I long to hear again
To bring back the memory
Of an old sweet song of love.


Most evenings we had supper in the *plateia* at Vangela's restaurant, where her two daughters were now helping her while Yorgo
sat in the back with his drinking buddies, all of whom soon became
friends of mine. One of them, a dock worker named Sotiri Peristerakis, was always accompanied by his wife Hermione, whom he
had met and married on Samos when he was in the Greek Navy.
Late in the evening, when he was in his cups, Sotiri would sing
'Samiotissa' (The Girl from Samos) in a voice so gravelly that my
friend Jim Lovett once said, 'If rocks could sing, they'd sing like
Sotiri.' Then Yorgo would sing a *cantada* from the Ionian isles,
where he had served with the Greek Navy during the war. It was
always the same song, 'Yialo, Yialo', and only the first two lines, for
his voice was so cracked and wavering that everyone broke up in
laughter, including Yorgo himself. I can hear him still: 'If the sea
were only wine and the mountains mezedes, / The *caiques* could
be the glasses for revellers to drink!'

There were days on Naxos when I felt that we were alone on a
small planet, floating between the blues of sea and sky, outside of
space and time, and nights when the island seemed to be orbiting
alone among the peacock constellations. I wanted to stay there
forever, and it saddened me to think that we would have to leave.

We stayed on Naxos till the end of July, for a family from
Athens had reserved our apartment for the month of August.
Rather than trying to find another place on Naxos, we thought
that it was time to move on, for we wanted to see some of the
other Aegean islands, particularly Skyros, southernmost of the
Sporades, the 'Scattered Isles' in the northern Aegean.

Three days before we left, Maureen celebrated her tenth birthday in the courtyard of Maria's house, and in one of our albums
there is a photo of her surrounded by a dozen girls her age from
the Borgo whom she befriended that summer. There is also a
photo of our last evening at Vangela's restaurant in the *plateia*,

showing us at a table with her and Yorgo and the many other friends we made that summer, most notably Sotiri and Hermione Peristerakis. They all come out to the pier the following morning to see us off on the *Despina*, and we stood at the rail waving to them until they disappeared from sight.

Since we were running short of money I had sent a cable to the college, asking that an advance on my fall salary be sent to the American Express office in Athens, where I would pick it up on the way to Skyros. We had to wait in Athens for a week for the payment to come through, by which time I was flat broke. We set off for Skyros the morning after the money arrived, boarding a bus that took us across a bridge over the Euripos Channel to Chalkis, capital of Euboea, the second largest island in Greece after Crete. The bus then continued across the island to Kimi, a little port on the western shore of Euboea, where we took a *caique* to Linaria, the port of Skyros. At Linaria we took a bus to Chora, the main town of Skyros, whose cubistic white houses clustered on the steep seaward slope of the acropolis rock, looking down on a long beach that stretched as far as the horizon.

We had lunch at a café in the *plateia*, where we decided that we would look for a place on the beach below Chora. I left Toots in the café with Eileen and Brendan while I went off with Maureen. We walked along the beach, passing a succession of seaside villas that appeared to be summer residences, with no indication that any of them had rooms to rent. I was about to give up when we came to an old windmill standing on a hummock above the beach, with a small concrete house directly behind it and a little porch in front that seemed to be a café-restaurant. I spoke to the owner, who introduced himself as Costa Balabanis, asking him if he had rooms to let, explaining that my wife and two other children were waiting in Chora. Costa said that he had just renovated the mill, which had been in ruins, and that it now had two rooms, one above the other, both of them with an old fashioned divan-bed extending around the periphery, the lower one with a circular table in the centre surrounded by half a dozen low wicker chairs. The price was 40 drachmas a day, the same as we had paid in Maria's place on Naxos, and so I agreed to take it, paying Costa a

1. Brooklyn, 1927: Peg

2. Brooklyn, 1927: John and JF

3. Ireland, 1931: JF, Tomas Murphy and Dorothy

4. Brooklyn, 1936: JF

5. US Navy, 1944: JF

6. Brooklyn, 1947: Toots

7. Red Bank, 1951: JF and Toots

8. Iona College, 1951: JF

9. Princeton, 1960: Brendan, Eileen and Maureen

10. Istanbul, 1960: Maureen, Brendan, Toots and Eileen

11. Spain, 1961: JF

12. Skyros, 1962

13. Cairo, 1962

14. Naples, 1963

15. Paris, 1963:
Toots

16. Athens, 1962

17.  En route to Naxos, 1965

18.  Venice,
1996: Toots

19.  Venice, 1996: JF

20. Istanbul, 2009: Toots on her 80th birthday

21. Istanbul, 2014: JF

week's rent in advance.

Then I asked Costa about the toilet and shower. He took us out to a cement-block outhouse with a brick partition that separated the toilet and the shower. The toilet was just a hole in the concrete floor and the shower was a rubber hose connected to a water tank on the corrugated metal roof of the outhouse. He saw the expressions on our faces, and he said he'd fix up something better before we moved in. He then got a friend named Stefanos to accompany us back to Chora with his donkey, which would carry our luggage when we returned to the mill with the rest of the family. We were back in the mill by mid-afternoon, and after we were settled we all took a nap, Toots, Brendan and me in the lower room, Maureen and Eileen in the upper.

When I woke up I went to the toilet, where the hole in the floor was now surmounted by a wicker chair with a circular orifice carved out of its seat. Then I checked out the shower, where a piece of sheet metal punctured with holes had been inserted in the roof, while the rubber hose was now attached to the bottom of the water tank, so that water came showering down on me when I turned on the tap. I was still dripping when I went out to the porch to have a beer, and when Costa served me I complimented him on the ingenious improvements he had made in the outhouse.

That evening at supper Costa introduced us to his wife Anna, who did the cooking, and their two teenage daughters, Frossa and Maria, who waited at table. There was no menu, so we just looked in Anna's pots and picked out whatever we fancied.

Costa was a fisherman and went out early every morning in his *caique*, setting his nets and lobster pots and spearing an octopus or two in the rocky shallows along the beach. So we had fish and lobster almost every day, and at drinks time before supper Costa always served me three or four tentacles of grilled octopus with my ouzo.

The other customers seemed to be Athenians who had summer cottages near the mill. One of them, a middle-aged gentleman who sat by himself at the next table, came over and introduced himself in perfect English as Spyros Yorgiades. I invited him to join us, and we quickly became good friends.

I didn't see Spyros the next two evenings, but then, just as were finishing supper on the fourth day of our stay, I saw him approaching across the dunes, wiping his eyes with a handkerchief, and when he joined us I could see that he had been weeping. I asked him what was wrong, but at first he could hardly speak. Then, after wiping his eyes again, he told me that he had just heard on the evening news that Marilyn Monroe had died.

That was the only news of the outside world that we heard during the month we spent at the mill. The only foreigner we met was a young Australian back-packer named Rory, who said he was spending a few days on Skyros, hoping to visit the grave of the poet Rupert Brooke.

One of the reasons why I had brought us to Skyros was its association with Rupert Brooke, who had been buried on the island after dying from blood poisoning aboard a French hospital ship on 23 April 1915, at the beginning of the Gallipoli campaign. I had read his poetry in my early teens, when he had become a hero of mine, and I had resolved to visit his grave during our stay on Skyros. I had read an account of his burial and thought I could find his grave, which was on the shore of Tris Boukis bay, south-west of Linaria.

Rory and I started off at dawn the next day, catching the morning bus to Linaria and then heading west along the rock-bound coast. We walked for hours without seeing a soul other than a goatherd tending his flock, and I began to lose hope. But then we finally found the grave, which was marked by a small monument in an olive grove above a rocky beach, where Brooke's companions had carried his body ashore and buried him. While we stood by the grave in the dappled shade of the olive grove I recalled the first stanza of 'The Soldier', the sonnet which anticipated his death in foreign parts: 'If I should die think only this of me: / That there's some corner of a foreign field that is forever England'.

The fifteenth of August is the feast of the Assumption, the most important Greek Orthodox holiday after Easter, and throughout Greece there are *paniyeria* at every church of the Panaghia, the Virgin Mary. On the morning of the *paniyeri*, Costa took us in his *caique* to a little cove north of Chora, where there was a tiny chapel of the Virgin set into a grotto. I learned that the cove was called Achilleion, from the myth that this was where the youthful Achilles was hidden by his father Peleus among the daughters of Lycomedes, King of Skyros, until Odysseus took him off to Troy.

There were a dozen other *caiques* in the cove and more arrived while we were there, everyone coming ashore in their bare feet, as we did, setting up blankets and straw mats on the beach and then filing into the chapel, where a white-bearded priest was just ending the liturgy. Then, after everyone had finished their picnic lunch, an old man took out his fiddle and began playing *nisiotika tragoudia*, as everyone formed up into a circle and began dancing barefoot on the sand in front of the chapel. They were led by a young woman waving her handkerchief as she guided her companions through the interwoven cycles of a *syrtos*, as if she was Ariadne, guiding Theseus and his companions out of the Cretan labyrinth.

We decided to leave Skyros at the end of August, for we wanted to see some of the islands in the northern Aegean before returning to Istanbul. So I sat down with Costa to make out our bill, which worked out to be less than $5 a day for all five us, including our rent, food and drink.

There was a weekly ferry from Linaria that threaded its way through the isles of the northern Aegean en route to Thasos. We booked tickets for the next voyage, and on the appointed day we said goodbye to everyone at the mill, promising to return the following summer. Stefanos loaded our baggage on his donkey and we headed off down the beach towards Chora, never to return.

When we arrived on Thasos we ran into the Greenwoods, who had spent the summer there. Keith had just about run out of money, but I was able to lend him $10 so that they could stay on for a few more days. We spent the following day exploring the town, particularly the ruins of the ancient city, which had been founded by Greeks from Paros in the mid-seventh century BC. One of the colonists was Archilochus of Paros, earliest of the archaic lyric poets, who earned his living as a mercenary soldier. As we sat there having a picnic in the ruins of the ancient city I recalled my favourite lines from Archilochus, which may have been written while he was on Thasos:

> Here I lie mournful with desire,
> feeble in bitterness of the pain gods inflicted upon me,
> struck through the bones with love.

We then took the ferry to Kavala, where we spent the night before boarding a bus to Istanbul the following morning. It was past midnight by the time we got home and fell into bed, ending another stage of our odyssey, which had now taken us entirely around the eastern Mediterranean.

# 5

# LOTUS EATING

Early in the fall semester in 1962 Bob Hall came to my office one afternoon and asked me if I intended to sign up for another three years, telling me to take a while to think about it. I had already been contemplating what we should do and had begun looking through *The Times* weekly educational supplement in the library, where I found interesting job openings at universities in the UK and in places that had formerly been part of the British Empire, such as Malta and Khartoum. I wrote to some of these universities and received very positive responses, and in the evenings Toots and I talked about them while we had our nightcaps on the balcony. Then one evening, when the full moon rose up from the hills of Asia, casting a silver path across the Bosphorus, she turned to me and said, 'Let's stay.' So the following afternoon I went to Bob Hall's office and signed a new contract. And so, during the autumn of 1962, we resumed our routine of exploring Istanbul on Saturday, going on to enjoy the evening at a Turkish *meyhane* or Greek taverna or one of the endless college parties.

My friend Cevat Çapan had an apartment on the Bosphorus just a short walk from ours, and one evening he invited us to a party there. There were a few other Americans from the college, but all the others were Turks, some of them academics from Istanbul University, where Cevat was professor of literature, while the others were writers, artists and theatre people. I had already met some of them at Aliye's parties including the actor Engin Cezzar, the painters Ömer Uluç and Ozer Kabaş, and the photographer Ara Güler, whom Henri Cartier-Bresson once referred to as 'my co-pilot above the Golden Horn'.

I was talking with some friends when a hulking bear of a man strode over and plucked a hair from my beard, which at time was still bright red, and took it back to show his companions, to their great amusement. I recognized him as the novelist Yaşar Kemal, for I had just read *Mehmet My Hawk*, which had his photo on the back cover. Yaşar had his shirt open to the waist, and when he and his group stopped laughing I walked over and plucked a hair from his chest, bringing it back to show to my friends. This brought the house down and began a friendship with Yaşar that continues to this day.

Not long afterwards we threw our first party. It was well under way when Cevat appeared with the American writer James Baldwin, who had just arrived in Istanbul. Earlier that day I had read a short story of his in the *Atlantic* magazine – 'This morning, this evening, so soon' – about two young black couples in Paris just after the war. It was a custom of ours that anyone who crashed one of our parties had to sing for his supper, so Maureen and Eileen, dressed in Toots' clothes, marched Baldwin into the living room, where he stood up on a table and sang an old black folksong called 'Tell Old Bill', and then I realized where the title of his story came from:

Tell old Bill when he comes home this morning,
Tell old Bill when he comes home this evening,
Tell old Bill when he comes home,
to leave them downtown gals alone,
This morning, this evening, so soon.

As the autumn vacation approached Jim Lovett and his wife Carla invited me and Toots to join them on a drive along the Aegean coast, and so we again left the children with Gulsun and set off. The first leg of our journey took us from Istanbul around the European shore of the Marmara to the Dardanelles, where we spent the night in Gelibolu, Greek Gallipoli. The next morning we took the car-ferry cross the strait to Çanakkale, where we had a morning dip in the Dardanelles before setting off to drive south through the Troad, the country around Troy. We had brought along food and wine, so when we crossed the upper reaches of the Scamander we stopped to have a swim and then a picnic lunch on the banks of the river, which flows through the Trojan plain on its way to the Aegean end of the Hellespont.

We had our third swim of the day at Ayvalık, on the Aegean coast just opposite Lesbos, where we checked into a hotel on the waterfront. That evening as we ate supper we looked across the strait to see the blue mountains of Lesbos after the moon had set, and I recalled a fragment from Sappho:

The Moon is down.
The Pleiades. Midnight.
The hours flow on.
I lie alone.

During the following days we drove down the Aegean coast through the regions known in antiquity as Aeolia, Ionia and Caria, and then back overland through Lydia, Phrygia and Bithynia to Istanbul. There were a few visitors at major sites like Ephesus, which had been empty when Toots and I had been there three months earlier, in the dead of winter, but most of them were Turks, for mass tourism had not yet engulfed Turkey. But lesser-known sites were completely deserted, with not even a watchman in sight, as at Euromus in Caria, which didn't even have a sign to identify it. I had read about Euromus in a book on the antiquities of Turkey and I spotted it as we drove by, its Temple of Zeus embowered in an olive grove a couple of hundred metres from the road.

We took our picnic lunch and a bottle of wine and sat under a gnarled old olive tree, which had entwined itself around one of the columns of the temple, as if embracing it. While we sat there, taking in the beauty of the site, we were joined by two old shepherdesses who bade us welcome and then sat watching their flock grazing in a nearby field. One of them said, pointing at the temple, 'Eski, çok eski!', meaning that it was very old. After Jim responded, for he was fairly fluent in Turkish, the other woman nodded and said that the temple was indeed very old, for it had been standing there when they were children.

I still have a photo of the temple that I took that day, and it remains as the enduring image of our early trips through Anatolia, which I later described in *The Western Shores of Turkey*, published in 1988. By that time the modern world had discovered this lost arcadia, spoiling it forever, but not in my memory, where it remains the same as it was when I first saw it in what now seems a golden age.

Towards the end of the day, as we sat at a little café on the waterfront in Bodrum, Greek Halicarnassus, watching the sunset, I recalled the lines written in the fourth century BC by Callimachus of Cyrene in memory of his beloved friend, the poet Heracleitus of Halicarnassus:

They brought me news of your death, Heracleitus, and I wept for you, remembering how often we talked the sun across the sky. Dear Halicarnassian friend, you lie elsewhere now and are mere ashes; yet your songs – your nightingales – will live forever. And never will the underworld, destroying everything, touch you with its ugly hand.

We decided to go to Paris for our winter vacation, and since Gulsun would be visiting her parents, we left the children under the care of a 60-ish Englishwoman named Rena Duren, known to all as Aunty. Numan Bey booked us tickets on the Orient Express, and as we boarded it at Sirkeci Station we could see that it had lost all its former glamour: there were no sleeping cars and no dining car, so we had to sit in an unheated and overcrowded compartment for nearly four days, getting our food and drink from little cafés in the railway stations where we stopped. The first half of the journey, though Bulgaria and Yugoslavia, was particularly grim, as border guards and policemen barged into our compartment at all hours of the day and night to check our papers, looking at the two of us with particular suspicion and hostility. But once we crossed the border into Austria the mood lightened and we sat back to enjoy the scenery as we passed through Lichtenstein and Switzerland into France.

It was almost midnight when we finally reached Paris, almost a day behind schedule. Numan Bey had booked us into a small hotel on the Left Bank, and as soon as we were settled we went out to eat in the first place we came to, for we hadn't had a proper meal since we left Istanbul. It turned out to be a Greek restaurant, which was just about to close for the night. But when I spoke to the owner in Greek he served us mezedes, souvlaki and a bottle of retsina, which was hardly what we expected to have on our first night in Paris, but we greatly enjoyed it nonetheless.

We spent the next week exploring Paris by day and by night, and as we walked around I couldn't help thinking of how much had changed since I had last been here in 1946, when some of the buildings were still scarred by bullet marks and everyone, myself included, was still recovering from the effects of the war. There were hardly any tourists, and we had Paris to ourselves, swept up in its gaiety, though we couldn't speak a word of French. In one of our albums there is a photo of Toots standing in front of Notre Dame with not another soul in sight, serene and alone in her beauty.

On the return journey we broke our trip to spend a day in Vienna, making a round of the night spots with friends from the college who were spending the holiday there. We then resumed our journey, but soon after we crossed the border into Bulgaria we ran into a blizzard that stranded us in Sofia for three days. When the blizzard stopped we continued, but on reaching the Turkish border found that the railway line ahead was inundated by a shallow lake formed by the melting snow. We were stuck there for the better part of a day until finally a Turkish Army helicopter flew in to ferry the women and children and older people across the lake, while we able-bodied men waded across the icy knee-deep lake with our luggage. We then boarded a bus that took us into Edirne for the night, and while there I sent off a telegram to

Bob Hall saying 'DELAYED BY FLOODS AT BORDER', for the spring term had already started. My message seemed to have been garbled in transmission, for when I checked in with Bob Hall after our return he showed me my cable, which read 'DELAYED BY FLOTARDS AT BORDER', which made him wonder what I had been drinking when I sent it.

The next two months passed rapidly, and as the spring vacation approached I went to see Numan Bey. He told me that a ship of the Turkish Maritime Lines, a post-boat called the *Tarı*, was scheduled to depart on the first day of our vacation, on an itinerary that would take us along the Aegean and Mediterranean coasts of Turkey as far as Antalya, from where it would go on at Larnaca in Cyprus before returning to Istanbul. I booked tickets for the five of us, and when I spread the word at the college half a dozen of our friends decided to join us.

The *Tarı* stopped briefly at several little ports in the Sea of Marmara and the Dardanelles before reaching Izmir, where it was scheduled to stay for two days before going on to its next stop, a little port called Güllük. Most of us had already visited Izmir, so we decided to travel overland in a convoy of three taxis and rejoin the *Tarı* in Güllük.

We set off early the next morning and by noon reached Bafa Gölü, a shallow lake that in antiquity had been the inner end of the Latmian Gulf, now silted up. The gulf was named after Mount Latmos, which towered over the eastern end of Bafa Gölü, its cloud-plumed peak mirrored in the still waters of the lake.

At the base of the mountain we could see the ruins of ancient Heracleia-under-Latmos, founded in the fourth century BC by King Mausolus of Caria. At that time there was no road to Heracleia, and the only way to reach it was by *caique* from a landing beside the road. The owner of the *caique* had set up a little outdoor eating place on the beach, and we had lunch there in the dappled shade of an olive grove before setting off across the lake.

I had been reading about the site, and so after we explored the temple of Athena, the theatre and the agora, I led the way to the necropolis and found the supposed tomb of Endymion. According to one version of the legend, Endymion was a young shepherd who

one night fell in love with Selene, goddess of the moon, who cast
a spell over him so that he would never grow old but would slum-
ber on in eternal youth. While we stood there beside the tomb I
recited the first lines of Keats' *Endymion*:

> A thing of beauty is a joy forever:
> Its loveliness increases; it will never
> Pass into nothingness; but still will keep
> A bower quiet for us, and a sleep
> Full of sweet dreams, and health, and quiet breathing.

We continued on through the region known in antiquity as
Caria, passing a succession of Graeco-Roman temples and tombs
embowered in olive groves. It was nightfall before we reached
Güllük, where we booked in at the town's only hotel, down at the
port. There were no other guests and so, since we had the whole
place to ourselves, we had a party in the hotel's outdoor café on
the pier.

The party continued the next day, which was Çocuk Bayram,
Children's Holiday, and all the schoolchildren of Güllük and their
teachers paraded up and down the waterfront following the town
band. Some of the townspeople joined us in the café, remaining
until the last call to prayer resounded from the minarets, leaving
us to continue the party by ourselves under the stars.

The *Tarı* arrived the next morning and anchored out in the
harbour, sending a launch to deliver the mail and take us back to
the ship. The other passengers cheered as we came aboard, and we
joined them in the dining room for lunch, which developed into a
continuation of the party that had started in Güllük.

A few hours later we docked in Bodrum, ancient Halicarnassus, where we were to remain until the following morning. We
explored the great Crusader castle of St Peter that dominates the
town from its sea-girt promontory, trying to decipher the coats of
arms on its walls, particularly the English Tower. My friend Evelyn
Lyle Kalchas had written a little book called *Bodrum Castle and its
Knights*, in which she pointed out that all the warriors mentioned
by Shakespeare in the address of King Henry V to the Earl of

Westmoreland before the battle of Agincourt in 1415 are repre-
sented by their coats of arms in the castle of St Peter:

> Then shall our names,
> Familiar in his mouth as household words,
> Harry the king, Bedford and Exeter,
> Warwick and Talbot, Salisbury and Gloucester,
> Be in their flowing cups freshly remember'd.

There were only a few remnants of ancient Halicarnassus to be
seen at that time, most notably the base of the Mausoleum, the
grandiose tomb of King Mausolus, erected in 354 BC. That was just
20 years after Alexander the Great had conquered Halicarnassus,
the birthplace of Herodotus, who at the beginning of his *History*
states the theme of his life's work:

> Herodotus of Halicarnassus, his researches are here put down
> to preserve the memory of the past by putting on record the
> astonishing achievements of both our own and other peoples,
> and more particularly to show how they came into conflict.

After leaving Bodrum, the *Tarı* stopped briefly at Marmaris,
Kalkan and Fethiye before arriving at Anatalya, where it would
spend the night before returning to Istanbul after stopping at
Larnaca. When we went ashore we ran into our friend and neighbour Matt Charles, who was driving along the coast with his wife
Norma and their little daughter Olive. They invited us to join
them, which we thought was a great idea. So I fetched our luggage
from the *Tarı* and said goodbye to our friends, and as soon as we
got aboard Matt drove off, heading eastward along the coast of
Pamphylia.

We revisited the places we had seen between Antalya and
Alanya, where we spent the night. Next day we explored the great
peninsular rock at Alanya, which marks the boundary between
the Pamphylian plain and the region known in antiquity as Cilicia
Tracheia, 'Rugged Cilicia', a rock-bound coast studded with the
ruins of ancient hilltop fortresses. We were told that we would

find no places to eat or sleep along the coast between Alanya and Silifke, 150 kilometres to the east, so we bought food, drink and blankets in case we were benighted.

The road was unpaved, parts of it had collapsed over the precipice on the seaward side, and we had to proceed very slowly and cautiously, so that by the time darkness fell we were still some 40 kilometres from Silifke. It was too dangerous to drive on, so we stopped at a sandy cove identified by a sign as Boğsak, where we spent the night in an abandoned shack on the beach.

When we got up the next morning I was able to identify where we were from the reading I had done about this coast. The cove was bounded to the east by the ruins of a medieval fortress and to the west by a promontory known to the Crusaders as Cape Cavaliere. Near the western end of the crescent bay there was an islet about 100 metres from the shore, which I identified as Provençal Island, another Latin name from the time of the First Crusade at the end of the eleventh century. I swam out to the islet and found it covered with the ruins of medieval buildings, most notably a chapel with Gothic arches, a relic of the Crusade that for a time had transformed this remote coast into an outpost of western Europe.

We drove on to Silifke, from where we headed back to Istanbul across the heart of Anatolia. We spent a couple of days in Cappadocia, exploring the extraordinary rupestrine churches round Göreme, most of them carved out of phallus-like cones known in Turkish as *peri bacaları*, or fairy chimneys. The predominant colours in some areas of Cappadocia are brick-red, rust, ochre or umber, while in others they may be ashen or even salt-white, but the sensuous rock surfaces subtly change their hues with the shifting patterns of sunlight and shadow, here and there deepening into pools of midnight blue, deep violet or even an ephemeral turquoise, and then at twilight the whole landscape is pervaded with an ephemeral pink and golden glow, fading into a pallet of pale pastels as night falls on this enchanted landscape.

We then spent a night in Konya and drove on from there to Istanbul. As always, we arrived home in the middle of the night exhausted, but after the children were bedded down Toots and I summoned up enough energy to have a nightcap on the balcony, celebrating the completion of yet another stage in our odyssey.

Later that spring the Robert College Players, a faculty theatre group founded in 1911, decided to put on a musical comedy called *Little Mary Sunshine* by Rick Besoyan. Toots auditioned, and after she sang one song she was given the lead role, for with her looks and voice she was perfect for the part of Little Mary. The play was a huge success and old timers said it was the best show ever put on at the college. For many years afterwards, whenever we gathered with old friends from the college they would always ask Toots to sing her opening line, 'It's nice to see you here again', to which they sang in response, 'It's nice to be here, Little Mary', all of which now seems an echo from a lost world.

We spent the summer of 1964 on Naxos, which by now I thought of as another world outside of space and time. Domina Sommaripa had found us an apartment in one of the towers of the Venetian Castro, with a large balcony looking out over the lower town and across the strait to Paros. The rent was only a bit more than we had been paying in Maria's place, and since I had received an increase in salary when I signed my new contract I figured we could stay there all summer if we were a bit more careful with our money.

When we went down to the *plateia* to have supper we were disappointed to find that Vargela had retired and had sold her restaurant to someone from Athens. But we met Yorgo Spiridakis, who took us back into the Borgo to show us two little tavernas where he and his pals always ate. The first one belonged to Vasili Voudias, where he usually ate lunch, and the other, a little further up the arcaded street, where he always had supper, was run by Vasili Mylonas, so we came to call them Lower Vasili's and Upper Vasili's.

We had supper that evening at Upper Vasili's, where the cooking was done by Vasili and his wife Nicoletta, while their teenage sons Marco and Costa waited at table, some of which were set up in the narrow side alley that led up to the Castro. We sat down with Sotiri Peristerakis and his wife Hermione, and as the evening went on other friends from the Borgo joined us. Then, as the retsina flowed, Sotiri began singing 'Samiotissa', followed by Yorgo's 'Yialo, Yialo', and soon we were back in our island micro-cosmos, oblivious to what was going on in the rest of the world.

The only other foreign family living in Naxos at the time was a Belgian artist named Theo with his wife and their two small children. Theo had just won an international contest to design a stained-glass window for a church in Bruges, which allowed him to spend the year painting in Greece. He had already spent several weeks painting on Naxos, and so I suggested that the two of us take the weekly boat that went to the little islands west of Naxos, the Lesser Cyclades, and then on to Ios and Santorini before returning to Chora, a three-day voyage. He agreed and we booked passage on the *Myrditiotissa*, travelling deck class.

During the first day the *Myrditiotissa* threaded its way through the Lesser Cyclades, seven of which have been inhabited since at least the fifth millennium BC. We stopped for about an hour each at Donoussa, Koufinissi, Schinoussa and Iraklia. At each of them two or three passengers came aboard or left in rowboats, all of them loaded down with chickens and goats, the new arrivals join-ing me and Theo on the fantail of the ship.

Dr Giovannis, the town physician in Chora on Naxos, had told me that he was sometimes called out to one or another of these islands, which at the time had no electricity, and so in medical emergencies, such as appendicitis, the islanders would light a large bonfire which would be spotted by a goatherd on Mount Zas, who would then ride on his donkey out to the main and only paved road and pass the news on to the driver of the daily bus into town, who would in turn tell one of his passengers to inform the good doctor. Dr Giovannis would then commandeer a *caique* and sail out to the island and perform the appendectomy, for which the grateful islanders would slaughter a sheep for him to take back to Chora, where he shared it with his poorer neighbours in the Borgo.

We stopped for the night in Ios, which tradition holds to be the last resting-place of Homer. Theo and I made our way up the immensely long stepped path from the port to Chora, capital of Ios, where we bedded down in our sleeping bags on the blue dome of one of the whitewashed village churches high above the sea. I was awakened at dawn by the brilliant sun rising out of the Aegean, and I saw that Theo had already completed a drawing in his sketch pad.

Just then I heard the *Myrditiotissa* sounding her horn, and so we joined a dozen villagers and their goats and chickens and made our way down to the port to be loaded onto rowboats that took us out to the ship. Before we boarded the rowboats Theo and I each bought a bag of the Greek pretzels known as *kouloueria*. This was the only food we had on our voyage except for the cheese and hard biscuits we carried in our back-packs, along with canteens that we refilled at a well on Ios and a straw-covered demijohn of home-made retsina that Vasili Mylonas had filled for me at his taverna.

The prevailing wind, the *meltemi*, was blowing from the north-east, just as it did for Odysseus and his crew when they were blown off course to the Land of the Lotus Eaters, but the chugging engine of the *Myrditiotissa* kept us on course towards Santorini, which we finally reached in the middle of a moonless night, tying up at a buoy connected to a weight on the ocean floor.

Once again I was awakened by the brilliant dawn, in what appeared to be the sea-filled core of a volcano. The first rays of the sun were reflecting with almost blinding intensity off the multi-coloured layers of the 1,000ft-high caldera, its rim crowned with a succession of white Cycladic towns that looked like troglodyte settlements, burrowed into the uppermost level of the striated mixture of volcanic rock, pumice, ash and solidified lava.

I was looking at part of the rim of a shifting and still active volcano, the fragmentary remnant of a larger island whose core was blown out in a cataclysmic explosion in c.1550 BC, creating the huge and almost landlocked bay of Santorini, its subterra-nean fires, which the islanders call Hephaestus, still smouldering through the cusped islet that had formed around its vent at the centre of the harbour.

The *Myrditiotissa* disembarked and embarked its usual collec-tion of chickens, goats and people, which here included two monks from the monastery of Profitis Ilias and a band of island musicians who has been playing at the *paniyeri* there on 21 July just past. When all were aboard the crew cast off the mooring lines and the *Myrditiotissa* sounded her horn, which echoed back and forth across the caldera as we steamed out of the calm waters of the bay headed for Naxos.

Once out of the harbour we found ourselves in the teeth of a Force 6 *meltemi*. The *Myrditiotissa* barely made headway in the gale, which was normal sailing weather for the Cyclades in midsummer, though all of us in deck passage on the fantail of the ship were shielded from the full force of the wind by the ship's superstructure. The two monks blessed themselves repeatedly and old women came over to kiss their hands. The musicians, still not sober after last night's *paniyeri*, took out their instruments and began to play *nisiotika tragoudia*, softly at first and then with more animation as they passed around a demijohn of retsina. Some of the younger passengers got up, all of them barefoot, forming a circle to do a *Kritikos Syrtos*, the ancient Cretan dance, the participants linked by handkerchiefs as they followed the steps of a young woman waving her kerchief in the air. Once again it was Ariadne leading Theseus and his companions out of the Cretan labyrinth, and as the music was carried away on the wind I let my mind drift and was once again transported out of space and time.

Eventually the gale wore everyone down as they huddled together for warmth in the lee of the superstructure, falling asleep as the food and wine took effect. It was well past midnight when we reached Naxos and steamed into the lee of the Palatia, the portico of Apollo's temple looming above us in the darkness. I was the only one awake, and I imagined that I was Theseus about to abandon Ariadne on the islet that is still sacred to the memory of the sleeping goddess.

One evening in the *plateia* I ran into an old friend whom I had last seen in graduate school at New York University. His name was Petros Protopapadakis and he was from the village of Apeiranthos high in the mountains of Naxos, founded by Cretan refugees in the nineteenth century. The people of Apeiranthos, as I knew from my experience with Mihali Zevgolis, were all *kleftis* (thieves). Petros was the first to admit that his ancestors had been sheep thieves, which someone has called 'the most arduous form of theft', but they were also poets, known for their *mantinades*, rhyming couplets sung to the accompaniment of the Cretan *lyra*, such as one that Petros recited for us: 'I'm glad to be Cretan, my word I do keep / with *mantinades* I sing, with *mantinades* I weep.'

One evening Petros invited us to a wedding in Apeiranthos, celebrated in the medieval *plateia*, with a band of musicians including my friend Mihali Karavoulas, the fiddler. Ordinarily the bride's father leads his daughter in the first dance of the evening, which is always a *balo*, the beautiful courting dance from Venetian times. But the bride's father had passed away the previous year, and so her uncle did the honours instead, and while they circled the marble dance floor the groom's sister sang a series of *mantinades*, beginning with this threnody addressed to the young *nymphe* (bride): 'If your father could see how happy you are as a bride / He would ask permission from Death to be at your side.'

Among the few foreigners who came to Naxos regularly in those years were Ralph and Eve Bates, an older couple who soon became good friends of ours. Ralph had served in the British Army in World War I, and afterwards published several novels, the last of them, *The Olive Field*, set in Andalusia on the eve of the Spanish Civil War, in which he had commanded the division organized by the commune of Barcelona. He is mentioned by George Orwell in *Homage to Catalonia*, who refers to him as Commandant Bates. After the war he went into exile in Mexico, where he had met and married Eve, a Jewish New Yorker, and through her connections he found a job in the School of Adult Education at NYU, though, like me, he had never graduated from secondary school.

The following year we were joined by Bob and Nora McCrae and their three daughters. Bob was dean of McGill University in Toronto and a noted Descartes scholar. He had been an officer in the Canadian contingent in the Dieppe Raid on France in August 1942, where he was wounded and then spent the rest of the war as a German prisoner.

Ralph was as interested as I was in the history, antiquities and culture of Naxos, and we began exploring the island systematically. Bob was as light-hearted as Ralph was serious, and so on our long hikes into the mountainous interior of Naxos he and I formed a two-man army led by Commandant Bates, who frequently lost patience with our frivolity. But that too is now part of a lost world.

That summer, while Toots and the children spent the afternoons at the Hagios Giorgis beach outside the town, I began taking long hikes through the interior of the island. Here I found another world altogether, as I trekked through the fertile farmlands of the coastal plain known as Livadia, the vast olive grove of the Tragaea, and the verdant river valley of the Potamia, from where I headed back to Chora through the lush vale of Melanes and the Flerio ravine.

It was in an olive grove in Flerio that I discovered the famous *kouros*, the colossal figure of a naked youth representing Apollo, carved in the mid-sixth century BC from the marble hillside in which he still lies, having been broken before he could be carried away. As I looked at him lying there in the olive grove I recalled the lines from the *Pythian Hymn to Apollo*, composed around the same time, that the *kouros* was carved as a votive offering to the gods: 'He is a youth, lusty and powerful in his full bloom, his hair spread over his shoulders.'

I wrote of the Flerio *kouros* in a book about Naxos that I began working on that summer. It was called *Naxos, Ariadne's Isle*, which was finally published in 1972. By that time Naxos had been discovered by the modern world, but most of the tourists who came to the island were only interested in its beautiful beaches, and so whenever I hiked across the thyme-scented hills to Flerio I found the *kourus* lying there alone in the olive grove, as if he were in an enchanted sleep, dreaming eternally while the seasons cycled over his recumbent form.

On one of my hikes I climbed Mount Zas, the highest peak on Naxos and in the whole Cyclades, its summit 1,010 metres above the Aegean. Naxiot legend has it that Zeus was raised by nymphs in the great cave under the summit of Zas after his birth on Crete, and that he was guarded there by flights of eagles. I have often seen a pair of eagles soaring over the summit of Zas, reminding me of the lines from Book 2 of the *Odyssey*, where Telemachus sees 'a pair of eagles from a mountain-crest / in gliding flight down the soft blowing wind, / wing-tip to wing-tip quivering taut'. From the summit of Zas I have seen all the encircling isles of the Cyclades floating between the blues of sea and sky against the background of the mountains of Asia Minor, whose peaks can be seen on the clearest of halcyon days.

Another of my hikes took me out to the beaches that fringe the south coast of the island, where I walked along the pink sand for hours without seeing a soul, stripping down every now and then to plunge into the glittering sea. Finally I climbed across a rocky promontory called Mikri Vigla, where archaeologists had discovered a fortress of the Late Bronze Age, dated about 1500 BC. There was very little left of the fortress, but I could see why it would have been built on the promontory, where it would have dominated the whole south coast of the island as well as the strait separating Naxos and Ios, whose blue mountains rose out of the Aegean to the south.

On the far side of Mikri Vigla there was another beautiful beach, which stretched for about a mile to the next promontory. There was a little taverna in the cove just under Mikri Vigla, and I decided that I would have lunch there before starting back to Chora. I was the only customer, and the owner, a farmer named Costa from the village of Filotii, just under Mount Zas, told me that he had just built the taverna, and that he and his family were living there for the summer. When I said that I'd like to bring my family for a visit he said that there was a rough track that led out to Mikri Vigla from the main road, so that we could drive to the taverna by taxi.

When I finished lunch Costa drove me out to the main road in his tractor and flagged down a passing car. The driver turned out to be a neighbour of his from Filotii, who drove me back to Chora, questioning me all the way about who I was and where I was from, for very few foreigners came to Naxos, he said, though he hoped that they would so that the Naxiotes could begin to cash in on the tourism boom that had enriched islands like Mykonos. I pretended to agree, and when he dropped me off in Chora I thanked him and said that when I returned to America I would tell all my friends about Naxos.

At the time there was only a single taxi on Naxos, an old Chev-

rolet owned by a friend of mine named Vasili, who preferred to
be known as Bill, for that's what he was called during the years he
had worked in Chicago. Bill said that he would be happy to drive
us out to Mikri Vigla for lunch the next day and that he'd come
back to pick us up late afternoon. So the next day he drove us to
the taverna at Mikri Vigla, where Costa was waiting for us with his
wife and their three daughters and two sons. We had a wonderful
day there swimming and strolling along the beach, and returned
several times that summer and in the years that followed.

# 6

# BEYOND THE PILLARS
# OF HERCULES

During the spring of 1963 we began planning the next stage of our odyssey, and with the help of Numan Bey I worked out an itinerary that would take us to the US and back on ships of the Turkish Maritime Lines and the Italian Lines, around the Mediterranean as well as back and forth across the Atlantic, beyond the Pillars of Hercules, so that I would once again cross the wake of Odysseus, this time with my Penelope and our children with me.

Early in June 1963 we started the first leg of our journey back to the US aboard the *Marmara* of the Turkish Maritime Lines, which would take us on a voyage around the eastern Mediterranean to Italy.

Our first stop was Izmir, where we would stay for a full day. We took the opportunity to visit the site of the ancient Greek city of Teos, whose ruins are scattered around a sea-girt peninsula completely enveloped in an olive grove. We had a picnic in the Temple of Dionysus, and while we sat there, Toots and I sharing a bottle of white wine, I thought of the lyric poet Anacreon, who was born in Teos in about 560 BC. After spending most of his life in exile he died here at the age of 87, choking on a grape-pit while drinking raisin wine. While I finished off our wine, pouring a libation to Dionysus, I recalled one of Anacreon's poems, of which only a fragment remains: 'Bring water lad, bring wine, bring me

garlands of flowers: aye, bring them thither, for I would try a bout
with love.'

Our next port of call was Rhodes, where again we stayed for
a full day. We spent most of our time exploring the Castle of the
Knights, which we had more or less to ourselves. In one of our
albums there is a photo I took of Toots and the children sitting on
a doorstep on the Street of the Knights, not another soul in sight,
a scene from our odyssey frozen in time.

Our next stops were Larnaca in Cyprus and Haifa in Israel,
after which we headed westwards through the Mediterranean on
the last stage of our voyage aboard the *Marmaris*, which would
bring us to Naples. Our route took us past the southern coast
of Crete, which I had last seen 18 years before when I had first
crossed the wake of Odysseus. Then the next day we went through
the straits of Messina between Sicily and Italy, and I told the children that this was where Odysseus had to pass between the terrible sea-monsters Scylla and Charybdis, who swallowed up six of
his men.

Night had fallen by the time we passed to the east of the Aeolian
and Lipari Isles, and we could see the volcano on Stromboli glow-
ing in the darkness. The following morning we passed the Gulf
of Salerno and entered the Gulf of Naples, and I again told the
children that we were crossing the wake of Odysseus, for this, I
was convinced, was Siren Land. Here, I told them, Odysseus had
his men tie him to the mast and stop his ears with beeswax so that
he couldn't hear the songs of the Sirens, who, as the nymph Circe
had warned him, were 'enchanters of all mankind', and those who
listened to them would never return home.

We disembarked in Naples and I checked in at a small hotel on
the waterfront, where Numan Bey had booked us a suite for three
days. As soon as we were settled in I hired a horse-drawn carriage
to drive us around the Amalfi coast.

The following day we went by ferry to the Isle of Capri, and on
the last day we explored the old Borgo Santa Lucia del Mare. That
evening we ate at a seaside restaurant near Castel dell'Ovo, where
an old man with a mandolin came and played for us. Of course he
sang 'Santa Lucia', first in Italian and then in English. I knew the

lyrics well, for Jean Caputo had often played it for me, in a record-ing by Enrico Caruso:

> On the sea glitters the silver star,
> Gentle the waves, favourable the winds.
> Come into my bounding barque,
> Santa Lucia! Santa Lucia!
> Come into my bounding barque!
> Santa Lucia! Santa Lucia!

The following day we took the train to Rome, where we stayed for three days in a small hotel near the Spanish Steps. The city was buzzing with excitement, for a papal election was under way to choose a successor to John XXIII, who had died on 3 June. We joined the multitude in St Peter's Square, waiting for a decision, till a puff of black smoke from a Vatican chimney brought a sigh of disappointment from the crowd. We then went on to explore the city, ending the day with supper at an outdoor restaurant in Trastevere.

The following day we returned to St Peter's Square, but a puff of black smoke again sent us away, and we resumed our explora-tion of the city, this time ending the day with supper in the Campo de' Fiore. On our third and last day we decided to forgo another visit to St Peter's Square and instead had lunch in the Campo Navona. We had just finished eating when a shout erupted around the square: a new pope had been elected who had taken the name Paul VI. A British couple at the next table bought balloons for Maureen, Eileen and Brendan, while Toots and I treated ourselves to a bottle of champagne, ending our sightseeing for the day.

Next morning we took the train to Florence, where Numan Bey had booked us for a three-day stay in a small hotel on the left bank of the Arno, just above the Ponte Vecchio. The city was far less crowded than we would find it on later visits, nor was there much traffic on the narrow streets of the old town. So we were able to get a sense of what Renaissance Florence might have been like, particularly since I had read works by Dante, Galileo, Petrarch, Boccaccio and Machiavelli in my Great Books programme, and so had Toots after I had passed the list on to her, as would the children in turn as they grew up, travelling with us on our odyssey until they went off on their own journeys.

After our three days in Florence we took the train to Genoa, where Numan Bey had booked us rooms in a hotel down by the Stazione Maritimme, for we would be boarding the *Leonardo da Vinci* there the following morning. As soon as we settled in we walked back along the docks of the Bacino Porto Vecchio, and from there made our way into the old town, where we sat down at the first likely looking restaurant, for we hadn't eaten since break-fast. After we finished the main course I was about to order a dessert, when the waiter served us a small cake with a large candle burning at its centre, and only then did I realize that it was my 37th birthday. After I blew out the candle Toots and the children joined in, saying, 'Goodbye to baby ways!', which had become traditional with us ever since Maureen's first birthday.

We boarded the *Leonardo da Vinci* next morning and by noon we were on our way, bound for New York. We stopped briefly at Marseilles and Barcelona to pick up passengers and then steamed through the Strait of Gibraltar into the Atlantic, which I was now crossing by sea for the 13th time. The weather was fine through-out the crossing and we spent most of the daylight hours on deck, usually on the fantail watching our churning wake and the seagulls who swooped down to pick up our garbage. Later on the voyage we began looking ahead from the prow, just as I remem-bered Peg, Dorothy and me doing as we approached New York 30 years before on our return from Ireland, waiting for our first glimpse of the Statue of Liberty.

We spent the first two weeks of our vacation in Red Bank with the Stanleys. We then took a bus from New York to California to see my parents, for they had moved there to be near my sister Nancy, who had just married for the second time. Peg and John were both on social security, but they had found that the payments were not enough to live on and so were working at a Jewish senior citizens care centre, which was far easier than digging graves at the Evergreens Cemetery or scrubbing floors at night in Rockefeller Center. They had a very nice studio apartment near the beach in

Santa Monica, and during the two weeks we were with them we swam nearly every day. I had never seen Peg as happy as she was then, for the years in Ireland and Brooklyn had been very hard for her, as they had been for John too. But when we left them I felt a deep sadness, for I knew that this late happiness could not last, and when we said our tearful goodbyes I wondered if I would ever see them again.

We then spent two more weeks in Red Bank before beginning our return journey to Istanbul, which brought us back through the Pillars of Hercules to the Mediterranean and Istanbul, where we arrived early in September 1963.

We were all happy to get back to our chalet on Arifi Pasha Korusu, but Toots and I had already decided that we would try to find a place closer to the college, for she would soon be taking Brendan to nursery school. I began looking around, and on the first Saturday of the fall term I walked up from the Bosphorus on the cobbled road that passes the Aşiyan Cemetery, the route we had taken the day we arrived at the college three years before.

There were only two houses on the side of the road opposite the cemetery, both of them almost hidden away amongst the trees that covered the steep hillside below the college. The lower house was occupied, for there was a car in its driveway, but the upper one seemed to be empty. The only approach to it was off the side road that led up to the house museum of Tevfik Fikret, the poet who had founded the Turkish department at Robert College. About halfway up the road to his house, which he had called Aşiyan, or 'the Nest', I came to an iron gateway wrapped in a coil of barbed wire, with the name 'NIGAR' carved on its lintel. I walked through the gateway and saw that the house was an old wooden Ottoman *konak*, or mansion, in three storeys, with an octagonal gazebo on its uppermost level. A balcony projected out from its *piano nobile* over an oval pool filled with tropical fish and surrounded by palmetto trees and a beautiful garden, at the back of which an immensely tall cypress was surrounded by a stone seat so as to form a little circular terrace looking out over the Bosphorus.

I made enquiries and found that the owner's name was Salih Nigar, whom I had met at a college reception, where he told me that his father Feridun had been one of the founding members of our Turkish department, a colleague of Tevfik Fikret. I called Salih Bey to ask him if the house was for rent, and when he said that it was we agreed to meet there in an hour's time.

Salih was waiting for me when I arrived and showed me around the house, which had been built in 1880 by his grandmother, the famous poet Nigar Hanım. Salih said that when she died in 1918 the *konak* had passed to his father Feridun, who had lived there up until a few years before his death, abandoning it after an angel appeared to him in a dream to warn him that the house was unlucky. Salih said that the house had been unoccupied since then and that he would be happy to rent it to me for the same amount that the college was paying for our apartment in Arifi Pasha Korusu.

Before returning home I had gone to the college library and found an English translation of one of Nigar Hanım's works in an anthology – a love poem called 'Tell Me Again' – and I read it to Toots that evening while we were having our nightcaps on the balcony.

Am I your only love – in the whole world – now?
Am I really the only object of your love?
If passions rage in your mind,
If love springs eternal in your heart –
Is it all meant for me? Tell me again.

Tell me right now, am I the one who inspires
All your dark thoughts, all your sadness?
Share with me what you feel, what you think.
Come my love, pour into my heart,
Whatever gives you so much pain.
Tell me again.

I had agreed to rent the house without consulting Toots, but when I told her the next day she was very excited, for the Nigar Hanım *konak* sounded like everything we had dreamed of when we had first moved into the Diamond of the Marshes.

The college executive committee approved our change of apartments, and at the beginning of October we moved to the Nigar
Hanım *konak*. It took a couple of weeks to settle in, and then on
the next Saturday evening we invited all our friends to a house-
warming party.

The party was well under way when we heard someone shouting
in the garden, and I went out on to the balcony to see who it was.
It was Jimmy Baldwin, bleeding from a cut in his forehead, and I
rushed down to help him into the living room, where everyone fell
silent as soon as he appeared. Toots took him to the bathroom and
helped him clean the blood off his face, and when they returned
I asked him what had happened. He confronted me in mock fury
and said that he had cut his head on our gateway, shouting, 'Moth-
erfucker, it's bad enough that you call this the Nigger House, but
then you go and wrap barbed wire around your gate!' Then he
smiled his brilliant toothy smile and kissed me and Toots as we
helped him to the punchbowl, where he was soon surrounded by
our friends, shifting the party into high gear.

It was nearly dawn before the last guests left. Jimmy was the last
to leave, and the two of us had a nightcap on the balcony, talking
and comparing notes about our past lives, which had been very
different but with many elements in common. He was a couple of
years older than me, but we had both grown up poor in New York
during the same period, he in Harlem and me in Brooklyn. He
had been a shoe-shine boy and worked in a sweatshop, whereas I
had been a scavenger and worked in a condom factory. Jimmy had
left the US and made a new life in France, just as Toots and I were
doing in Turkey.

We finished our nightcaps just as the sun rose above the hills
of Asia across the Bosphorus, the first call to prayer echoing from
both sides of the straits, along with the clamour of barking dogs
and crowing roosters. Jimmy got up to go and said, 'We've come a
long way, buddy!'

Early in the fall of 1965 Bob Hall asked me whether I wanted
to stay on for another three years, once again suggesting that I
think about it for a while. I had already been pondering over it,
and one possibility that occurred to me was to request a sabbati-

cal so that I could study the history of science for a year, since my lectures in the humanities programme had made me deeply interested in that field.

I had read Alistair Crombie's two-volume *Augustine to Galileo*, a pioneering work on the development of European science, which had stemmed from his researches at Oxford. I applied to the National Science Foundation (NSF) in the US for a fellowship to study with Crombie for a year, so that I could start a course in the history of science at Robert College.

I was astonished when my proposal was accepted, and the NSF gave me a grant of $12,000, payable in 12 monthly instalments, which was more than Harold Wilson's take-home pay as prime minister of the UK. The executive committee at RC granted me a year's leave of absence, and so early in September 1965 we set out for London, for I had decided that we would live there for the year and that I would commute to Oxford for Crombie's seminars.

We found a large furnished apartment in Hampstead, the top floor of an old mansion on Frognall Gardens, with a roof terrace from which we could see the dome of St Paul's. We registered Maureen and Eileen at Hampstead Comprehensive and enrolled Brendan at the Hampstead primary school.

A few days later I took the train from Paddington Station and presented myself at Oxford University, where they didn't quite know what to do with me at first, for they had never had a National Science Fellow from the US before. But they duly signed my fellowship forms and then directed me to Professor Crombie's office at the old Bodleian Library.

After I received a reader's ticket at the Bodleian, I went to All Souls College and found the library there. Then I went to a nearby pub and had a pint of Guinness, and as I drank it, and another, the euphoria kicked in, for here I was, among the dreaming spires of Oxford, something I couldn't have imagined 20 years before, a high-school dropout just returned from the war.

Crombie was very pleasant and said that he would be happy to have me join his seminar, which he and his colleague Rom Harré gave every Wednesday afternoon from three to five in the old library at All Souls, starting the following week. He invited me to have dinner with him at All Souls that evening, but I regretfully declined, saying that we were living in London, which seemed to surprise him, but we shook hands and he said that he would see me next week.

That evening we celebrated with a champagne supper at our apartment in Frognall Gardens, for the children were happy at their schools, Toots was excited about living in London, particularly in Hampstead, and my day at Oxford had opened up a new world for me.

The apartment had a television set, something which we had never had before, neither in the US nor in Istanbul, and so after supper Toots and the children decided that they would see if they could find an interesting programme or film to watch, which left me free to go out and explore the local pubs.

The first one I tried was on the high street just down from the tube station. It was called The Bird in Hand, and it appeared to be a bit more plebeian than the many other pubs in Hampstead, which was what drew me there. It was Friday evening, and the pub was so crowded that I could hardly get in the door. I was wondering how I could make my way up to the bar, which was four or five deep with customers, all of whom seemed to know one another, when suddenly a small space opened up and I quickly moved in and waited to be served, for the governor of the pub and his wife were very busy. I gathered that his name was Charles and hers was Kathleen, and from her soft brogue I guessed she was from County Kerry, which turned out to be correct, when we spoke for a while after she served me a pint of Guinness.

'And will you be having another, Bryn?', she said to the man on my right, who seemed to be the only one in the pub besides me who was not there with a group of friends. He was quite drunk, which was probably why a space had opened up next to him at the bar. We got talking and he introduced himself as Bryn Fugue, saying that he was from the Rhonda Valley in Wales. He had served in the British Army in Burma during World War II, and it turned out that he and I had been in Mykitkina at the same time in the summer of 1945. That formed a bond between us and we quickly became friends, though Bryn demanded full attention from me, for my mind sometimes wandered as I took in the convivial scene around me in the pub. 'Are you listening to me, John?', he asked repeatedly with some annoyance. 'I am, Bryn,' I assured him, and then he said, 'You're a fucking liar. I've been speaking in Welsh for the past ten minutes!'

The following morning Toots went shopping in Hampstead and I waited for her in The Bird in Hand so that I could help her carry things home. Bryn was there, a bit more sober, and introduced me to another Welshman, the poet Keidrych Rhys, who soon became a close friend. Keidrych was the founder of *Wales* magazine, where Dylan Thomas had first published his poetry, and he himself had published two volumes of poetry at Faber when it was headed by T.S. Eliot. Through Keidrych I came to know a number of other local writers and characters, all of them, like my literary friends in Istanbul, alcoholics to varying degrees.

Every Wednesday I took the train to Oxford to attend Crombie's seminar, which took me deep into the world of medieval science as it had developed after the collapse of Graeco-Roman civilization. During the week I thought and read about these things, browsing in the bookshops and libraries of London.

I was also exploring London through its pubs, from the Isle of Dogs to Greenwich, the Elephant and Castle, Chelsea, Soho, Bloomsbury and the West End and every Friday I took Toots to the most interesting ones I had found during the week. With my generous grant we could also afford to go to the theatre, opera and ballet on Saturdays, always taking the children along.

Besides all that, I managed to spend several hours each day writing, working on my *Broken-Down Paradise*, the huge work on Istanbul that I had started soon after we arrived at Robert College.

As the mid-year break approached, Toots and I decided that we would try to take a brief holiday in Dublin, which I had not seen during my childhood in Ireland. I had met an American couple who were studying in Oxford, and they agreed to move into our apartment in Hampstead and look after the children while we were away.

And so early in January Toots and I took the train to Holyhead in Wales, where we boarded the ferry for Dun Laoghaire in County

Dublin. The sea was very rough, so Toots took to her bunk in our cabin while I went straight to the bar. The only customers were five bearded Irishmen who were quite drunk and singing loudly in Irish. I recognized them immediately as the famous group known as The Dubliners, and the Irish barmaid, seeing my red beard, thought that I was with them, for she moaned, 'Jesus, Mary and Joseph, not another one!' But I set her at ease by ordering a Guinness and sitting there quietly, listening to The Dubliners singing songs I hadn't heard since my childhood.

We checked into an old hotel on the Liffey, and though we arose late the next morning it was still dark outside, for we were only two weeks past the winter solstice. We were near the Moore Street market, where the pubs open at 8am, and so after breakfast at the hotel we went into the first pub we came to, which was as dark inside as it was on the street outside. When my eyes adjusted themselves to the darkness I could see that the booths and benches were packed with men and women from the market who were sitting there quietly drinking pints of Guinness, so I went up to the bar and ordered one for myself and a shandy for Toots, who said she was saving herself for the evening.

As I listened to the conversation around me I learned that Stephen Behan, father of Brendan Behan, had died the previous evening, after being run over by a taxi. Brendan himself had died just two years earlier, and so it seemed like the end of an era, or so we gathered from the talk we heard all day in the pubs.

Early that afternoon, in a pub on Grafton Street, I met an American writer named Harry Ruber, who was drinking there with his British wife Joan. Harry said that he had written only one book, a novel called *The Cook*, which had sold so well that he never had to write again. He and Joan had moved to Dublin and bought an apartment there, since the cost of living was much lower than in New York or London, and the talk was much better too, although the Irish writers he knew, including a number we met in the week that followed, were given to 'talking their novels away', as he put it.

Harry then took us on a tour of the Joyce pubs in Dublin, all of which appear in *Ulysses*, explaining the architectural and artistic features of each of them and classifying the types of customers they attracted, which seemed to be much the same as it was in Joyce's time.

The only decent restaurant in Dublin at that time was Jammet's, but that was far too expensive, so Harry and Joan had us for supper every evening and we brought along the wine. And so during our brief holiday in Dublin the only sites we saw were its pubs, but by the end of our stay I felt that I had gotten to know the city that I had read about in *Ulysses*, the last of the Great Books that I had read in the year after the war.

At the end of our last evening we said goodbye to the Rubers, thanking them for their hospitality and inviting them to stay with us when they came to London, which they did, though separately, but I couldn't help feeling that the pubs of Hampstead were no match for those in Dublin, particularly when it came to what the Irish called 'the talk', as I well knew from my childhood.

We were glad to see the children again, and they said that the American couple who had looked after them had been very dull. We stayed up very late with them the night after we returned, telling them all about Dublin and promising to take them there in the summer.

I soon got back into our old routine, as I took the train to Oxford every Wednesday, spending the rest of the week exploring London and enjoying its theatre, opera and ballet with Toots and the children, studying the history of science and working on my *The Broken-Down Paradise*, as well as hobnobbing with Keidrych and my other pals at The Bird in Hand.

On Sunday Toots took the children to mass in the French Church just off Church Row, where Charles de Gaulle had worshipped when he was living in London during World War II. We then had lunch in the garden of Jack Straw's Castle, the only pub in Hampstead where children were allowed, after which we spent the rest of the afternoon strolling on Hampstead Heath.

As the academic year neared its close Toots said to me wistfully that it was a pity that we had to leave London, but then she sighed, knowing we were committed to return to Istanbul.

We had decided to spend the summer in Ireland, from where

we would return to Istanbul by way of New York, travelling by sea all the way. This would give me the opportunity to visit the places in Ireland where I had lived when I was boy, and we would have a chance to see our parents while we were in the New York area, for Peg and John had moved back there after my sister Nancy had remarried again and left California.

We left London with great regret late in May 1967 and took the train to Holyhead and then the ferry to Dun Laoghaire, from where we took a taxi into Dublin. We spent three days there, and during that time I went on a round of all the pubs I had read about in *Ulysses*. In one of them, The Old Bailey, I saw Joyce's son Giorgio, who was there to dedicate a James Joyce cocktail lounge, for literary tourism had discovered Dublin.

We then took the train from Dublin to Ballyhaunis and checked in at the Central Hotel, the only one in town. The next morning we took a taxi to Scragg, my father's birthplace, which was about five miles from Ballyhaunis, asking the driver to pick us up there later in the afternoon. Scragg was just a few scattered cottages, most of them abandoned, and it took us a while to find the Freely cottage.

I knew that my uncle Jim and his wife Agnes had returned from the US to run the farm after my grandparents died. They were living there with my cousin Eileen, daughter of my uncle Luke, for her mother had died and her father had remarried and was living in London, where I had visited him earlier that year. I had written to my Uncle Jim and told him that I hoped to see him early in the summer, and so it wasn't a total surprise when we appeared in the taxi.

The cottage was just as I remembered it, and though it now had electricity, running water and plumbing, the turf fire in the huge hearth was still used for heat and cooking. The curtained 'hags' in the walls where my father and his brothers and sister had slept were still there, but they were no longer used, since two bedrooms had been added to the cottage, one of them now used by Jim and Agnes and the other by my cousin Eileen.

I hadn't seem Jim and Agnes since I was a boy, for they had lived in Boston rather than Brooklyn, but still I had fond memories of them, for they had always been very loving to me, as they were to Toots and the children during the three happy days we spent with them. We also got to know my cousin Eileen, a very pretty and intelligent girl of around 18, and when we left Ballyhaunis we took her with us to Dublin, where she stayed with us for two days.

The following day we took a train from Dublin to Tralee and then a taxi to Anauscaul, where I had rented an apartment for the summer. The apartment was above a general store run by Nora Ashe, whose husband Tom Ashe turned out to be a cousin of mine, for we were both great-grandsons of Thomas Ashe, the Crimean War veteran.

We bought groceries in Nora's store and Toots prepared supper, for we hadn't had anything to eat since breakfast. There was a brand-new TV set in the apartment, and so after supper Toots and the girls decided that they would spend the evening watching Irish television, which was very different from what they had seen in London, with much more music and dancing.

It was still broad daylight outside, for there were two weeks to go before the summer solstice, so I decided that I would take Brendan for a walk and explore Anascaul, which I hadn't seen since I was his age. We strolled down the main street of the village, which was actually its only street, the main road from Tralee to the town of Dingle, flanked by what seemed to be as many pubs as there were houses. The only pub I remembered was the South Pole Inn, at the far end of the village, founded by Tom Crean, the Arctic and Antarctic explorer, to whom my grandfather Tomas had introduced me when I was a boy.

Just beyond the South Pole Inn there was a dirt road leading off to the left, marked by a signpost that read 'Inch 3 miles'. It was only 6pm, and I figured that it would take us no more than an hour to walk to Inch, for Brendan had reassured me that he had 'feet that never tired'. And so off we went, as the road took us along the crest of the hill above Dingle Bay. Soon I could see the great transverse sand spit of Inch stretching for more than three miles across the bay, a sight that caught me by the heart, for I had last looked upon it more than 36 years before when we left the Murphy cottage, thinking I would never return.

It was about 7:15 when we reached Inch, where we saw a new hotel and restaurant that seemed to have just opened at the head of Inch strand. We walked on for a bit and then we came to the tiny hamlet of Inch, a couple of cottages clustered around an old church opposite a seaside graveyard, where, as I told Brendan, some of our ancestors were buried. And there, all by itself at the side of the road was Foley's pub. I told Brendan that his grandmother Peg had worked there as a girl, looking after Jerry Foley, the son of the publican, who had now inherited the pub, for his name was on the sign over the door.

The pub was packed, but I found a space at the right-hand corner of the bar and sat Brendan down on the stool there. While I waited to be served I looked around the room and listened to the flow of talk and bursts of laughter, the older people speaking Irish and the younger ones English, with the melodious Kerry brogue that reminded me of my nocturnal dialogues with Peg. I gathered that the two people behind the bar were Jerry Foley and his somewhat younger wife Bridey. Bridey came over to serve me and I ordered a pint of Guinness for myself and a lemonade for Brendan.

I had not said a word to anyone, but when I ordered another Guinness, Bridey asked me if I was Peg Murphy's son, and when I said that I was indeed I realized that Nora Ashe must have spread the word that I was back. Jerry Foley came over to welcome me back, and he was very pleased when I told him that Peg had sent her love, for he had very fond memories of her.

Bridey introduced me to the gentleman on my left, a man about my age named Pat O'Connor. Pat said that his mother had heard that I was back and wanted very much to see me, for she had known me when I was a boy and was a close friend of my mother and grandparents. Pat said that the two of them lived just down the road beyond the church, and so Brendan and I followed him as he led us there. He told us that his mother was past 90 and had recently suffered a stroke, so that she was partially paralyzed, though she was still able to speak.

The O'Connor cottage was just as small as the Murphys', as I remembered it. Pat's mother was propped in bed beside the fire-

place, where a turf fire was still glowing, for although it was early
June there was a damp breeze off the sea just across the road. She
had been dozing, but she woke up as soon as we entered and Pat
told her that Jackie had come to see her, for that was the name
by which I was known as a boy. She embraced us and then began
speaking in Irish, but to Brendan and not to me, for he was about
the same age as I was when she last saw me, and so in her fading
memory he became Jackie. We stayed with her for only about
ten minutes before she drifted off to sleep, so we left quietly and
returned to Foley's.

The pub was even more crowded than it had been before, but
the conversation was more muted, for an old man was playing the
fiddle and a beautiful young woman was singing in Irish, a song
that I knew in English as 'The Land of the Heart's Desire', one of
Peg's favourites. I ordered another Guinness and let my mind drift
with the music, imagining that I was the disguised Odysseus back
in Ithaca, with Brendan, my Telemachus, at my side.

The next morning we received a visit from Larry O'Shea,
husband of my mother's dearest friend and next-door neighbour,
Peig Callaghan. Larry had heard that we were staying at the Ashes,
and he had come with his car to take us to see Peig, who was
immobilized by rheumatism. So we drove off with Larry, and
after we passed Inch I ticked off four milestones until we came to
Lach, which now had just two cottages, those that belonged to the
Murphys and the Callaghans. Larry said that the Sayers cottage
had been demolished and that a retired Irish-American and his
wife were now living in the Murphy cottage, but they would be
away for the next few months.

After Larry parked his car he opened the door of his cottage
and said, 'Who do you think I have here, Peig?' Then a voice
called out 'Would it be Jackie?', and I went in and embraced Peig,
who was sitting in a chair by the fireplace, and when I introduced
Toots and the children to her she embraced and kissed each one of
them in turn. I told her that Peg was fine and sent her love, which
pleased her very much, for they had been the closest of friends.

Larry showed me a feather from the American Indian war
bonnet I had worn on St Stephen's Day in 1932, when I had 'hunted

for the wren' with the other local boys. He told me that their son Lawrence had worn the bonnet several times on St Stephen's Day when he was a boy, but the festival was no longer celebrated, for only a few of the cottages up in the hills still had thatched roofs, and there was nary a wren to be seen on the Dingle Peninsula these days, he said. So he had kept the feather as a souvenir to remind him of the 'old ways' that had now vanished.

Peig said that she missed the old ways, though life was much easier now and both their son Lawrence and their daughter Moira had graduated from university and had good jobs in England, and Larry was driving a car instead of a donkey cart like my grandfather Tomas.

Such was the beginning of a memorable summer in Ireland, which ended when we departed from Cork Harbour on 15 August 1967 aboard a ship of the US Lines, the *United States*, bound for New York. As we did so I recalled that more than 34 years had passed since Peg and I and Dorothy had sailed from the Cobh of Cork to begin a new life in America, to which I was now returning only briefly before resuming our life of exile in Istanbul.

A week later we landed in New York, where we were scheduled to spend ten days before embarking on the last stage of our journey back to Istanbul. My brother Jimmy and his wife Jane were waiting for us when we cleared customs and immigration control, and they drove us to their home in Hasbrook Heights in New Jersey, where John and Peg were living with them for the time being. We spent four days with them and four more with the Stanleys in Red Bank before embarking on a ship of the Italian Lines, the *Marco Polo*, bound for Naples. Our brief return to the US was both happy and sad, for though it had been wonderful seeing our families, we left them in tears, wondering if we would see one another again.

The *Marco Polo* took us across the Atlantic and through the Pillars of Hercules before docking in Naples. We spent a day there and then boarded a ship of the Turkish Maritime Lines, the *Marmara*, which two days later landed us at the passenger terminal in Galata. Some of our friends from the college were waiting there to welcome us home, for that was what Istanbul had become in our life of exile.

When we returned from my sabbatical at Oxford in the fall of 1967 we moved into an apartment on the top two floors of the Tower House, so called because it stood across the road from one of the towers of Rumeli Hisarı. Our downstairs neighbours were Ali and Süheyla Artemel, a colleague of mine at the college, and their son Mehmet, who was Brendan's age, and we soon became good friends.

Maureen graduated from the American College for Girls in Istanbul in June 1970. She had applied for early admission at Harvard and received a full scholarship, but Toots and I were a bit concerned about her being there all on her own, for her family and friends were all in Istanbul, and since she hadn't grown up in the US she would be a total outsider in American life.

I decided that I would apply for another sabbatical and try to find a position as a visiting professor at some university in the New York area, where we would be near Maureen during her first year at Harvard. I applied to the physics department of the City College of New York (CCNY), now part of the City University of New York (CUNY), since some friends from NYU were teaching there. But I wasn't very optimistic, for although I had published several scientific papers in *Physical Review* while at RC and was now a full professor, I had been out of the mainstream of physics for a decade and was now a complete unknown in the American scientific community.

And so I was quite surprised when, almost by return mail, I received a letter from the chairman of the physics department at CCNY, Professor Harry Winston, offering me a visiting full professorship. He said that I was a perfect fit, for he was going off on a year's sabbatical at UNESCO in Paris and had been looking for someone of his academic rank to replace him and at the same time to sublet his apartment while he was away. I cabled him immediately to accept the job and also to sublet the apartment, which seemed just right for us.

We spent the summer on Naxos and then at the beginning of September flew to New York. We spent a few days with the Stanleys in Red Bank, while I took the train into Manhattan to check in at the physics department at CCNY, where Professor Winston introduced me to the colleague who would be acting chairman while he was away. He then took me to look at his apartment, which was in the Inwood section at the northern tip of Manhattan, just across a park from the Hudson. He gave me the keys and said that we could move in the following week after he and his family left for Paris.

After we moved into the apartment we all took a train to Boston, where we stayed with friends in Cambridge while Maureen registered at Harvard and moved into her dorm. When we returned to New York we registered Eileen in George Washington High School in northern Manhattan, where the students were predominantly black, while we signed up Brendan at the local primary school in Inwood, which was almost entirely white.

I didn't know what to expect at City College, whose alumni included eight Nobel laureates, including the playwright Arthur Miller, all of them of eastern European Jewish origin. CCNY was now part of the City University, which a year earlier had adopted an open-admission policy. Incoming students were only required to have a sixth-grade reading ability, greatly increasing the enrolment, and everyone expected that academic standards would drastically decline.

The physics department, in adjusting to the open-admissions policy, had started a course called 'Physics for Poets', which would satisfy the science requirement for new students with inadequate preparation in science and maths. No one in the physics department wanted to take on the course, so I volunteered, figuring that I could teach it in terms of the history of science.

More than 750 students signed up for the course, and the only space large enough to hold them was a huge lecture hall in the form of a theatre. When I stepped in front of the class for the first time I really had no idea what I was going to say. But then I started talking about the first Greek philosophers of nature in Asia Minor, working my way up to Socrates, Plato and Aristotle in Athens, and when the bell rang at the end of the period I could tell that most of the students had been with me all the way. A black girl came up to me after class, saying, 'Thanks, Professor, you taught us some really interesting shit this morning!'

It was great being back in New York, for Toots and I hadn't

spent much time there since her family moved to Red Bank in 1950. So we set out to reacquaint ourselves with the city, particularly Greenwich Village, where our dear friends Buck and Kay Rogers had settled after they left Istanbul in 1963.

Maureen frequently came down from Cambridge to stay with us on weekends at our apartment in Inwood, where relatives and new and old friends gathered for parties reminiscent of those we had thrown in Istanbul. And so at the end of the academic year we left New York with some regret, returning from beyond the Pillars of Hercules to our life of exile in Istanbul, our home far away from home.

# 7

# THE ODYSSEY
# CHANGES COURSE

After our return we resumed our old routine, strolling through Istanbul on Saturdays and exploring Anatolia and Greece on school vacations, spending most summers on Naxos, though we often extended our travels further afield.

We had bought an old secondhand car from the Greenwoods, an Opel that was in such bad shape that we called it 'the Opeless'. Toots had learned to drive in Princeton and had an international driver's licence, so she drove while I rode shotgun as I had on the Burma Road, but now armed with roadmaps as we travelled around Anatolia and Greece.

We spent the summer of 1969 on the island of Skiathos, one of the northern Sporades, where we rented a villa belonging to a Greek poet named Aris Economides, who lived in an adjacent cottage. The villa was on an isolated seaside promontory, so we had to park our car in the Chora of Skiathos and make our way on foot over the headland. Our landlord had a *caique* called *Delphini* (Dolphin) and Aris let me use its dinghy, which I rowed into town whenever we needed groceries.

There was a radio in the villa on which I was able to get the BBC, and I followed the news of the US Apollo 11 mission to land a man on the moon, which would be attempted on the night of 20-21 July 1968. Aris had been following the news too, and he invited us to go with him in the *Delphini* that evening to a

161

lighthouse on the south-easternmost promontory of Skiathos, 'so that we could look at the moon for the last time before it was profaned by the footsteps of mankind'. Others had the same idea, and about a dozen *caiques* had landed at the lighthouse jetty by the time we arrived. We all sat on the barren cape and gazed at the full moon, as if it was a sacred occasion. I laughed when I noticed a number of rabbits doing the same thing, apparently transfixed as they stared up at the brilliant lunar disk, as if all of nature was aware of what was happening. I recited a fragment from Sappho: 'The glow and beauty of the stars are nothing near the splendid moon / When in her roundness she burns silver around the world.'

We remained there for an hour or so before Aris took us back to our villa and said goodnight. Then I turned on the radio and tuned in to the BBC, and we listened to the live transmission from the Apollo spacecraft, cheering when we heard that it had landed safely and that Neil Armstrong had set foot on the moon.

The following spring vacation Toots and I left the children with Aunty, while we drove to Greece with our friends Allan and Susan Ovenden. Allan had been talking to me about going with him to Mount Athos, the semi-autonomous monastic state on the easternmost of the three peninsulas of the Halkidiki, the barren coastal region east of Thessaloniki. Women were not permitted on the Holy Mountain, as it was called, but they could stay at a simple beach resort on Ouranopolis (City of the Heavens), a tiny hamlet on the isthmus joining the peninsula to the mainland.

Allan and I had made the rounds of the civil and religious authorities in Thessaloniki to obtain the necessary papers, which allowed us to stay on the Holy Mountain for three full days as guests in one or other of the 20 monasteries.

After spending a night in Ouranopolis, Allan and I left Toots and Susan and boarded a *caique* that took us along the western shore of the peninsula to Dafni, the main port of Mount Athos. There we boarded an old bus driven by a monk and were taken to Kariyes, the capital, where we presented our papers before heading off on our own.

The oldest and most famous monastery on Athos is the Grand

Lavra, founded on the far end of the Holy Mountain in 963 by the Byzantine emperor Nicephorus II Phocas, so we decided to take the trail leading in that direction. But since it was already past noon we had to spend the first night in Karakoulu, a smaller monastery halfway out along the peninsula, where we arrived just before sunset.

We climbed up the stone ramp that led to the gate of Karakoulu, which, like all the other foundations on the Holy Mountain, looked like a medieval fortress, with a towered defence wall enclosing the monastery itself. An old monk, the *hegumenos*, or hospitality master, was sitting outside the gate, and as we arrived he handed each of us a glass of raki and a piece of *loukoumi*. Hearing us speaking American English, he laughed and said, 'Used to work in Ford Motor Company Detroit, couldn't stand the noise.' He showed us our room in the guest quarters, and after we dropped off our back-packs there he took us to the refectory, where about 50 monks were eating at a long table.

We helped ourselves to the food, which was cold potatoes and lentils and stale, hard bread. One of the monks was standing at a lectern reciting prayers in a grating monotone voice, ducking every now and then when one or another of the brethren pelted him with a potato, which I gather was done for our amusement.

It was dark by the time that Allan and I got back to our room after supper, but the *hegumenos* had given us an oil lamp, so we lit it and stayed up for a while talking. We then sacked out with our clothes on, for it was freezing and our cots were as hard and cold as mortuary slabs, and the paper-thin mattresses bristled like steel wool. But each of us had brought along a quart bottle of Johnny Walker scotch, and after a couple of swigs we fell off to sleep, which in my case was deep and dreamless.

We left the next morning after breakfast, which was the same hard bread and even harder cheese, reminding me of the K rations that I had been issued on the Burma Road. We said goodbye to the *hegumenos* who pointed out the trail to the Grand Lavra, sending us off with a *Kalo dromos*, which literally means 'Good road'. But the rock-strewn mountain path proved to be so rough that whenever I spoke of it in later years Allan always groaned and said,

'John, there are miles and then there are Athos miles.'

The last stretch of the trail brought us down to the little port of the Grand Lavra, a crescent-shaped cove where a *caique* called every day on its way around the end of the peninsula, picking up passengers from the several monasteries en route to Dafni and Ouranopolis. A long and steep rock-hewn stairway led up from the port to the Grand Lavra, which was perched on the top of a sheer cliff several hundred feet above the sea, reminding me of a scene from the film *Lost Horizon* with Ronald Coleman, which I had seen with Peg at the Colonial Theater in Brooklyn, where the hero gazes from afar at a Tibetan monastery.

There were several other monks slowly ascending the stairway ahead of us, and when we caught up with them we learned from their conversations that they were from other monasteries on the Holy Mountain. It seems that the following day was the annual *panayeri* of the Grand Lavra, and they had come to join in the celebration.

The *hegumenos* served us raki and *loukoumia* and then led us to our rooms, after which we joined the other monks, more than a hundred of them, on a terrace hanging over the sea, which was beginning to turn golden as the sun sank into it on the western horizon.

I heard two old monks on the bench beside us speaking Turkish, so I figured that they must have been part of the exchange of minorities between Greece and Turkey of 1923. I greeted them in Turkish, saying that we were teachers at the American college in Constantinople. They were very excited by this and called over several other elderly monks, all of whom bade us welcome in Turkish. This welcome continued after we filed into the huge refectory, where the abbot himself greeted us in Turkish, seating us on either side of him at the high table. He also told us that we would be moved from our present room to a more spacious and comfortable one reserved for visiting dignitaries, because we were honoured guests from the holy city of Byzantium.

Our new room was above the entrance to the *katholikon*, the monastic church, with a balcony overlooking the courtyard. The abbot and his acolytes had just begun the prelude to the *panayeri*, a liturgy unchanged since the founding of the monastery more than a thousand years earlier. As the antiphonal chant echoed up to us through billowing clouds of incense I was transported back to medieval Byzantium, and at the same time I thought of serving as an altar boy at a solemn high mass at Fourteen Holy Martyrs Church in Brooklyn, such were the layers of imagination and memory evoked on this sacred evening, far away from the modern world on the Holy Mountain, a Greek Tibet.

The liturgy went on for hours, as we received a succession of visitors with whom we conversed with in English, Greek and Turkish. The older English speakers were usually widowed Greek-Americans who had retired to spend their last years in the monastery, where they felt more at home than they would have in senior-citizen housing in Chicago or New York, where even after half a lifetime they still felt like exiles, or so they told us as they helped us drink the bottle of Johnny Walker we had brought along.

The most interesting visitor was a monk who introduced himself in Greek as Yorgo, to which I replied 'O pou Yorgo kai malama', which means 'Where you find Yorgo (George) you find gold!' Yorgo was carrying a circular tray about a metre in diameter, in which he had baked a cake decorated in coloured sugar with a bust of Christos Pantocrator (Christ the All-Powerful). During the evening the abbot and many of the other monks dropped by to have a ritual piece of the cake, greeting me and Allan as if we were co-emperors of Byzantium. Subsequent visitors helped us finish off all the cake and most of the Johnny Walker, though we managed to save enough whisky so that we could have a night-cap the following evening, which would be our last at the Grand Lavra.

The next day a group of Greek academics arrived from the University of Thessaloniki, and we joined them for a tour of the famous library of the Grand Lavra, which the Emperor Nicephorus II Phocas had stocked with many ancient Greek manuscripts from Constantinople. Among those that I saw and inspected was a fifth-century manuscript of St Paul's *Letter to the Galatians*, and an even older copy of Diosorides' *De Materia Medica*, one of the works I had studied at Oxford in my seminar with Alistair Crombie. We were told that the tour would also include the monastery's treasury, which included its precious reliquaries, but the monk in charge would not permit me and Allan to enter, since we were not members of the Greek Orthodox Church. I could have told him that I had seen relics of some of the very same saints in Catholic churches in Italy and Brooklyn, including two almost intact skulls of St John the Baptist, while the Grand Lavra had only a fragment, according to its catalogue.

The following morning Allan and I walked down to the port to board the daily *caique* on its way to Dafni and Ouranopolis. The only other passengers were three old monks who came aboard at Dafni, and when I took out my camera to photograph a monastery one of them said to me, 'Put that camera away or I'll arrest you!' Then he laughed and introduced himself, saying that he was a retired detective from the Chicago police force and that he and his two companions were going to Thessaloniki to cash their American social security cheques. He was pleased when I told him that I was an Irish-American from Brooklyn, saying that many of his best friends in Chicago had been small-time Irish gangsters, and we shook hands on that when we said goodbye to one another at Ouranopolis.

At the beginning of the academic year 1966–67 the Board of Trustees at Robert College had appointed a new president, Dwight Simpson, who turned out to be a total disaster, and before the year was over had had a nervous breakdown and was permanently relieved of his duties. Bob Hall was appointed acting president, while the trustees began a search for a new president of RC and its sister institution, the American College of Girls (ACG) in Arnavutköy.

The trustees finally chose Dr John Scott Everton, a retired American diplomat, who took office in the summer of 1968. Everton had accepted the position on the understanding that either RC or ACG should be shut down, for they were both operating at a loss and the endowment had shrunk to the point where only one of the two campuses could be kept open.

Meanwhile the political situation in Turkey had degenerated into violent anarchy, and left-wing students at RC denounced the American administration of the college as an example of 'cultural imperialism', demanding that the school be taken over by the Turkish government. The anarchy led the Turkish Army to intervene, and on 8 March 1971 the government of Prime Minister Süleyman Demirel was forced to resign under pressure from General Cevdet Sunay, as the Turkish military took over control of the country, imposing martial law.

Three months later Dr Everton announced that the Board of Trustees had reached an agreement with the Ministry of Education, in which the latter would take over the campus of Robert College, the collegiate division of which would become a Turkish institution called Bosphorus University. At the same time Robert Academy would be amalgamated with the American College of Girls in Arnavutköy as a co-educational secondary school under the name of Robert College, administered by the American Board of Trustees. The transition took place in the summer of 1971 and that September our campus began a new existence as Bosphorus University. The first rector was my friend and colleague Aptullah Kuran, an alumnus of RC and a distinguished historian of Ottoman architecture, who was committed to perpetuating the bi-cultural Turkish-American tradition of the old Robert College.

Soon after the fall semester began, Aptullah gathered together the American faculty and told us that our RC contracts would be honoured by the Ministry of Education and that he would try to raise enough money to keep us on at the university for as long as possible. Many of the Americans on the faculty of Bosphorus University had departed at the end of the previous academic year and now there were only six of us left, including Bob McMickle, who had been replaced as head of the physics department by Erdal Inönü, son of Ismet Inönü, Atatürk's successor as president of Turkey and later prime minister.

Among the remaining Americans in the community were several members of the American Board of Missions, which had been responsible for the founding of Robert College in 1863. One of them was my friend and neighbour Bill Edmonds, editor of

Redhouse Press, a publishing house run by the American Board. Bill had heard that both Hilary Sumner-Boyd and I had been writing huge books on Istanbul that were as yet unpublished, referring to Hilary's *Seven Hills of Constantinople* and my *The Broken-Down Paradise*. He suggested that we combine and condense our manuscripts so that Redhouse could publish a single book as a scholarly guide to the city, for there wasn't an adequate work of that kind on the market. I talked about it that evening with Hilary and he said, 'Why not, my dear', whereupon I informed Bill and he gave me the go-ahead.

Such was the genesis of *Strolling Through Istanbul*, which was published in 1972. It received rave reviews, with *The Times* rating it 'the best travel guide to Istanbul' and William Buckley in the *International Herald Tribune* describing it as 'a guide book that reads like a novel'.

Among the new friends we made were Jim Burkart, who worked at the US Consulate, and his Irish-American wife Briget, who along with their eight children would play an important part in our lives for years to come. About the same time, we also met Bruce and Kate McGowan, whose son Joshua was the same age as Brendan. Bruce had a PhD in Ottoman History from Columbia University and had just been appointed head of the American Research Center in Turkey (ARIT). ARIT had been founded by a score of universities in the US as a residence and study centre for American and Turkish scholars doing research in Turkey.

Bruce was a talented singer, and while in graduate school had sung in the chorus of several productions at the Metropolitan Opera. Kate was a professional dancer and had become a member of the Turkish National Folkdance Group, with which she had been on tour throughout Europe.

One winter Sunday we all had lunch at our apartment in the Tower House and then sat around the fireplace talking. Brendan had been reading a book I had given him about Vlad the Impaler, the Romanian prince who was the historical prototype for the fictional Dracula of Bram Stoker's novel and the film with Bela Lugosi, which had left an enduring impression on me when I had seen it together with Jimmy Anderson as a boy. Bruce had also seen the film and read the novel, and we began playing with the dramatic possibilities of Lugosi's portrayal of Dracula, which, as we saw it, sitting around a blazing fire after an alcoholic lunch, had elements of both tragic drama and high-camp comedy.

Bruce and I talked more about the idea in the days that followed and decided that *Dracula* would make a great musical comedy. I would write the book, which would be set in Vlad the Impaler's castle in Transylvania, and Bruce would compose the music, which he felt should have an authentic Romanian quality to it. And so as the winter vacation approached, we decided that that we would drive to Romania, where Bruce would attune himself to the sound of the local music and I would absorb the feel of the Transylvanian countryside. Bruce said he would drive the four of us in his car, since it was in far better shape than ours, and he was familiar with the pot-holed and often perilous roads we would encounter on our journey up through the Balkans, where he had travelled extensively during his researches on Ottoman history.

Our route took us up through Turkish Thrace and Bulgaria, where we crossed the Danube into Romania. We spent several days in Bucharest before going on across the Transylvanian Alps to Kluj, the site of Vlad the Impaler's castle, which embedded itself indelibly in my memory, as did the ululating Romanian melodies we heard wherever we stopped for the night, and on our way back to Istanbul I could hear Bruce humming softly as he drove. We had caught Dracula's lost world on the wing, and now we would try to recreate it on stage, though in a way that Bram Stoker could never have imagined.

Jim Lovett agreed to direct the play, which we put on at the old Robert College Theatre, where many of Turkey's leading actors and playwrights had started their careers. Donald Hoffman played Dracula and Bruce took the part of Dr Kreutzer, the Viennese psychiatrist who struggles to save Lady Caroline, the victim of the vampire lord's blood lust, a role played by Barbara Frey, wife of my colleague Donald Frey, while Toots and Kate had supporting roles, as did a number of our friends.

The play was a huge success, and a visiting director from the UK tried to find backing to put it on in London, though to no avail. But as far as I was concerned it didn't really matter, for we had travelled to a fascinating part of Europe we hadn't seen before, and I had also revisited a fabulous character from the cinematic wonderland I had known in my youth.

Eileen graduated from the American College for Girls in June 1973. She had applied for early admissions at Wheelock College in Boston, which granted her a full scholarship. Meanwhile, with the help of the Burkarts, Brendan had been admitted to Rock-well College, a Catholic secondary school for boys at Cashel, the capital of County Tipperary in Ireland. The two of them flew off in early September 1973, leaving me and Toots alone for the first time in more than 21 years.

During the spring vacation of 1973 Toots and I drove to Athens, where we spent a couple of days before driving around the entire Peloponnese, looking at both its ancient and Byzantine sites. The high point of that tour was our visit to Mistra, the ruined city that had once been capital of the Despotate of the Morea, one of the last outposts of Byzantium.

I remember my first sight of Mistra, when we finally came upon it an hour or so before sunset after a long drive through the mountains of the Peloponnese. I could see the conical acropolis hill crowned with the crenellated walls and towers of a Crusader castle, with the remains of the Palace of the Despots and a score of Byzantine churches clustering below it on the western slope. The ruins were shrouded in a mist that clung to the spectral cypresses on the northern ridge of the hill, the surrounding Vale of Sparta embowered in olive groves and fruit orchards, five snow-capped peaks of Mount Taygetos catching the golden equinoctial light of the falling sun.

We made our way to the cathedral church of St Theodore, where in the nave we saw a relief slab bearing the double-headed eagle of the Palaeologues, the dynasty that ruled Byzantium through its last two centuries. Constantine XI Dragases Palaeo-logus, fated to be the last emperor of Byzantium, was crowned on the spot on 6 January 1449, only to die defending the fallen city of Constantinople on 29 May 1453. Mistra itself held out until 1460 and Trebizond until 1461, but after they fell Byzantium became just a golden memory, which still clings to this ghost city in the heart of what Homer called 'Hollow Lakedaimon'.

We drove back to Istanbul via northern and central Greece, stopping in Ioannina, Kalambaka and Trikala. The beautiful old city of Ioannina, set at an altitude of some 500 metres on the western shore of Lake Pamvotis, is capital of Greek Epirus and was part of the Ottoman Empire until 1913, when it joined Greece after the Balkan Wars. Byron, who visited Ioannina in 1809, when it was ruled by the legendary Albanian warlord Ali Pasha, the 'Lion of Yannina', described it as being 'superior in wealth, refinement and learning' to any other Greek town. The city still retains evocative monuments of its distinguished Byzantine and Ottoman past, particularly the Kale (castle) in the centre of the old town and the six monasteries on Nisaki, the little islet on Lake Pamvotis.

After seeing the old town, Toots and I took a boat out to Nisaki, where at a lakeside tavern we drank the sparkling zitsa wine of Ioannina and dined on its famous lake eels, which are said to mate only in the Saragasso Sea and to be a cure for rheumatism. We then made a pilgrimage to the Monastery of St Panteleimon, where in 1822 Ali Pasha made his last stand against an Ottoman army under Hurşid Pasha, who shot Ali Pasha and then cut off his head and sent it to Sultan Mahmut II. That evening, while we drank our zitsa wine, I offered a toast to Ali Pasha, quoting Byron's memorable lines from *Childe Harold's Pilgrimage*:

I talk not of mercy, I talk not of fear
He neither must have if they serve the Vezir.
Since the days of our Prophet the Crescent ne'er saw
A chief ever glorious like Ali Pasha.

We then drove across the Pindus Mountains to Kalambaka, where we visited the famous monasteries of the Meteora ('Suspended in air'), one of the largest and most important Eastern Orthodox complexes in Greece, second only to Mount Athos. The six intact monasteries are built on natural sandstone rock pillars at the north-western edge of the plain of Thessaly; four of them are inhabited by monks and two by nuns, each of them with fewer than ten inhabitants.

The oldest and largest monastery, the Grand Meteoron, was erected in the mid-fourteenth century by the Abbot Athanasios Koinovitis from Mount Athos, who dedicated its *katholikon* to the Transfiguration of Jesus. The second largest is the Holy Monastery of Varlaam, founded in 1541, whose *katholikon* is dedicated to All Saints. The stepped stairway to each of the six monasteries was far too long and steep for us with the limited time at our disposal, so we had to content ourselves with admiring them from below. As we stood below the Monastery of Varlaam, I realized that it was the difficulty of access to these monasteries that kept them inviolate during the long centuries of lawless Turkish rule, and I recalled the old folksong entitled 'Moni Varlaam':

I hear the wind arguing and moaning.
It argues with the mountains, goes on arguing:
'You mountain of Grevena, trees of Metsova,
You know well this man, this Papayiorghis,
backwards at letters, backward at his tables,
and now in his old age risen to be chief kleft.
He's raided all the strongholds, all the monasteries,
But there was one church he couldn't raid, All Saints.
Round and round he went and found no steps.
He called to the abbot, shouted to him:
"Come down, come down and give me absolution,
I have committed sins, I am a sinner,
I killed a priest while he was at the altar."'

We then drove south to Trikala and the great Thessalian plain, described by both Homer and Herodotus as the homeland of Achilles and Jason as well as of the mythical centaurs and lapiths. At Trikala we came upon the annual market fair of the Vlachs, a semi-nomadic people who speak a Latin language akin to Romanian. It is estimated that there are about 30,000 Vlachophones in Greece and another 20,000 in Albania. The fair, known in Greek as *to Pazari* (the Market), lasts for three days, celebrated with cultural activities during the day and in the evening with singing and dancing.

On the first day of the fair we went to an exhibition of primitive paintings by a middle-aged artist who had set up his canvases along a concrete aqueduct in the fields. Some of his paintings depicted the Greco-Italian War (28 October 1940–23 April 1941), in which he fought as a young soldier, so he told me proudly. The paintings were technically excellent and highly original, particularly his depiction of legions of winged centaurs flying down from the heavens to aid the Greeks in their battle against the Italians.

That evening wooden tables and benches were set up in the fields, and we joined hundreds of Vlachs at their festival, all of them dressed in their native costumes. Sheep roasted on spits and roast lamb was heaped in front of each of us along with flagons of white wine. A young woman sang in Vlach, Albanian, Greek and Turkish to the accompaniment of a ten-piece band, while circles of celebrants danced barefoot in the fields. Among the songs, I recognized one, an old love song of Trikala and the Thessalian plain:

> The plain thirsts for water
> the mountains for snow
> the falcons for meat
> and I, Despo, for you,
> for your plump hand
> with strong knuckles.
> Let me have it as a pillow
> Let me come to it with rent
> Every morning one gold florin
> Ten gold florins every week.
> My Trikalian partridge,
> My Larissian dove.

Early in 1973 I signed a contract with George Philips publishers in London to write a guide to Greece. Maureen agreed to help me, and during July and August of 1973, while she was on her summer vacation from Harvard, she joined us on Naxos to complete the book with me. The *Complete Guide to Greece* was published on 15 May 1974. So when Toots and I flew back to Boston for Maureen's graduation from Harvard early in June, I was able to present her with a copy of the book the day she took her degree.

We had picked up Brendan in Ireland on the way back to the US, and since Eileen was already in Boston all five were reunited for at least a few days. I had written to my parents inviting them to join us in Cambridge for the graduation, and I asked my aunt Nell to come too, since she lived in Boston.

At Maureen's suggestion we agreed to meet at nine o'clock on the morning of graduation day in the bar of the Wursthaus, an old restaurant directly opposite the entrance to Harvard Yard. Maureen was waiting for us at the Wursthaus with her boyfriend Paul Spike, a young American writer she had met on Naxos when we were finishing our book on Greece. A few minutes later Nell and Peg arrived, but there was no sign of John, and when I asked Peg where he was she told me she'd left him for good, after 50 years of marriage. He had started drinking heavily again and she'd simply had enough, so she'd gone to live with my sister Dorothy and her husband Frank Lehner in Albany, New York, leaving John behind with my brother Jimmy and his wife Jane, who had moved to Seabrook Heights, New Jersey. She would talk no more about it, she said, for her mind was made up, so we crossed over to Harvard Yard and proceeded to the graduation.

After the opening remarks by Derek Bok, the president of Harvard, the various speakers droned on, none of us paying much attention, until one of them, a Protestant minister, concluded his remarks by saying, 'God Bless You', which led Peg to shout, 'God should be abolished!' This caused a stir among those seated around us, though the rest of the audience and the dignitaries onstage seemed not to have heard Peg's blasphemy, which led Nell to cross herself repeatedly.

After the graduation Peg and Nell said goodbye, for they were taking a bus to my uncle Gene's house in south Boston. Peg would spend the night there before taking the train back to Albany, and so we said our tearful goodbyes, as I wondered once more whether I would ever see her again.

The next day we said goodbye to Maureen and Paul, who were getting ready to move to New York, while Toots and I flew to Athens with Eileen and Brendan. We spent the summer together on Naxos before returning to Athens, flying off on our separate ways, Eileen to Boston, Brendan to Ireland, Toots and I to Istanbul. And so in mid-September 1974 we moved back into our apartment in the Tower House, which seemed very empty without our children.

A month later Maureen and Paul suddenly showed up and moved in with us, for they hadn't been able to find suitable jobs in New York. They thought they might be able to teach English at a Turkish school in Istanbul, but since the fall term had already begun there were no openings. They tried again at the beginning of the spring semester, but again to no avail, so they moved to London after Paul's mother had lent him enough money to support them for a while. They were married shortly afterwards, but as it was during the school term Toots and I couldn't be there for the ceremony, which saddened us, as I realized that this was yet another price to be paid for living a life of exile.

Eileen and Brendan rejoined us on Naxos during the summer holiday. We looked forward to settling back into our old routine, but tourism had now discovered Naxos and we no longer had it to ourselves. Later that year Lycabettus Press in Athens published my *Naxos, Ariadne's Island*, an evocation of the place as we first knew it, before it had lost its innocence to the modern commercial world.

Soon after the beginning of the spring semester in 1976, Aptullah Kuran called in the six remaining Americans on the faculty of the university to meet with him in his office. He said that the Turkish Ministry of Education had cut the budget for foreign faculty salaries for the next academic year, and so there would only be enough money for five of us. He looked around the room, waiting for one of us to speak, until finally I volunteered to be the odd man out.

Toots wasn't at all surprised or upset when I told her, for we had been expecting this to happen sooner or later. I said that I would try to find a job in Athens, which she thought was a great idea. I wrote to several international schools, all of which said they were interested, so we drove there during the spring vacation. After inconclusive interviews at two schools I finally accepted an offer from the Hellenic International School (HIS) in Kifissia, the fashionable garden suburb of Athens beneath Mount Pendeli, where the marble for the Parthenon had been quarried.

The directors of HIS, two Americans named Bob Betts and Lloyd Pawkett, showed me around the school, which they had founded three years before. HIS had several levels: primary and secondary schools as well as collegiate and graduate divisions, the latter two run in association with La Verne University in California, which also offered courses at the US Navy base at Nea Makri in Marathon, site of the battle in which the Greeks had defeated the Persians in 490 BC. I would teach in both the secondary school and the collegiate division, which also offered evening courses as well as Saturday study tours of the monuments of Athens and its environs, for which I would be paid extra.

Brendan had one more year to go at Rockwell but wasn't very happy there, and so we thought that he could complete his secondary schooling at HIS. When I asked Bob and Lloyd about this they said that it would be fine and that he could go free of charge. We shook hands and they said they expected me on the first Monday in September, by which time their assistant, a young Lebanese Druze named Samir, would have found a suitable apartment for us.

We spent the rest of the spring semester preparing to leave, and by the time I finished teaching my last classes we had packed up our belongings, which were mostly books. Brendan had joined us by that time and he helped me load our things into a wooden crate, which we were having shipped to Athens.

Istanbul had never been more beautiful than it was in the last days before we left, with blossoming judas trees purpling the hillsides above the Bosphorus and in the evening nightingales serenading one another in the valley behind our house. We finally left early in the morning of 15 June 1976, driving down the same road by the Bosphorus along which we had come to the college nearly 16 years earlier. And so we left Istanbul, and I wondered if we would ever return. Our odyssey was changing course, a fate that had befallen Odysseus when his men had opened the bag in which Aiolus had tied up the contrary winds.

# 8

# THE ODYSSEY
# INTERRUPTED

We spent the summer on Naxos and then took the car-ferry to Piraeus on 14 September, driving up to Kifis-sia, where Samir took us to the apartment he had found for us, about half an hour's walk from the school.

From nine to three I taught secondary school courses in phys-ics, mathematics and astronomy, as well as filling in for Bob Betts in his history course. From three to five I gave university-level courses in physics, mathematics, astronomy and the history of science. Then from seven till ten I offered graduate-level courses in Byzantine and Ottoman history. During the week I also taught afternoon courses at the US Navy base at Nea Makri, and on Saturdays I led study tours of the monuments of ancient Athens and its environs.

My tours of Athens eventually led to *Strolling Through Athens*, published in London by Penguin in 1990. Like *Strolling Through Istanbul*, it comprises a series of interconnected walks through the city, including its ancient Greek and Roman periods and through the Byzantine and Turkish eras up to modern times. In one of my strolls I pass the Temple of Olympian Zeus at a point where the Ilissos River is canalized beneath the modern highway. I recalled that this was the scene of Plato's dialogue *Phaedrus*, where Socrates congratulates his companion for having led him to such a beauti-ful spot, 'a fair resting place full of summer sounds and scents. My dear Phaedrus, you have been an excellent guide!'

One of the friends I made that year was Nikos Stravroulakis, founder and director of the Jewish Museum in Athens. Nikos was from Chania in Crete, where he was restoring a thirteenth-century Venetian tower-house, and he said that he hoped to have us as his guests there when work was completed.

The closest friends we made were a young British couple, Roddy Conway Morris and his wife Christine, who were beginning their own life of exile, and in the years that followed our paths crossed several times in the course of our odysseys.

Among the other good friends we made in Athens were Rosemary Engman, who took my graduate course in Byzantine history. Her husband Larry Engman was a CIA officer in Athens who had come as a replacement for Robert Welch after he had been assassinated by Greek terrorists the previous year. Through Larry I met a number of other CIA agents, including Ernie Tzicagos and Gust Avrakatos, both Greek-Americans. Ernie was known as 'the Mad Bomber', a name he had earned when serving with the OSS in China during World War II blowing up bridges. It turned out that one of those he had blown up was over the Salween River between Burma and China, which my truck convoy had crossed early in August 1945 after waiting for the damage caused by Ernie's bomb to be repaired.

Gust Avrakatos was later involved in the coup that overthrew the government of Andreas Papandreou, and later still he was portrayed by Philip Seymour Hoffman in *Charley Wilson's War*, starring Tom Hanks, a film based on Gust's clandestine exploits in Afghanistan.

Brendan graduated from the HIS secondary school in June 1977. He received a full scholarship from Yale, which was a pleasant surprise, for his school record was somewhat less than brilliant. He flew off to the US at the beginning of September to enrol at Yale. Shortly afterwards we were joined by Eileen, who had graduated from Wheelock College with a degree in early childhood education. She had applied for a job at the HIS elementary school, where she was hired to teach first grade.

That September the secondary school and collegiate division of HIS moved into the old Hotel Cecil in Kifissia, where we had much more room. The kitchens in the basement had been converted into science laboratories, and I was joined there by two new teachers, both of them in their late 20s, a Brit named Tony Baker, who would teach chemistry, and an American, Faye Breslin, who would teach biology. Tony had a car, and since he lived near us I asked him if he could give Eileen a lift to the elementary school, which was some distance away. Tony said that he would be happy to do so, and within a few weeks he and Eileen began going out together.

We had been worried about Brendan, for he hadn't lived in the US since he was a baby and we had no family or friends in New Haven to look out for him. He was a complete outsider and we could tell from his letters that he was having trouble. At the end of the semester he received failing grades in all his subjects and was dismissed from the university. He flew back to Athens to rejoin us at HIS, where he was given a job helping Samir around the school.

We spent the summer on Naxos again before beginning the fall term at HIS. Brendan seemed all right for a while, but as the fall went on he became increasingly depressed. Then one Friday evening we were having dinner when we received a call informing us that Brendan had slashed his wrists and was in the emergency ward at a hospital in Athens. We rushed to find him in no immediate danger, but the doctor in charge said it was imperative that he be placed in a psychiatric clinic where he could be kept under observation and treated. We placed him in a private mental hospital in Kifissia, where his condition improved enough to be able to bring him back to our apartment.

But it was obvious that Brendan needed more extensive treatment, and so Toots decided that she would have to take him back to the US. She called her dear friend Ann Couch, who was living in the Boston area, and asked her for help and advice. Ann said that Toots and Brendan could stay with her while they were getting settled, and so early in the spring semester they flew off to Boston.

Toots called me every weekend to let me know how things were going. The second time, she called to tell me that Brendan had been admitted to a state psychiatric hospital and that she had found a secretarial job at the Windsor Girls' School in Boston. She would be staying with Ann until she could find her own apartment. I said I would fly to Boston to see her during the spring vacation and that I would contact our old friend Neil Bull, former headmaster at Robert College who now ran an academic placement agency, to see if he could help me find a teaching job in the Boston area.

Neil arranged an interview for me at the Noble and Greenough prep school near Dedham, a suburb of Boston, where there was an opening for a teacher of science and maths. I went there during the spring vacation and met the headmaster, the Reverend Ted Gleason, and the head of the science department, Fred Sculco, both of whom were good friends of Neil. I seemed to have just the qualifications they had in mind, for after a very pleasant interview I was offered the job and accepted it immediately.

Toots was overjoyed, and she said that she would try to find an apartment for us in Dedham, and so when I left her to fly back to Athens we were hopeful for the future, though also sad, for in the 28 years of our married life we had never before been separated for more than a day.

I finally left Athens in late August, by which time Eileen had moved in with Tony Baker. As I flew away I could see the Parthenon and then all of Athens receding in the distance as the plane gathered height over the Aegean and its encircling isles. I felt that our odyssey had ended and that circumstance had forced us back to the country of our birth, where we no longer felt at home.

After Brendan was released from the hospital Toots had rented a house in Dedham and had borrowed money from Ann Couch to buy a secondhand car so that she could commute to the Windsor School, while I could either walk to the Noble and Greenough School, which was about three miles away, or ride on the school bus. Brendan found a job at a petrol station in Dedham while he lived with us for a while, but then found a better position in Boston delivering flowers and moved into his own apartment.

I enjoyed teaching at Noble and Greenough and made a number of good friends in the faculty, as Toots did at the Windsor School. Our social circle included new friends, particularly Peter and Connie Oliver and Bob and Ellen Kaplan as well as our old friends Ann Couch, my former student Jacob Maya and his wife Mimi, Roddy and Olga O'Connor and Peter and Rosemary Shiras. So we soon began enjoying life as much as we had in Greece and Turkey, which we still missed terribly, and on evenings when we were on our own we always played Greek and Turkish music.

Meanwhile our dispersed family was growing. On 10 December 1979 Maureen gave birth to a son, whom she and Paul called Matthew. They moved to El Paso, Texas, in 1982, when Paul joined the creative writing department of the University of Texas, El Paso. They were still living there on 1 May 1983 when their daughter Emma was born. Toots and I were able to attend the christening, where the god-parents were Pandelis and Eirene Bamias, Greeks who had met and married in the US when they were at university.

Eirene was from the Greek island of Samos, and so at my request she sang for us 'Samiotissa' (The Girl from Samos), which I had last heard Sotiri Peristerakis sing to Hermione on Naxos. Pandeli was a Vlach from the mountains of northern Greece, and we talked with him about the festival we'd been to at Trikala and the songs we'd heard there. Next day he took us across the border to a Greek restaurant in Juarez, where we listened to Mexican songs on the juke box. Such were the journeys we took on the wings of song.

Eileen and Tony Baker moved from Athens to London in 1980, when Tony found a job teaching at Dulwich College. They were married in Bristol on 30 August 1980, and in London on 3 October 1981 Eileen gave birth to a girl, whom they called Ariadne because of the association of the goddess with Naxos. Then on 23 April 1985 Eileen gave birth to a son, whom they named Alex.

Meanwhile we had lost some of those who were dear to us, for my father had died in 1978 while we were in Athens, and Toots' father passed away in 1985. Two years later my mother died and I felt a profound desolation, for with John and Peg gone I had lost all living connections with my childhood and youth, which had passed into what Homer in the *Odyssey* called the Country of Dreams.

My *Companion Guide to Turkey* was published in 1979 by Collins
(later HarperCollins) in London. It received a number of excellent
reviews and I began writing to other publishers in the UK to see if
they were interested in my work. I received a very positive response
from A. and C. Black, publishers of the Blue Guides, and so over
the mid-year break I flew to London to see Paul Langridge, the
chief editor. Paul offered me a contract to write the *Blue Guide
Istanbul*, which I accepted immediately. Then he said that A. and
C. Black were extending the Blue Guide series to the US and had
recently commissioned a guide to New York City. He suggested
that since I was now living in the Boston area I might be interested in writing a guide to that city. I said that I certainly would,
and at that same meeting signed a contract to do the *Blue Guide
Boston and Cambridge*. I would first write the *Blue Guide Istanbul*,
which would take little effort, for I used *Strolling Through Istanbul*
as the principal source. Meanwhile I would get to know Boston
and Cambridge, and when the Istanbul book was finished I would
start working on the new book.

The *Blue Guide Istanbul* was published in 1983. By that time
I was already working on the *Blue Guide Boston and Cambridge*,
which was published in 1984. The distinguished scholar Bernard
de Voto wrote an 18-page review of the book in *New England Magazine*, in which, among other things, he pointed out that in my
description of the residences of famous authors I noted the books
they wrote when they were living there, and that in describing the
mansion of Henry Wadsworth Longfellow in Cambridge I had
quoted his translation of the line from Dante's *Purgatorio* that he
had inscribed on the sundial in the garden: 'Think that this day
will never dawn again.'

By that time I had received a commission from Weidenfeld and
Nicolson in London to write a book on Crete. I had accepted with
some hesitation, for although I knew a great deal about Crete from
a lifetime of reading about it, I had seen it only from the deck of
a troopship in 1945. We planned to go there during the coming
summer, for the advance I had received was enough to pay for our
airfare and expenses, but I had no idea where we would stay. So
I wrote to my friend Nikos Stavroulakis saying that we hoped to

spend the summer in Crete. He answered by return mail, inviting us to be his guests at what he called his 'cottage' in Chania. He said that he would be there when we arrived but would be away for most of the summer, but that his housekeeper Maria would look after us. Brendan quit his job so that he could join us, and so at the beginning of the summer vacation we flew off, spending a week with Maureen and Paul at Daya in Majorca before going on to Athens and from there to Chania.

Nikos was waiting for us at his 'cottage', a magnificent three-storeyed Venetian *pyrgos*, or tower-house, which he had restored from near ruin when he bought it. We had the whole of the top floor, and he said that we would have the run of the entire place while he was gone. He introduced us to his housekeeper Maria, who served us supper in the *piano nobile* of the *pyrgos*, where the Venetian lord of the manor had dined with his retinue in the thirteenth century. The following morning Nikos departed, saying he would be back late in August and wishing me well with my writing.

We had lunch that day on the huge balcony on the top floor of the *pyrgos*, which looked out over the whole town and its harbour to the White Mountains, whose peaks were still covered with snow. That evening we walked along the seafront promenade, which extended around the Turkish port to the old Venetian one, where we had supper in the taverna of Yorgo Drakakis. After we finished eating, Yorgo took down his *lyra* from the wall and began to play softly. Soon another man took his *lauto* and a third his guitar and when they had picked up Yorgo's tempo all three began to play a haunting Cretan melody. This was followed by a livelier tune that brought a group of customers to their feet in a *Kritikos Syrtos*, the beautiful circle-dance headed by a young woman waving her handkerchief as she leads the way through a series of interwoven loops – the symbolic recreation of the Cretan myth in which Theseus and his companions are led out of the labyrinth by Ariadne.

We spent the next two months exploring Crete, visiting sites from its Minoan, ancient Greek, Byzantine, Venetian and Turkish past, as well as getting to know the Cretans themselves, including their music, dance and folk poetry, particularly their *mantin-*

*ades*, the extemporaneous rhymed couplets they recite even when passing one another in the street. The *mantinade* I recall most vividly is one that Cretans in exile recite to one another, referring to Mount Psilorites, one of the lordly mountains that form the spine of the great island: 'When you go to Crete, Cretan, greet her from the mountain, aged Psilorites!'

Our last excursion took us to the remote south-western corner of the island, to visit the Monastery of the Chrysoskalitissa, Our Lady of the Golden Steps. The monastery is on a hilltop site above Cape Elefonissi, the south-westernmost promontory of Crete, where we spent the afternoon swimming on a beautiful beach of pink and white sand. Afterwards I stood out at the end of the cape, looking at the ships passing far to the south where the Aegean merges with the Libyan Sea. As I watched them I thought of my troopship passing through that same stretch in mid-October 1945, when I looked north from the flying bridge to see this very cape where I was now standing. This brought to mind the lines from Chapman's translation of the *Odyssey*, where the disguised Odysseus tells Penelope a lying tale about his voyage home from the Trojan War:

> In the middle of the sable sea there lies
> An isle called Crete, a ravisher of eyes,
> Fruitful, and mann'd with many an infinite store;
> Where ninety cities crown the famous shore ...

Nikos returned at the end of August, and a couple of days later we left the *pyrgos*, thanking him for his truly Homeric hospitality. The following day we flew to Athens and from there to Boston, where we arrived just in time for the opening of the fall semester. Brendan had found a much better job working with the Social Services Bureau in Boston, where he and a young woman named Anne Taylor ran a house for patients suffering from Down's Syndrome.

That fall I received copies of my book *The Cyclades*, published by Jonathan Cape in London. Reading through it, as well as working on my book on Crete, renewed my longing for the Aegean. I remembered the line from Keats' *Hyperion*: 'I dream of thee and of the Cyclades'.

We celebrated my 60th birthday on 26 June 1986 with a big party at our house in Dedham. One of the guests was a Greek musician I had met in Boston, and he played and sang Greek music for us all evening, including *nissiotica tragoudia* from the Cyclades, to one of which Toots and I danced a *balo*, the old Venetian courting dance we had learned on Naxos. After the party was over the two of us began reminiscing about Greece and Turkey and began wondering if we would ever get back to our old world. We had made a new life for ourselves in the Boston area but still felt out of place in our native country, for our hearts were half a world away.

Shortly after the beginning of the fall semester, on 1 October 1986, I was scheduled to give a lecture at the hour-long morning assembly, the subject being the new comet that had appeared in the evening sky. When I arrived at school that day I suddenly decided that I wouldn't give the lecture and instead went to my office and wrote a letter of resignation, saying that I would be leaving the school at the end of the academic year. I made copies of the letter for the headmaster, the dean and the departmental chairmen, which I put in their mail boxes and then went back to my office.

When the assembly ended the headmaster, the dean and the department chairman came in turn to my office, all of them a little puzzled by my decision, but I could tell that they weren't too unhappy about it, for although I had been a very popular teacher I hadn't really fit into the ethos of a New England prep school.

It was a beautiful autumn day, and while walking home after school I whistled all the way, something I hadn't done since I was a boy. When I told Toots what I'd done she was overjoyed, and that evening we celebrated with a bottle of champagne.

We then began to think about what we could possibly do and asked Maureen and Eileen if they had any ideas. Maureen said that she would keep her eye out to see if a teaching job came up in London. Eileen and Tony Baker had moved to Istanbul, where he was teaching chemistry at the Robert College secondary school in Arnavutköy and she was teaching first grade at the Community School in Rumeli Hisarı. They had bought a flat in London and were renting it out, but if we moved there they would make it available to us.

Just before Christmas Maureen called to say that there was an opening for a science and maths teacher at the Southbank International School in London. She make an appointment for me, and during the mid-year break I flew to London and met with the headmaster, who hired me right away, to begin in September.

Our friends Roddy and Olga O'Connor had made the same decision as us. They had been hired to help run an American art school at Lacoste in France, beginning in September, and so they resigned their teaching jobs in the Boston area. They thought they would try to book passage on a ship that would take them and their belongings to France, which I thought was a great idea. And so I began checking the shipping news, until I finally booked passage for us and our car on a Polish ship, the *Stefan Batory*, which would sail from Montreal in late June, bound for Tilbury docks on the Thames outside London.

Brendan would not be coming with us, for he was now engaged to Anne Taylor and doing well at his job in Boston. Late in June we packed our belongings and drove to Montreal, where we spent the night in a hotel before boarding the *Stefan Batory*. It was the first time that Toots and I had been in Montreal since our weekend honeymoon in July 1951, and here we were 36 years later, about to resume the odyssey which had been only a dream when we signed our blood pact after we had first met.

We boarded the *Stefan Batory* the following morning. Then, when the PA announced 'All ashore who're going ashore', we said goodbye to Brendan and Anne. They stood on the dock and we waved to one another as the *Stefan Batory* moved slowly out from the pier, finally losing sight of them as the ship steamed down the St Lawrence towards the Atlantic.

The voyage, which took 12 days, was extremely pleasant. A string quartet played in the dining room during meals, which were excellent, and in the evening after dinner a band played dance music in the ballroom. The weather was fine and we spent most of the day on deck, seeing the occasional iceberg and spouting whale as well as the flotsam of the Gulf Stream, all of which was new to me, for this was by far the most northerly of my 21 crossings of the Atlantic by sea.

Maureen and Paul Spike were waiting for us at Tilbury, and together we drove off to Tony and Eileen Baker's flat in London. The flat was in Shepherd's Bush, on the top floor of a three-storey house, looking out over the yard of an auto repair shop towards the viaduct of the District Line, whose trains went roaring by every few minutes. Maureen and Paul helped us unload our things and then Paul went to a Turkish kebab restaurant and had them deliver us a take-away meal for supper.

I had gathered from talking with Paul that his marriage was on the rocks, and when he had gone out to order our supper Maureen confirmed this, saying that she would be filing for a divorce before she left for the US. And so our first evening in London ended sadly, dampening the excitement we had felt in beginning a new life.

We talked for a while after supper before Maureen and Paul drove back to Oxford, where they had been living since the fall of 1984. By then Maureen had published two novels, *Mother's Helper* in 1982 and *The Life of the Party* in 1986, both of which had received excellent reviews. She said that in the fall she would be going off to teach in the creative writing department at the University of Miami, while Paul remained in Oxford with Matthew and Emma.

As soon as we were settled in I reported to the Southbank School, which was near Victoria Station. The headmaster, a very pleasant gentleman who asked me to call him Milton, showed me around the school, which was housed in two buildings, the second of which, the annex, as he called it, was a block away from the main site. He told me that I would be teaching courses in general science, physics, mathematics, astronomy and the theory of knowledge, and that I would teach my physics course in the annex, where I would be expected to set up a laboratory. He handed me a scientific apparatus catalogue and I spent a couple of hours ordering equipment for the lab. Then Milton and I shook hands as he told me that he looked forward to seeing me again at the beginning of September.

The O'Connors had invited us to spend the summer with them in Lacoste in Provence, east of Avignon. And so in late June we drove down to Dover and took the ferry to Calais, and from there we followed a circuitous route through the west and south of France to Lacoste, where the O'Connors were waiting for us.

Lacoste is perched on the top of a steep hill above the surrounding plain, the houses in the upper village clustering round the ruined chateau of the Marquis de Sade. The art school, which had been founded by the American artist Bernard Frame, was designed for American students who wanted to study art in France. The faculty were mostly American artists, and the O'Connors had been hired to help run the school and also to teach French.

We lived with the O'Connors and ate with them and the students and faculty in the school refectory, which was housed in the ruins of the Marquis de Sade's chateau, and in the evenings we went down to the lower village to have a drink at the Café de France, a raffish old hostelry built on the precipice of the medieval defence walls of Lacoste.

During the day I usually hiked through the surrounding plain and up into the Luberon, the low range of hills separating Provence from the French Riviera. At weekends we accompanied the O'Connors on school outings, one of which took us to Arles, where we had supper in a café that I recognized from a painting by Vincent van Gogh, stars blazing in the midnight-blue sky.

And so the summer passed, as we and the O'Connors resumed the good times that we had enjoyed with them in Istanbul and Boston, as our paths crossed again in our lives of exile. When we said goodbye to them at the end of August they invited us join them again the following summer, to which I responded by saying 'Inshallah', which in Turkish means 'God willing', for our lives had become just as unpredictable as that of Odysseus on his long journey home to Ithaca.

I began at the Southbank School in mid-September. My teaching load was very heavy, 33 periods a week, which, with a 90-minute commute on the Underground each way, left me exhausted by the time I arrived home. Then in good weather I began walking home through Hyde Park and Holland Park, which took about the same time as the Underground, but I arrived home exhilarated rather than worn out.

Most weekends we drove to Oxford to be with Paul and the children. On one of our first weekends there we met a publisher named Derek Johns and his wife Jane. Paul had submitted a synopsis to Derek and had invited him and Jane to dinner so that they could talk about the proposed book. Toots and I hit it off immediately with Derek and Jane, and in the weeks that followed we saw them frequently in London.

One sunny Sunday that autumn we ran into our dear friends Roddy and Christine Conway Morris while strolling along the Thames Embankment from Hammersmith to Chiswick. They had left Athens and were now living in London not far from us, and so we saw a great deal of them in the months that followed, usually going to a little Greek taverna to recreate the good times we had enjoyed together in Athens.

Toots and I often went to Soho on Friday evenings, where we usually had a bottle of champagne at happy hour in a French café and then went on to have supper in a Greek taverna. We also went to some of the pubs we had frequented during our previous stay in London, but we were saddened to find that The Bird in Hand had closed and that both Keidrych Rhys and Bryn Fugue had passed away.

I had signed a contract with John Murray publishers to write *The Western Shores of Turkey*, which was scheduled for publication in the spring of 1988. Despite my heavy teaching schedule, I managed to spend an hour or two each week at John Murray's offices in Albemarle Street, Mayfair, the same house where the first John Murray had published Byron's debut work in 1811. The present director was the seventh John Murray, whom I came to know along with his father, the legendary Jock Murray. My editor was Grant McIntyre, who became a good friend, and I worked with him in his office on the illustrations and proofs of my book.

*The Western Shores of Turkey* received good reviews, as did *Crete*, which was also published in the spring of 1988. As a result of that

I received a contract from Penguin to do a book called *Classical Turkey*, which I spent all my spare time writing, even during school hours when my students were doing experiments or solving problems.

During the spring vacation we drove to Connemara in Ireland, where our friend Briget Burkart had given us the use of her old cottage outside the coastal village of Roundstone. Briget had inherited the cottage from her parents and was going to renovate it, so it was still without modern conveniences other than electricity, running water and plumbing, but we didn't mind at all and greatly enjoyed the two weeks we spent there.

While we were in Roundstone I ran into my old friend Tim Robinson, a former colleague of mine at Robert College, whom I hadn't seen since he and his wife Muraide left Istanbul in 1962. He told me that he and Muraide had gone to live in the Irish-speaking Aran Islands off the coast of Connemara in 1972, an experience that he wrote about in *Stones of Aran, Pilgrimage*, published in 1986. A reviewer described this as, 'One of the most original, revelatory and exhilarating works of literature ever produced in Ireland.'

I recalled that Tim and Muraide had spent the summer of 1961 on Naxos, and that it was his description of the island that persuaded me to go there the following summer. And now a quarter of a century later we were resuming our life of exile while they were continuing theirs, with Tim and I both writing about the historic landscapes of our adopted homes.

Late in the spring I received a letter from John Chalfont, another former colleague at Robert College. John had been the first headmaster of the new Robert College co-educational secondary school at Arnavutköy after the merger in 1971 and had done such a good job that he had been hired to set up a number of schools in the Gulf states. He was now working for the wealthy Turkish industrialist Vehbi Koç, for whom he was setting up a school in the Asian suburbs of Istanbul.

John offered me a job as head of the science department at the Koç School and said that Toots could work in the English language lab. The school was scheduled to open in mid-September 1988, by which time the faculty housing would be ready for occupancy. My salary would be significantly more than I was earning at the Southbank School, and since Toots would also be working and we'd be living rent free, the offer was too good to refuse and I accepted immediately.

We were sad at the thought of leaving London, for we had greatly enjoyed living there, but we had barely got by and had no savings, facing a precarious future. I gave my notice at the Southbank School and called Eileen and Tony Baker to give them the news, telling them that we would be leaving the flat in Shepherd's Bush in mid-June and expected to arrive in Istanbul at the beginning of September.

We spent a month with the O'Connors in Lacoste and then began the long drive to Istanbul. Our route took us down through Italy to Brindisi, from where we took the ferry to Corfu, northernmost of the Ionian Islands, where we stayed for a couple of days before taking another ferry to Igoumenitsa on the Greek mainland.

We continued south, crossing the entrance to the Ambracian Gulf on a car-ferry. In doing so we passed the site of the battle of Actium, where on 2 September 31 BC, Octavian, the future Augustus, defeated the combined fleets of Antony and Cleopatra. Just south of the gulf we drove across a causeway to reach the Ionian island of Lefkas, where we spent a day before continuing southwards to Astakos, the port for Ithaca, stopping along the way to pay brief visits to the Ionian isles of Paxos and Lefkada.

We spent the night in Astakos before taking the ferry out to Ithaca, which for me was the culmination of a lifelong quest that began when I first read Homer. We checked into a little hotel in Vathi, the capital, and set out to explore the island, whose topography was engraved on my mind from years of reading about it. But, like Byron, I had little interest in supposed Homeric sites, such as the Fountain of Arethousa, which had been identified by the imaginative speculations of nineteenth-century antiquarians. (After Byron had been shown the supposed fountain he said, 'Enough of this antiquarian twaddle, I'm going for a swim.') I then recalled the lines from Book 9 of the *Odyssey*, where Odysseus identifies himself to Alkinoös, King of the Phaeacians:

I am Odysseus son of Laertes, known before all men for the study of crafty designs, and my fame goes up to the heavens. I am at home in sunny Ithaka. There is a mountain there that stands tall, leaf-trembling Neriton, a rugged place, but a good nurse of men; for my part I cannot think of any place sweeter on earth to look upon.

We went on to see two more of the Ionian Islands, Cephalonia and Zakynthos, spending only a few days on each, for time and money were running out and our overloaded car had difficulty on the steep mountain roads. We resolved to come back again and explore the islands in more detail, which we did, and ten years later my book *The Ionian Islands* was published in London by I.B.Tauris.

We took a ferry from Zakynthos to Patras and drove from there to Athens, where we spent a couple of days before beginning the long and familiar drive back to Istanbul. The final stretch took us along the coast of the Sea of Marmara, which was far more developed than when we had last seen it 12 years before. Then the magnificent ruins of the Theodosian Walls appeared, marching across the downs of Thrace from the Marmara to the Golden Horn, and as we drove around the seaward periphery of the city to the Bosphorus I felt that our odyssey was almost back on course, at least for the moment.

# 9

# THE ODYSSEY
# RESUMED

We spent our first day in Istanbul with Eileen and Tony Baker and our grandchildren Ariadne and Alex, who were living in a faculty apartment at the Robert College secondary school in Arnavutköy. That afternoon I walked up the Bosphorus to Rumeli Hisarı and the lower gate of Bosphorus University, but I couldn't bring myself to enter, feeling like an unwelcome stranger.

The old fortress of Rumeli Hisarı was unchanged, though I saw from a sign over its main gate that it was now being used as a venue in the annual Istanbul Summer Festival. A short way upstream from the fortress the Bosphorus was now spanned at its narrowest point, between the villages of Rumeli Hisarı and Anadolu Hisarı, by the Fatih (Conqueror) Mehmet Sultan Bridge, which had just opened to traffic. It was built across the same stretch of the strait as the bridge of boats constructed by the Persian king Darius in 512 BC, exactly 2,500 years before, an incident mentioned by Herodotus.

As I walked back from Hisar to Arnavutköy I could see the first Bosphorus Bridge, between the villages of Ortaköy in Europe and Beylerby in Asia, which had opened on 27 October 1973, the 50th anniversary of the founding of the Turkish Republic, a ceremony that Toots and I had watched from a hilltop above the Asian side of the bridge.

I called John Chalfont that evening, who said that he would be meeting with the foreign faculty of the Koç School the following day at an office of the Koç company in Ortaköy. We would be going out to the site of the school, which was some 40 miles east of the Bosphorus, near a place called Kurtköy, the Village of the Wolf. Neither the school building nor the faculty housing were quite ready for occupancy, so for the time being we would stay at a hotel in Bostancı, a small town on the shore of the Marmara, about 15 miles from the school.

Besides ourselves, there were about a dozen foreign faculty at the meeting, including three whom we knew from our earlier years at Robert College: Rita and Tony Carey and Dan Parrish. Tony had been hired as the dean of studies, while Rita and Dan would be in the English language preparatory division, in which Toots would teach in the language laboratory. Most of the subjects at the school would be taught in English, and the English prep classes would be given in parallel with the regular courses.

The other teachers drove off with John in a mini-van, while Toots and I followed in our car, crossing the Bosphorus Bridge and heading eastwards through the Asian suburbs of Istanbul. We went first to Bostancı and checked in at the hotel, then joined John and the others in the mini-van to drive out to the school. We passed through Kurtköy, a very lively and ramshackle village with a Wild West atmosphere about it, probably because most of its inhabitants were Kurds and other refugees from the Kurdish rebellion that was raging in south-eastern Anatolia.

The school was several miles beyond Kurtköy, set in barren and virtually uninhabited countryside that seemed to stretch all the way to the Black Sea. The school was just north of the new approach highway to the Fatih Mehmet Sultan Bridge, which John said should be ready for use in a few months, much diminishing the driving time to Istanbul.

The school building was almost ready for occupancy, though the furniture, plumbing, electrical wiring and gas supply for the science labs had not yet been installed, and it would be my responsibility to supervise the school workmen in doing this, as well as unpacking, assembling and testing the scientific equipment for the student experiments and lecture demonstrations I would have to design. I would also have to write the curricula for the various courses in general science, biology, chemistry, physics and mathematics, as well as go over them with the other science and maths teachers, all of this in the two weeks before the school opened in mid-September. I would be teaching only in the three-year secondary school programme, which would start with 100 students – 50 boys and 50 girls – and I would continue teaching the same group as they moved up from Lise I to Lise II and then Lise III.

The faculty housing was ready for occupancy a week later. It consisted of a double row of two-storey apartments on the hillside above the school, each apartment with a kitchen, dining room and sunken living room on the ground floor, and above a bedroom, office and bathroom, with small balconies on both floors. We drove into Kurtköy to buy groceries and other supplies, while for faculty without cars there was a regular shuttle service.

Classes began at 9am on Monday 15 September, when the first of four successive groups of 25 students each filed into my lecture room. I had asked John Chalfont for advice on what to teach, and he said that it was entirely up to me, for the main purpose of my course would be to introduce students to the terminology of science and maths as well as teaching them the fundamentals of physics, which I thought was easier said than done.

So without thinking further about it I gave essentially the same lectures in elementary physics as those I had given my students in Istanbul, Athens, Boston and London. Most of the students knew some English and some were fluent, and they translated for the others as we went along, slowly at first and then more rapidly as time went on. I gave frequent demonstrations during the morning classes, and then the students themselves did experiments during the afternoon laboratory sessions. They were eager and bright, and before long the classes were up to the same level as those I had taught at other secondary schools.

I was also expected to supervise some of the student extra-curricula activities, and so I started physics and astronomy clubs. As I had been taking long walks in the countryside around the school, I also founded a hiking club, for which more than 50 students signed up. I led them on hikes which took us far out of sight of the school, where the only people we saw were a few shepherds grazing their flocks on distant hillsides, and we waved to them as we passed.

Toots enjoyed her work too, teaching the younger students of the Middle School in the English language laboratory. Although she had never taught before, her gentle manner made her very popular among her students, many of whom had never been away from home till they came to the school.

We made a number of good friends among both the Turkish and foreign faculty, as well as with the school staff, all of whom were Turkish. There was a community centre just above the faculty apartments, and on the first Saturday after the school started John Chalfont threw a big party there. Everyone employed at the school was invited, including the watchmen and workers, most of whom were from eastern Turkey. One of them had brought along a *saz*, the traditional stringed instrument of Anatolia, and while he played, his companions circled around the room in some of the beautiful Turkish and Kurdish folk dances of eastern Turkey, with a few of the Turkish faculty joining in. It was a memorable evening, and as Toots and I were having a nightcap on our balcony after the party we felt that we were most fortunate to have landed on our feet once again in a pleasant community. Then as the late rising moon emerged from behind the hills to the east, casting its ashen light on the barren landscape around us, I could hear the unmistakable howling of wolves, which reminded me that we were now living in the vicinity of Kurtköy, the Village of the Wolf.

Most Fridays after school we drove into Istanbul, crossing the Bosphorus on the new Fatih Mehmet Sultan Bridge to the village of Rumeli Hisarı, spending the weekend with the Bakers. We often had parties on Saturday evenings, socializing with old pals of ours as well as new friends from Eileen and Tony's circle.

The old friends included Tony Greenwood and his wife Gülen Aktaş. Tony was the director of ARIT, the American Research Institute of Turkey, for which I led several tours of Istanbul in the months that followed. Another old friend was Emin Saatçi, one of the first Turks I had met other than colleagues when we came to Istanbul.

During the spring vacation I led an ARIT trip to the ancient Graeco-Roman city of Aphrodisias, western Asia Minor. We were guided around the site by Professor Kenan Eren, the young Turkish archaeologist who had spent years excavating the ruins of the half-buried city, restoring its major monuments and unearthing the magnificent statues that had given Aphrodisias the reputation of being 'the Florence of the ancient world'. Shortly after our trip we learned that Professor Eren had died of a sudden heart attack, an irreparable loss to Turkish archaeology. He was buried next to the magnificent Roman gateway that he had finished restoring not long before he died, and on subsequent trips to Aphrodisias I always made a pilgrimage to his grave.

The next academic year was uneventful, and the completion of the approach highway to the Fatih Bridge across the Bosphorus made it much easier to go to Istanbul at weekends. We spent most of our time there with the Bakers, although sometimes they stayed with us at the school. Other Istanbul friends came too, and we put them up in the guest rooms at the community centre. So we began to feel less isolated in Kurtköy, though the completion of the highway seemed to have driven the wolves away, for we no longer heard them howling in the evening.

Among the new friends were Memo Sağıroğlu, a Turkish businessman, and his Irish wife Ann Marie, who worked as a nurse at the old Robert College Community School, where Eileen was now head of the Lower School. We had many other acquaintances in the city, old and new, but Tony Greenwood, Gülen, Emin, Memo and Ann Marie would be, in the years that followed, the most steadfast of all our Istanbul friends. Meanwhile I carried on with my writing, working on an expanded second edition of *The Companion Guide to Turkey*, which would be published by Harper in 1993.

Brendan and Anne Taylor were married in a civil ceremony in Boston late in the fall of 1988. A week later they flew to Istanbul, where we had made arrangements for them to be wed at a nuptial mass at the Catholic church of San Antoine in Beyoğlu. We had a big party for them at the Bakers' apartment at Robert College and a few days later they flew back to Boston.

Meanwhile we heard from Maureen that she and Paul Spike had divorced and that she had custody of Matthew and Emma. Not long afterwards she told us that she was now living with Frank Longstreth, an American academic who had also just been divorced and had custody of his children, Kimber and Rachel. Frank was teaching at the University of Bath, and he and Maureen moved there from Oxford in 1992, a year after their daughter Helen was born. Two years later another daughter, Pandora, was born in Bath, so that their household now included six children, which forced them to move to a larger house in a suburb of the city in 1996. That same year Maureen began teaching creative writing at the University of Warwick, by which time she had published six books, including four novels.

We spent the summer of 1989 in Naxos, where Toots celebrated her 60th birthday on 30 July. Tourism had now completely transformed Chora. Vangela's restaurant had closed, so we spent our evenings with our old friends at the taverna of Vasili Mylonas, who had been forced to move from the Borgo to a place outside town on the barren west coast of the island, where there were no beaches to attract tourists.

During the mid-year break Toots flew to the US to see her family, who were still living on Red Bank, New Jersey, while I stayed with the Bakers. This gave me a chance to get to know Istanbul again, and I spent my days strolling through the old city as well as revisiting my old haunts in Beyoğlu, where I found that all the old Greek tavernas had gone, for most of the Greeks in the city had by now moved to Athens, taking their music and dancing with them.

Even Çiçek Pasajı had lost much of its colourful character, for it had been rebuilt and modernized after a structural collapse had closed it for several years. The collapse had occurred just after we left for Athens in June 1976, which had led a young journalist friend of mine, Mustafa Gursel, to write an article in the *Milliyet* newspaper, in which he said that 'Çiçek Pasajı collapsed last night out of sadness for the departure of John Freely.'

We spent the summer vacation of 1990 with Maureen and Frank Longstreth and their children in Oxford. I took the train into London a couple of times to see my publishers, and on one of those trips I signed a contract with Penguin to write *Strolling Through Venice*, which would be a companion volume to my books on Istanbul and Athens. The only problem was that I didn't know Venice, but I thought that Toots and I could move there after we completed our three-year contract at the Koç School, and in the interim we could make an extended visit there at the first opportunity so that I could start working on the book.

When we returned to the Koç School in mid-September we found the O'Connors waiting for us. They said that a change of administration at the Lacoste school had forced them to resign, and the letters that they had received from me had led them to write to John Chalfont, who had hired Roddy to teach literature and Olga to teach biology and set up a greenhouse. Their apartment was just down the block from ours, and that evening we had dinner with them there to celebrate our reunion, as our lives of exile intersected once again.

Toots and I spent the spring vacation in Venice, exploring the city and buying books on its history and monuments. We looked up our friends Roddy and Christine Conway Morris, who had moved there the year before and who would once again be our neighbours.

We had been living rent free during our time at the Koç School and had saved up $20,000, far more than we had ever had in the bank before. I had also signed contracts with a French publisher, Didier Millet, to write four books, three of which were profusely illustrated guide books, and the fourth the text for a book on the great Ottoman architect Sinan, with photos by my friend Ara Güler. I would receive $5,000 for each of these, half of which would be given as an advance before we left for Venice and the other half paid when I submitted the completed manuscript. I would also receive an advance from Penguin for my *Strolling Through Venice*, as well as one from Harper for the second edition of my *Companion Guide to Turkey*. Besides that I would be receiving a monthly cheque from the US Social Security Agency, for I would turn 65 on 26 June 1996. So all in all we thought that we could manage to retire to Venice.

The remainder of the spring passed rapidly, as we gradually carted all our things to Istanbul and put them in the Bakers' apartment. After the graduation ceremony at the Koç School we said goodbye to all our friends there, including the O'Connors, who were flying back to the US to see their children. We spent the summer with the Bakers, and then early in September 1991, after packing all our belongings into our car once again, we said goodbye to them and drove off, beginning yet another stage of our continuing odyssey.

We took a car-ferry from Istanbul to Izmir, where we spent the night, before boarding another bound for Venice. We landed at the Tronchetto, the docks at the western end of Venice. There we boarded yet another ferry that took us across the Venetian Lagoon to the Lido, the most populous of the barrier islands that separate the lagoon from the Adriatic.

On the Lido we drove to the Grand Viale, where we parked our car and walked to the first real estate office we could find. The agent spoke English, so we told him what we were looking for and he said that he had something we might like. It turned out to be on the third floor of an apartment house at 28 Via Bragadin, just behind the Hotel des Bains, the grand old hotel on the sea-front promenade where Thomas Mann's *Death in Venice* is set.

The owner, a very pleasant local who introduced himself as Tino Giada, showed us the apartment, which was fully furnished and just what we wanted, and since the rent was reasonable we said that we'd take it, paying a month's rent in advance. Tino helped us unload our belongings from the car and by late afternoon we had moved in.

Tino had recommended a restaurant named Andre's, which was around the corner from Via Bragadin on Via Lepanto, a street that extended along the side of a canal to the Grand Viale. We had dinner at Andre's, which was excellent, and afterwards went for a nightcap at one of the cafés on the Grand Viale, which was just a ten-minute walk from our apartment. And so ended our first day in Venice, which we could already tell would be very different from the many other places in which we had lived.

As soon as we settled in we had dinner with Roddy and Christine Conway Morris at their apartment, which was in Castello, one of the six *sestiere*, or quarters (actually sixths), of Venice, three on either side of the Grand Canal. San Marco and Canneregio are on one side, while Santa Croce, San Polo and Dorsoduro are on the other, as is Giudecca, which is part of Dorsoduro administratively, but separated from it by the Canal de la Giudecca, which is much wider than the Grand Canal.

After dinner we walked to the Piazza San Marco, where we sat in Quadri's Café and ordered proseccos, looking at the magnificent spectacle before us, with the basilica of San Marco and the Doges' Palace floodlit at the eastern end of the piazza. After another round of proseccos, they put us on the *vaporetto* at the San Zaccaria station and said goodnight to us there, as our ferry took us back to the Lido, a routine we followed repeatedly in the months to come.

Our apartment had two bedrooms, the smaller of which I set up as my office, getting to work on the several books for which I had contracts. The four books I was doing for Didier Millet wouldn't take much work, nor would the second edition of *The Companion Guide to Turkey*, for I was so familiar with the material involved. So I worked a couple of hours a day on those books and the rest of my time researching *Strolling Through Venice*, which involved reading about its history and monuments as well as exploring the city itself.

In mid-October I came down with a serious cold and went to see an English-speaking doctor on the Lido named Piccolotto, who said I had bronchitis and gave me a prescription for an antibiotic. But the bronchitis continued to get worse, even though Dr Piccolotto came to the house and prescribed additional medication.

Then at 6:05 on the morning of 21 October I woke up feeling light-headed and was unable to use my left arm. I thought that I must be having a stroke, so I woke Toots and told her what was wrong. She dressed immediately and helped me dress as well, and then drove out around the Hotel des Bains and raced at top speed down the coastal road to the Ospedale del Mare, the public hospital at the north end of the seaside promenade.

We drove in through the emergency entrance, by which time I had regained the feeling in my left arm and was able to move it, though I still felt somewhat light-headed. The doctor on duty spoke English, and Toots told him what had happened. He examined me and found that my blood pressure was very high and so had me taken to the intensive care department for observation.

I was given medication that within an hour reduced my blood pressure to normal. A more extensive examination revealed nothing obviously wrong, and so I was moved to a regular ward where Toots was allowed in to see me. The physician in charge of the ward, who introduced himself as Dr Casalino, told us that I would be kept under observation for some days and that I would be taken to the main hospital in Venice, the Ospedale Civile, so that a CAT scan of my brain could be taken to determine whether I had suffered a stroke.

Two days later I was taken in a water ambulance to the Ospedale Civile, a monumental edifice that had been erected in the fifteenth century as the hospital of the Scuole Grande de San Marco, directly adjacent to the great Dominican church of Santi Giovanni e Paolo, built at the same time as the hospital. The water ambulance entered the emergency entrance from a canal beside the hospital and I was taken up to the radiation lab where my brain was scanned. The following day Dr Casalino came to tell me that the scan showed no evidence of a stroke. When I asked him if the scan had revealed anything else amiss, he shook his head, saying, 'Just the usual atrophy.' This alarmed me, so I began solving complex mathematical problems in my head, such as computing the Fibonacci numbers, after which I silently recited the names of all the Byzantine emperors, Ottoman sultans and Venetian doges I had been reading about as part of my research. But my memory seemed as good as ever, which greatly relieved me, since my brain was my only resource, the machine that powered my cottage industry of writing books.

Poor Toots had been terribly worried, and she breathed a deep sigh of relief when I told her that I was OK. My bronchitis was finally getting better too, and Dr Casalino told us that if all went well I could expect to be discharged from the hospital in a few days.

The hospital fare was basic but good, and Toots always brought me a treat after supper in the evening. I was surprised to find that wine was served at both lunch and supper, but I wasn't allowed to have any because of my condition. I had made several attempts in the past to give up alcohol, but to no avail. But now, as I'd had nothing to drink for a week, and it might be the better part of another week before I was discharged, I decided that that would be a good start to giving up alcohol completely, and so I did, and this time it proved to be permanent.

Soon afterwards our old friends Peter and Rosemary Shiras came to Venice for a week, checking into a hotel, the Atlanta, just around the corner from us on Via Lepanto. We had dinner with them at Andre's on the evening of their arrival and we decided that the next day I would give them a tour through the Castello quarter.

We took the *vaporetto* to Isola de San Piero, where we visited the beautiful fifteenth-century church of San Pietro. We then crossed a bridge over the very wide Canal di San Pietro, turning left at the first intersection on the other side, where a narrow *calle* led us to a little square called Campo dei Do Pozzi, the last two words meaning 'two well-heads'.

One of the two eponymous well-heads in the campo had vanished, but I had found that the other one was decorated with a relief showing the square when both were still in use. I led the way to the well-head, whose spigot was dripping water that had formed a slippery green slime on the pavement below. I tried to sidestep the slimy area, but my feet skidded out from under me and I fell flat on my back as a terrible pain flashed through my left leg, and I knew immediately that it was broken.

Two men who had been working in a furniture-making shop near the well-head rushed out to see if they could help me, and when they saw the state I was in one of them called the emergency number of the Ospedale Civile, as they told Peter, who spoke some Italian. The two men then brought out a half-finished couch for me to lie in, taking care not to move my broken leg. The pain was not too bad, and as I waited there I was able to joke a bit with Toots and the Shirases, at one point quoting D.H. Lawrence's putdown of Venice, which he had called 'a slippery, green, abhorrent city'.

After about half an hour two medics appeared with a stretcher, and when they reached the well-head both of them slipped and fell in the same slime that had downed me. They were unhurt, but the pavement was so slippery that they had some difficulty getting me into the stretcher. They also had trouble getting the stretcher through the very narrow alley leading to the canal where the water ambulance was waiting. Toots and the Shirases said they would see me later at the hospital, for they weren't permitted to go in the ambulance.

The only other person in the ambulance, besides the two medics and the driver, was a little old lady who had apparently broken her right arm, which was in a sling. As my stretcher was set down next to where she was sitting, she let out a laugh at the sight of my beard and said, 'Eh, Signor Emingway!', and I couldn't help laughing with her.

An X-ray examination showed that my left tibia was broken in several places. I was taken directly to surgery, where a young physician who introduced himself as Dr La Bombarda said in basic English that he and his team would set my leg and pin the fragments together. I was given a spinal anaesthetic and was only vaguely aware that my leg was being operated on. When I was fully awake after the operation, Dr La Bombarda showed me an X-ray photo of my mended leg, which had six metal pins holding it together, and he laughed as he pointed out that it looked exactly like the bronze emblem on the prow of a gondola, where each of the six strips symbolized one of the *sestiere* of Venice.

Toots and the Shirases came to visit me in the hospital that evening, and they were relieved when I told them that the operation had gone well. Toots had brought along my things, including a copy of *Canali, Ponte e Campi* (Canals, Bridges and Squares), a book of maps of the whole of Venice as well as the islands of the lagoon, which I had been using while designing the itineraries for *Strolling Through Venice*, and so I was able to continue working on the book while I was in hospital.

By the time I was discharged I was able to hobble about on crutches. I hardly ventured out of the apartment for the next few weeks, for the weather was rainy and the streets and bridges wet and slippery. So I spent all my time writing the four books I had contracted for with Didier Millet, as well as working on the itineraries for *Strolling Through Venice*.

We flew back to Istanbul in mid-December to spend Christmas with Eileen and Tony Baker and the children. While we were there we were invited to the Bosphorus University Christmas party, the first time I had set foot on the Rumeli Hisarı campus in more than 15 years. I found myself surrounded by old Turkish colleagues and former students who were now on the faculty, some having risen to the post of departmental head and dean, and, in one case, vice-rector. All of them asked me why I didn't rejoin them, for the situation had greatly improved since I left. The university was now allowed to have as many as 50 foreign faculty, who weren't subject to mandatory retirement at 67, as were Turkish citizens. I was very flattered and said I would certainly consider the possibility, though Toots and I were very happy in Venice.

By now we had made a number of good friends in Venice, some of them through living on the Lido and others in the historic centre through Roddy and Christine Conway Morris and from my own explorations of the city. The first of our friends on the Lido were Michael Gluckstern, the British consul-general in Venice, and his Neapolitan wife Liliana, who introduced us to Patricia Bonelli, an Irish musician whose husband Alessandro was first violinist in the La Fenice Teatro orchestra. We also got to know Adolfo and Sheila Rodigheri, and through them a charming group of women I called 'the Lido Ladies', including Pat Liani, Muriel Alvaise and Lesley Court. Together they welcomed us into their very congenial social circle on the Lido, where life was so very different from the labyrinthine microcosmos of Venice's historic centre.

Through the Glucksterns we got to know Lady Frances Clarke, widow of Sir Ashley Clarke, former British ambassador to Italy and founder of the Venice in Peril Fund. Frances introduced us

to a number of interesting Venetian and ex-pat scholars, many
of whom we met at monthly meetings of the Circolo, a society
devoted to Anglo-Italian cultural interchange.

Through Roddy and Christine we also met a number of ex-pat
writers and artists, beginning with the British photographer and
journalist John Brunton and his wife the French painter Marie, and
soon afterwards Tony Cepeda and her husband Craig Manley, two
American vagabonds who had acquired a little *palazetto* in Cannaregio. Soon afterwards they introduced us to Geoffrey Humphries,
a British painter, whose American wife Holly Snapp had opened a
gallery in the San Stefano parish. Through the Humphries we met
the American painter Geoffrey Leckie and his wife Liz, and the
distinguished Irish-American sculptor Joan O'Connor, who had
been a member of Ezra Pound's circle in Venice.

Geoffrey and Holly invited us to a number of parties at their
palazzo in Giudecca, and at the first of them I met Peter Lauritzen,
an American historian, whose books – *A History of Venice* and *The
Palaces of Venice* – I had read with great interest. Peter and his Irish
wife Rose lived on the *piano nobile* of a sixteenth-century palazzo in
the Ghetto Nuovissimo in the Cannaregio quarter, where at their
elegant dinner parties we met a succession of writers and artists as
well as members of the old Venetian aristocracy, of whom Roddy
Conway Morris said, 'they can be lured from their palazzi with the
promise of a free meal'.

Eileen and Tony Baker joined us later in the spring, along with
Ariadne and Alex. Tony spent much of his time taking photos for
me, which I used as illustrations for *Strolling Through Venice*. The
weather was so pleasant during their stay that we explored several
islands in the lagoon, including Murano, Mezzorbo, Burano and
Torcello, where Tony took a superb photo of the eleventh-century
church of Santa Fosca.

There were hardly any other tourists on Torcello the day we
were there, and we had the site pretty much to ourselves. One of
the lesser-known sites that I pointed out was a rough-hewn marble
seat known as the 'Throne of Attila', traditionally associated with
Attila the Hun, who in 452 sacked and destroyed Aquileia and
Atinum and other towns on the mainland, forcing thousands of

refugees to seek shelter out on the then uninhabited isles of the lagoon, beginning the history of Venice. That brought to mind the elegiac lines that John Ruskin wrote in *The Stones of Venice*, at the end of his description of the view from the campanile of San Fosca, looking out over the deserted site of Torcello:

> Thirteen hundred years ago the grey moorland looked as it does this day, and the purple mountains stood in the deep distance of evening, but on the line of the horizon there were strange fires mixed with the light of sunset, and the lament of many human voices mixed with the fretting of the waves on their ridges of sand. The flames rose from the ruins of Altinum, the laments from the multitudes of its people seeking, like Israel of old, a refuge from the sword in the path of the sea.

Through the Lauritzens we were invited to half a dozen palazzi, including two that were still owned by direct descendants of doges and one, the Palazzo Mocenego on the Grand Canal, where Byron had lived in 1818-19 with his tempestuous housekeeper-mistress 'La Fornarina', whom he described as having a body 'fit to breed gladiators from'. It was here that he began writing *Don Juan*, somehow finding time to write despite his romances and carousing. As he wrote to the Irish poet Thomas Moore on 1 June 1818: 'Good night, or rather good morning. It is four, and the dawn gleams over the Grand Canal and unshadows the Rialto. I must be to bed; up all night – but as George Philpot says, "It's life, though, damme its life."'

The Ghetto Nuovissimo where the Lauritzens lived was the latest addition to the Venetian Ghetto, the oldest in Europe, which had been founded in 1516 to give refuge to the Jews of the Veneto when they were in danger of being slaughtered by the marauding troop of the League of Cambrai. The Venetian Jews were confined to the Ghetto until the conquest of Venice by Napoleon in 1797, and on 19 July of that year its gates were demolished, 'with music and dancing by Jews along with Christians', as reported in the Venetian press.

By the beginning of May 1992 I had finished the final drafts of
the four books I was doing for Didier Millet, and after I sent them
off spent all my time on *Strolling Through Venice*. By the end of the
summer I had finished my explorations of the six *sestiere* of the
historic centre of Venice as well as the islands of the lagoon. Then
in the autumn I began writing the final draft of the book, and, in
checking the details, Toots and I wandered all over the city, stopping in the various little restaurants and cafés that had become
our favourites during the past months.

Sometimes late in the evening we wandered through the
more remote parts of the city, particularly when there was a full
moon to light our way along the *fondamenta* of side canals that
led into one silent little *calle* after another, the only sounds being
the echoing footsteps of other nocturnal strollers. At times like
this I recalled the bewitching lines that Proust wrote in *Albertine
disparue*, describing a solitary dreamlike stroll through the moonlit
Venetian labyrinth:

> I had plunged into a network of little alleys, *calli* dissecting
> in all directions the quarter of Venice isolated between a
> canal and the lagoon, as if it had crystallized along those
> innumerable slender capillary lines. All of a sudden, at the
> end of one of these little streets, it seemed as if a bubble had
> occurred in the crystallized matter.

Early in the spring of 1993 we received a visit from Tony
Greenwood and Gülen Aktaş. Gülen was now a full professor of
physics and had been appointed vice-rector by Üstün Ergüder, a
friend and former colleague of mine who was rector of Bosphorus
University. She said that one of my former students, Ayşe Soysal,
was now the dean of the School of Science and Languages and
that the two of them had talked together with Üstün and decided
to offer me a position as a full professor of physics, with rent-free
faculty housing.

The thought had been in the back of my mind since our Christmas visit to Istanbul, and I had talked about the possibility with
Toots. She loved living in Venice and would have been happy to

spend the rest of our lives there. But she could see that our money was fast running out, despite the payments, advances and royalties I had earned from my books. The only steady income we had was my monthly social security cheque, which was barely enough to pay our rent.

Toots was reluctant to leave, and it was only after I said that we could return to Venice during university vacations that she finally agreed. So I told Gülen that I would accept the appointment, and she said that she would make all the necessary arrangements, including a suitable faculty apartment.

I finished the final draft of *Strolling Through Venice* early in July, sending it off to Eleo Gordon, my editor at Penguin in London. Then we began making arrangements for leaving, hiring a moving company to pack into a crate all that we would not be taking with us by car. I booked tickets on a ferry of the Adriatica Line, which would depart from Venice early in September, bound for Igoumenitsa, from where we would drive across northern Greece and Turkish Thrace to Istanbul.

We spent the last couple of weeks saying goodbye, not only to our many dear friends but to the places in Venice we loved most, such as Quadri's Café in Piazza San Marco, where, as always, we had a nightcap before boarding the *vaporetto* to the Lido for the last time, though now I drank orange juice rather than prosecco.

On the morning of our departure we took the ferry from the Lido to the Tronchetto docks in Venice, where we boarded the Adriatica Line ferry. We stood out on the foredeck as the ferry steamed down the Giudecca Canal and through the Bacino San Marco, as we watched the familiar domes and spires of Venice slip by as we passed them in succession. Then the ferry headed out into the lagoon to pass through the Porto de Lido, the ship channel leading out into the Adriatic. Our friend Patricia Bonelli had said that she and her teenage daughter would be waiting there beside the entrance to the channel, by the monastery of San Nicolo. And so they were, and as the ferry passed we waved to them until they faded from sight, along with the city where we had just spent two of the best years of our life.

But we were going home, for that's what Istanbul had become, and as we drove up the Bosphorus and into the university campus I felt like a returning exile, though I knew that Toots would always miss Venice.

We parked our car outside the faculty house in which we would be living, in a somewhat gloomy valley inside the back gate of the university that I had always called 'The Slough of Despond'. We had planned to unpack the car there and then drive to Arnavutköy to spend the night with the Bakers. We had just about run out of petrol, so Toots thought that perhaps we should fill up the tank on the way to Arnavutköy. We had just about run out of money too, so I checked my pockets to see how much I had left, which turned out to be the Turkish equivalent of about $5. 'Then we could have stayed in Venice for another day,' she said, which I realized was the spirit that had kept us going through the more difficult days of our life of exile.

# 10

# THE ODYSSEY
# CONTINUES

T he Slough of Despond lived up to its name, for our return
to the university campus began on a dismal note. The
guard at the back gate said that our apartment had not yet
been vacated by its summer occupant, an official from the Turkish Ministry of Education, who was away at the moment. So we
decided to drive to the Bakers and spend the night with them, but
our poor old car refused to start. I asked the guard to call a taxi,
and when it arrived we just took our hand baggage with us and left
the rest of our belongings in the car. The $5 in Turkish liras I had
left was only about half the taxi fare, so I had to borrow the differ-
ence from Tony when we arrived at his apartment.

We had a wonderful evening with the Bakers, who had just
returned from a summer on the Greek island of Euboea, where
they had built a seaside cottage. The next day Tony drove us back
to the Slough of Despond with a mechanic who managed to get
our car started, though he said it needed some serious attention.
The guard said that that there was still no sign of the occupant of
our apartment, so we drove back to the Bakers, where we stayed
for several more days.

Gülen Aktaş eventually found us a much nicer place in one of
the faculty houses further up the hill near the old south campus.
We were given an apartment on the second floor, embowered by
trees through which we could see the Bosphorus flowing past the

towers of Rumeli Hisarı, and we knew that we had truly come home.

The physics department was now in the new north campus at the top of the hill, along with the library and the other science and engineering departments as well as the School of Education. When I left in 1976 the enrolment was about 1,000, but now there more than 10,000 students, including the graduate school. The physics department now had 27 faculty, including eight of my former students, who insisted on calling me 'Sir'. When I tried to get them to call me 'John', one of them said to me, 'Once a sir, always a sir', though some of them eventually addressed me by my first name.

During the first semester I taught a course in astronomy and another in the history of science, both with about half a dozen students. The history of science course proved to be very popular, and more than a hundred students signed up for it in the second semester, so that my class was shifted to the largest lecture hall in the department, though extra chairs had to be brought in to seat the overflow. I also gave a course on Saturdays and in the summer school on the Byzantine and Ottoman monuments of Istanbul, which had as many as 80 students enrolled. It was great to be teaching in a university again after a 17-year absence, and I was very pleased that I didn't seem to have lost my touch.

Toots and I quickly settled into our old pattern of life in Istanbul, getting to know the city again, renewing old friendships and starting new ones. Tony Greenwood asked me to begin leading tours of Istanbul and Anatolia for ARIT, and in the spring of 1994 I led an ARIT tour to Venice. Toots and I rented our old apartment on the Lido, so that we were able to stay on for the whole of the university's spring vacation, renewing all our old friendships. While we were there the first copies of my *Strolling Through Venice* appeared and I had the pleasure of seeing it displayed in the window of my favourite bookshop, on the Bacino Orseolo, just off the Piazza San Marco.

The last time that Toots and I returned to Naxos was in the summer of 1994. During the years we'd been away several of our dearest friends had died, including Yorgo Spiridakis, Sotiri Peristerakis and Vasili Mylonas. Vasili's widow, Nikoletta, continued running their taverna outside of town with the help of her three sons, and we spent every evening there with our old friends, for Chora was now overrun with tourists.

On our second day Toots and I had a picnic in the archaic temple of Apollo on the Palatia, the tiny offshore islet in the port where Dionysus discovered Ariadne after Theseus abandoned her while she slept. Then we walked up to the Castro, where we found that all the old Venetian families had gone except for Nikos Dellarocca, who had turned the family's thirteenth-century tower-house into a museum devoted to the Venetian heritage on Naxos. Nikos was overcome with emotion when we ran into him at the gateway of the Castro, for our two families had been very close in the early 1960s, long before mass tourism had discovered Naxos and changed its old way of life.

Next day we took a taxi to Mikri Vigla, though we were hesitant to go there after such a long absence for fear that it would be swarming with tourists, spoiling the memory of the summer days we had spent there in the past. But we were relieved to find that it had hardly changed, other than for a few summer cottages that had been built along the shore. Toots and I walked out to the taverna and sat down, looking out on the turquoise waters of the cove, feeling as if we had been permitted to have one last glance at our paradise lost.

Niko and Marco, Costa's two sons, were still running the taverna, and they came over to welcome us back. Their parents had passed away and their sisters had married and moved to Athens, they said, but they themselves still lived in Filoti and came down to Mikri Vigla in the summer months to run the taverna.

After we finished lunch Marco came over to sit with us, talking of how much Naxos had changed since we had first come to Mikri Vigla. The conversation was entirely in Greek, which I had no trouble understanding, though I hadn't conversed in it for years.

I remembered that when we first saw Marco he was just four, a year younger than Brendan, and that sometimes Costa would give the two of them a ride on his donkey. This prompted me to ask him if there were any donkeys left on Naxos, for I hadn't seen one since we returned. 'Interesting that you should ask that, Kyr Yani [Sir John],' he said, smiling, and went on to relate a pair of incidents, separated in time by 30 years, which together said everything about the effect of the modern world on Naxos during the time we had known the island.

He said that on the day that we first came to the taverna, Bill had honked the horn of his taxi as he approached the cove, and Marco had asked his mother about the strange sound. She told him that it was an *aftokinito*, or automobile, the first one he had ever seen, which made a great impression on him. He then went on to say that earlier this summer a child in Filoti had heard a donkey braying and asked his mother what it was. She explained that it was a *gaidouri*, or donkey, and showed him the animal as it passed their house carrying an old farmer to his cottage high up on the slope of Mount Zas, where the modern world was still very far way.

We laughed when we heard the horn of our taxi returning to pick us up, and we told Marco and Niko that we hoped to see them again before too much longer. But I feared that I would return to Mikri Vigla only on the wings of daydreams that the Greeks call *lotophagoi*, lotus eating, which since childhood had been my means of escape from the real world.

Meanwhile, during the mid-year break we had flown to the UK to see our new granddaughter Pandora in Bath. We also spent a few days in London, where I went to see Eleo Gordon, my editor at Penguin. Our friend Derek Johns was now working as a literary agent at A.P. Watt, and through him I submitted a proposal to Eleo for a book about the history of Istanbul. This was the genesis of *Istanbul, the Imperial City*, published by Penguin in 1998, and still selling steadily after more than 16 years in print.

Brendan and Anne Taylor were divorced in 1995 and he came back to join us in Istanbul, working as Eileen's assistant at the Community School. He lived with us for a while but then found an inexpensive apartment in Hisarüstü, the ramshackle village that had developed around the north campus, where he soon made a new life for himself. Ten years later he married Yelda Turedi, a Turkish girl from south-eastern Anatolia who had graduated from Bosphorus University, and the two of them moved into her apartment in Beyoğlu, where they supported themselves by doing translations while they worked on their own writing.

Among the new friends I made was Rick Blakney, who had replaced Bill Edmonds as head of the Redhouse Press. Rick suggested that I write a series of illustrated historical guides to the various regions of Turkey. I thought it was a great idea, particularly since Tony Baker had been taking photos for me on excursions around Turkey during school vacations ever since we returned to Istanbul, and I had been accumulating information on the history and monuments of the country during the years I had been living in the city. Tony and I began making trips to fill in the gaps, and within four years after our return to Istanbul, Redhouse published seven of my regional guides to Turkey.

Another new friend I made in Istanbul was Selcuk Altun, a graduate of Bosphorus University who was now head of Yapı Kredı Bank, one of the largest in Istanbul, which also ran a publishing house and cultural centre. Selcuk had read a number of my books, and when he asked me what I was going to work on next I said that I was thinking of doing a history of Robert College and Bosphorus University. But there was a problem, for the Robert College archives had been taken to New York when Bosphorus University was founded in 1971. Selcuk said that Yapı Kredı Press would publish the book and that their cultural centre would pay for my expenses to go to New York and work in the archives.

I received permission from the American trustees of Robert College to examine their archives, which would be made available to me in their New York office. I was then given a sabbatical leave from the university for the spring semester of 1998.

I had been in touch with my friend Kevin Kehoe, a banker we had known when he was working in Istanbul, and he offered to let us use his apartment in New York, for he and his wife B.A. would be in London until early June. So Toots and I packed our things and on 1 February flew off to New York on THY, Turkish Airlines. For the first time in our lives we travelled first class and without charge, for the president of THY, my friend Jem Kozlu, was a Robert College alumnus and this was his way of supporting my project.

The Kehoe flat was in an apartment house on Broadway and West 84th Street. B.A. was waiting for us when we arrived and had the building superintendent, a Puerto Rican named Jose, help us take our things up to the apartment. After showing us where everything was, she left to fly to London that evening to join Kevin.

The New York office of Robert College was in the Helmsley Building, near Grand Central Station at the beginning of Fifth Avenue. On the first Monday morning after our arrival I took the subway downtown to 42nd Street, where I changed to take the cross-town shuttle to Grand Central.

The head of the Robert College office, a very pleasant woman named Lynn Prevo, had gone to a great deal of effort on my behalf. The archives had been taken from the warehouse where they had been stored and were now in the waiting room of the office, in more than 200 large cardboard cartons. During the course of the next four months, working eight hours a day, five days a week, I examined all the documents in every one of these boxes, as well as photos, maps and architectural drawings, and if they looked at all interesting I made photocopies and took them away in my briefcase.

Meanwhile Toots and I found it very exciting being back in the heart of Manhattan, seeing old friends and going to places that we hadn't been to for many years, including a bar in Greenwich Village where I had proposed marriage to her 50 years before. We also made a number of new friends, beginning with Barbara Porter, an old school friend of Maureen's who was a curator at the Metropolitan Museum of Art. Barbara in turn introduced us to a number of her friends, most notably Nina Köprülü and her husband Murat, who would play an important part in our life after we returned to Istanbul.

By the beginning of May I could tell that at the rate I was going I would finish my examination of the archives with time to spare. So one particularly nice morning, when I was on my way downtown on the subway, I suddenly decided I would pay a visit to my old neighbourhood in Brooklyn. I continued past the 42nd Street stop and got off at 14th Street, where I changed to the Eighth Avenue–Canarsie line to Brooklyn.

Forty-seven years had passed since my last ride on that subway line, but I knew every stop along the way, and as we approached the Wilson Avenue station I knew that the train would emerge from the tunnel and surface just briefly there before going on underground. I got out there, and as the train pulled away I looked across the tracks to see the tombstones and mausoleums of the Evergreens Cemetery, where my father had dug graves for so many years and where I had worked briefly after coming home from the war.

I left the station and walked down Wilson Avenue just as I had on 26 May 1946, the day I came home from the war. But Paul Hesse's bar was no longer there, nor the Italian barber, nor the German pork store where a three-piece band used to play on Saturday mornings, nor any other place I had known except the Halsey Street park, my Siren Land, and I remembered a girl calling to me from there as I passed the evening before I went off to war. But now the voices coming from the park were all in Spanish, for my old neighbourhood was completely Latino and the Irish bars were Pentecostal churches.

Hellman's grocery store at the corner of Wilson Avenue and Cornelia Street was now a Spanish *bodega*, and in passing it I thought of Mr Hellman calling out to welcome me home the day I returned from the war. All the other houses on the block were in good repair, but the brownstone at 225 Cornelia Street where we had lived was abandoned and in bad shape, its broken windows boarded up and a FOR SALE sign posted on its wall. I stood there looking at it for a moment, thinking of us all sitting on its steps of a summer evening, recalling my nocturnal dialogues with Peg, whose soft Irish brogue I could still hear, speaking to me from the Country of Dreams. Then I turned and walked away, feeling like Odysseus leaving his mother behind in the Underworld, walking back in desolation to the Wilson Avenue station.

My course in the history of science had by now become so popular that I had as many as 250 students enrolled in the class. I also gave a course on the historic monuments of Istanbul, with 70 students. Most of the course was not given in a classroom, but in Istanbul itself, in the form of walking tours of the city on Saturday. I later learned that three marriages had resulted from this course – couples who had met while strolling through the city with me.

I also led a number of ARIT walking tours of Istanbul, and on one of these met Steven Kinzer, a journalist on the *New York Times*, who did a profile of me that appeared in the *International Herald Tribune*. I also appeared in several television documentaries about Istanbul by the BBC, the National Geographical Channel and Turkish National Television.

The publicity I received from this exposure led to a number of very interesting contacts, particularly a telephone call from someone who identified himself as Ahmet Çakmak. He said that he had graduated from Robert College in 1958 and had been a student of Hilary Sumner Boyd, with whom I had written *Strolling Through Istanbul*. He was now professor of architectural engineering at Princeton University and had co-authored a book on the architecture of Haghia Sophia, which I had read in connection with the course I was giving on the historic monuments of Istanbul.

Ahmet suggested that we collaborate on a book about the Byzantine monuments of Istanbul, which I thought was a great idea. He said that he had talked about this with a former student of his, Beatrice Riehl, senior editor at Cambridge University Press in New York, who was interested in the project.

Ahmet said that if I could obtain a sabbatical from Bosphorus University for the spring semester of 2001, he could arrange for me to have a research fellowship at Princeton University. He said that he and his wife could put us up at their house in Princeton, and we could also use their condo on the Jersey Shore so that he and I could work together on the book.

Such was the genesis of the *Byzantine Monuments of Istanbul*, published by Cambridge University Press in New York in 2004. Toots and I spent the spring of 2001 with Ahmet Çakmak and his

Japanese wife Nuriko at their house in Princeton and also their seaside condo in Island Beach, enjoying an extremely pleasant time in both places, particularly on the shore, where I walked for miles every day along the beautiful white sand beach.

While we were in Princeton I made an appointment to see Beatrice Riehl at the offices of Cambridge University Press, which were on West 22nd Street between Broadway and Eighth Avenue. I took the bus to the Port Authority Bus Terminal, and since it was a nice day and I had time to spare I decided that I would walk to her office along Eighth Avenue, turning left on to West 22nd Street.

As I did so I suddenly realized that I was in very familiar surroundings, for halfway down the block and on the left, directly opposite the entrance to Cambridge University Press, there was a loading dock with a truck parked next to it. Two young blacks were unloading a freight elevator, carrying big cardboard cartons out to the dock and stowing them in the truck, just as Nathan Cohen and I had done at the same place many years before. For this was the back entrance to the building at 123 West 23rd Street, where in the two years before I went off to war I worked at the Eagle Druggist Supply Company. I stopped to look at the scene for a few minutes, looking up at the grim building where I had slaved for 50 cents an hour for two years, daydreaming of the travelling I hoped to do one day, and here I was, 57 years later, still pursuing the dream. But now I had Toots waiting for me in Princeton to share my dreams and my travels, whereas then I was all alone, and I realized just how far I had come.

At the end of May we called the Kehoes in London, telling them that we would be leaving the apartment in a couple of days and thanking them for their hospitality. We rented a car, and on 1 June Toots parked it in front of the apartment house, while Jose helped me carry our things down. There was barely enough room, for I had accumulated 19 cardboard boxes of documents that I had photocopied in the Robert College archives. We then drove to Newark airport, where on 15 June we boarded a THY flight to Istanbul, again first class, with my 19 cartons of documents stowed in the hold as free excess baggage, thanks to Jem Kozlu.

We spent the summers of 1998 and 1999 with the Bakers on Euboea, where I worked on my *History of Robert College* as well as swimming every day and exploring the island with Tony. I also worked on the book during the academic year 1998–99, and it was published as a two-volume work early in 2000.

That same year Penguin published my *Inside the Seraglio: Private Lives of the Sultans in Istanbul*, while Art and Archaeology Press in Istanbul put out my *Galata: A Guide to Istanbul's Old Genoese Quarter*, both of them based on my many years exploring Istanbul and studying its history and monuments.

Late in the spring of 2000 Jem Kozlu, together with his colleagues at Turkish Airlines, held an event to honour me for all the books I had written about Turkey. I was awarded two free round-trip, first-class tickets so that Toots and I could go to any city in the world to which THY operated flights.

I had always wanted to go back to Kunming in China, for I had never forgotten the promise that Ching Ging Too and I had made to seek one another out again after the war. I knew that it was very unlikely that I could ever find him again, but at least I would be able to show Toots a part of the world that I had been telling her about since we first met.

I looked through the THY schedules and saw that they had direct daily flights from Istanbul to Beijing and Shanghai, and that the Chinese national airlines had direct daily flights between Kunming and both Beijing and Shanghai. So I worked out an itinerary that would take us from Istanbul to Beijing, then in turn to Kunming and Shanghai, from where we would fly back to Istanbul. Then I found that there were daily flights between Kunming and Lijiang, a beautiful medieval town near Dali, the old caravan city which our truck convoy had passed along the Burma Road in late August 1945. So I added Lijiang to our itinerary, which I figured we could complete in the fortnight we had set aside for our trip in mid-September, for that would get us back to Istanbul just in time for the beginning of the fall semester at the university.

The first leg of our journey took us almost the whole width of Asia, and as I looked down on the bleak Tibetan Plateau and the ochre sands of the Gobi Desert I recalled looking at the maps on the blackboard during geography classes at Fourteen Holy Martyrs School, daydreaming of the places I was now looking down upon.

My memories of war-torn and starving China were hard to reconcile with what we saw during our three days in Beijing, where bulldozers were demolishing the last pagodas of old Peking, with cranes erecting skyscrapers in their place. The streets were thronged with well-dressed younger people and one-child couples, filing into the same brand-name shops and fast-food restaurants that we ourselves had avoided in New York, so that we had trouble finding a simple Chinese eating place.

Our hotel was within walking distance of the Forbidden City and Tiananmen Square, so we spent the first two days of our stay sightseeing in that part of the city. On the third and last day we went on a tour that took us to a stretch of the Great Wall of China known as the Simatai, at Mutlangu, some 50 kilometres north-east of Beijing. This was a sight I had been longing to see ever since I first read about the Great Wall in *A Pictorial Journey Around the World*, and the long line of crenellated walls and watchtowers marching along the crest of the wooded hills looked just like the lithograph I had looked at in that long-lost book nearly 70 years before.

The next day we flew diagonally across virtually the whole of China from Beijing to Kunming. As we came in to land I recognized the ring of mountains that encircled the city on its mile-high plateau, and I could see that the airport was in exactly the same place it had been when I was last in Kunming. But then it had been an unpaved military airstrip in an open field, whereas now it was a modern international air terminal. The date was 15 September 2000, 55 years to the day since I had left Kunming from this same field on a C40 troop transport, with half a dozen US Army mules among my fellow passengers.

Kunming had changed profoundly since I last saw it. Then it had still been a medieval town, whereas now it was to a large extent a modern city, though far less developed than Beijing and had not completely lost its old Chinese character. It was different from Beijing in other ways too, for its remoteness had spared it

from Mao's Cultural Revolution, and also because its native population was not Han Chinese but one or other of the 26 ethnic
minorities that inhabit Yunnan and Sichuan provinces, each with
its own distinctive language and culture, most notably the Miao
and Naxi, who were still matrilineal, as I had learned from my
reading.

By now I knew there was no hope of finding Ching Ging Too
in Kunming, for I had been advised not to mention my wartime
service in SACO during our visit to China – our outfit had since
been demonized by the communist government. In any event,
he had been from the more tribal areas near the Tibetan border,
which was why I had decided that we should spend a few days in
Lijiang.

The flight to Lijiang took just 45 minutes, landing us in a beautiful valley within sight of the snow-covered mountains of easternmost Tibet, which I remembered from the last days of the war.
A taxi took us to a modern hotel on the edge of the old town
of Lijiang, a labyrinth of ancient wooden and adobe houses with
pagoda roofs, built along the cobbled banks of a maze of canals
spanned by stone bridges, the crystal-clear water flowing down
from the Jade Dragon Snow Mountain to the north.

The market square in the old town was filled with Naxi women,
distinguished by their blue blouses and trousers covered with blue
or black aprons, a T-shaped cape with crossed straps holding up
the huge wicker basket hanging on their back. They were formidable women and obviously ran the town, the men apparently
relegated to a secondary role.

The town was filled with tourists, most of whom were pros-
perous Chinese who seemed to be from elsewhere in the country. Toots and I were continually being photographed, sometimes
being asked to pose with the companions of the photographer,
who usually thanked us with a thumbs-up sign.

On our second evening in Lijiang we went to a performance by
the Naxi Classical Orchestra, which was given in a beautiful old
theatre on the main street of the old town. We arrived early so as
to get a good seat, finding a place in the second row, left of centre.

I sat back to look at the members of the orchestra as they came from the wings to take their seats on stage and tune up their instruments. I counted about 50 musicians, most of them old men with long white beards, dressed in traditional embroidered robes, along with a number of somewhat younger players, including a woman with a broad moonlike face who kept staring at me, just as I was transfixed by her, the two of us looking at one another across a cultural gulf as wide as the world itself.

Then the master of ceremonies came on stage, introducing himself in both Chinese and perfect English as Xuan Ke. He explained that the members of the orchestra were all Naxi and would be playing a type of Taoist temple music that had been lost in the rest of China. As he introduced some of the older musicians he described their instruments, many of which had also disappeared elsewhere in the country. It was left unsaid, but I knew that the Cultural Revolution had destroyed much of the precious heritage of ancient Chinese culture, and only the remoteness of Lijiang had allowed these old masters to preserve the music we were about to hear.

Xuan Ke then introduced each of the musical pieces in turn, in one of which a young woman sang the 'Love song of the walking marriage', referring to the temporary matrimony that a girl from one of the matrilineal tribes such as the Naxi goes through with her first lover. This was followed by a number of orchestral compositions whose haunting melodies put me into a trance, which was suddenly broken when I heard Xuan Ke say, 'The next piece of music our orchestra will play for you is "Waves Washing the Sand". This song was written by the last Tang Dynasty Emperor, Li Ya.' I was astonished and deeply moved, for this was the song that Ching Ging Too had sung for me during our little party in Kunming on 2 September 1945, celebrating the end of the war. Though 55 years had passed I recalled Ching Ging Too's explanation of the song, which was that time passes like the waves of the sea lapping upon the shore, and memory is the faint pattern left by the ripples on the sand, soon to be washed away, another sepulchral voice speaking to me from the Country of Dreams.

Toots and I celebrated our 50th wedding anniversary in Istanbul on 21 July 2001, where we and all our family and friends who were in town had a party at a tavern in Beyoğlu called Kallavi. The tavern was owned by our dear friend Aziz, whose six-piece gypsy band played and sang for us non-stop all evening, serenading us as we drove away in a taxi at closing time. The two of us sat out on our balcony for a nightcap at the end of the evening, talking of our brief honeymoon in Montreal and of our first night together in the Diamond of the Marshes. We had indeed come a long way.

Ever since my boyhood I had walked immense distances, and one of my students once calculated that the total distance I had travelled on foot in my lifetime would have taken me a third of the way to the Moon. I had thought that all this walking would be good for my body, which I'm sure it was, but I hadn't counted on the wear and tear on my joints, which early in the fall of 2001 forced me to undergo the first of two hip replacements, the second of which followed early in 2002.

As a result, I was given a year's medical leave from the university, which left me completely free to write. Besides working on the books I had already contracted for, I turned my attention to a project I had been thinking about for some time, a textbook for my history of science course. Entitled *The Emergence of Modern Science, East and West*, it was published by Bosphorus University Press in 2004. I used it and all the material I had accumulated in researching it as a quarry for other books on the history of science that I would subsequently write.

I resumed teaching full-time at the university in the fall of 2002, travelling at every opportunity, usually in connection with a book I was writing. Toots had started painting again, using watercolours rather than oils. We had the idea of doing a book together about our travels, illustrated with her paintings. The paintings were based on her colour photographs, which she continued to take on the new trips we made in connection with my books. These journeys were in both space and time, since they not only took us to interesting and out-of-the-way places but also carried us back into the past, both of the world and of our own lives.

The first of these was for a book I had agreed to write for

Penguin – *The Lost Messiah: In Search of Sabbatai Sevi* – which was published in 2002. This was a book I had been thinking about for many years. Toots and I had already been to all but one of the places that Sabbatai Sevi, a self-proclaimed messiah from Izmir, had been during his astonishing career, the exception being Albania, where he had died in exile in 1676. So when the opportunity presented itself I set out to look for his grave, an excuse for visiting a country I had wanted to see ever since I was a boy.

Toots and I and our friend Emin Saatçi flew to Tirana, the capital of Albania. Our time was very limited; because of visa restrictions we could only stay in the country for three full days. We had been told that travel was difficult and dangerous, for the roads were in appalling condition, and because the spillover from the war in Bosnia had increased lawlessness in Albania. We received a great deal of help from the Turkish ambassador, Ahmet Rifat Okçun, who arranged for us to hire a car with an armed driver who spoke some Turkish.

My researches had indicated to me that Sabbatai had been buried in Berat, a beautiful old town in southern Albania, and so on the day after our arrival we drove there and back. From the accounts of earlier travellers I was able to find what I believed to be the site of Sabbatai's grave, now the shrine of a supposed Muslim holy man who was still worshipped there clandestinely, as evidenced by the talismanic cloths tied to the iron grillwork of the tomb. After the book was published I received several messages from followers of Sabbatai Sevi, saying, in effect, 'We still believe, and await the return of our Lord.'

The next literary journey was made in connection with a book I was doing for HarperCollins in London, entitled *Jem Sultan: The Adventures of a Captive Turkish Prince in Renaissance Europe*, which was published in 2004. Jem, the younger of two surviving sons of the Turkish sultan Mehmet II, the Conqueror, was 22 when his father died in 1481. Jem fought two brief wars of succession with his elder brother Beyazit II, who won both conflicts and succeeded his father as sultan. Jem took refuge with the Knights of St John on Rhodes, who soon shipped him off to one of their castles in France. This began an exile in which the Turkish prince was used as a pawn in negotiations between the Christian powers of Europe and Sultan Beyazit, ending only when Jem died of a fever in Naples on 25 February 1495, after having spent more than a third of his short life in ignominious exile.

Toots and I had already seen the apartment in the Palace of the Knights on Rhodes where Jem had begun his life of exile, as well as the one in which he lived when he was imprisoned in the Vatican. So in the summer of 2002 we flew to France with Brendan and his Austrian girlfriend Ulricke Ammicht. We rented a car and with Ulricke driving, since she was the only one with a valid licence, we followed Jem's journey in France, which eventually took us to Bourgeneuf in the Auvergene.

There in the centre of the town we found the tower in which Jem had been a prisoner for seven years and which had now been converted into a museum devoted to his memory. After visiting the museum we had lunch in a café across the square from the tower where everyone was watching a huge television screen showing the finals of the football World Cup, in which Turkey was playing South Korea. A group of men behind us were cheering for Turkey, and I learned that they were working as wood-cutters in the forests around Bourgeneuf. The Turkish community had been established in Bourgeneuf in the early 1970s, but there was a completely baseless local legend that they were descended from children who had been fathered by Jem while he was imprisoned here. I asked one of the Turks about this and he was amused but said that he and the other members of the community did nothing to dispel this legend, for Jem was still a hero to them.

We embarked on another literary journey early in the summer of 2005 when we went to Spain in connection with a book for Alfred Knopf in New York. This was *Aladdin's Lamp: How Greek Science Came to Europe Through the Islamic World*, which was published in 2009. Toots and I had been to some of the centres of medieval Islamic science, most notably Cairo, Damascus and the cities in southern Spain that had been under Muslim rule. We had never been to Baghdad, but the political situation there as well as in the rest of the Arab world was such that we decided to go to Spain instead, which we hadn't seen since 1961.

Once again we were accompanied by Brendan and Ulricke, who drove a rented car that we picked up at the airport in Madrid. From there we drove in turn to Toledo, Seville, Cordoba and Granada, spending a few days in each, visiting some of the surviving Islamic monuments and catching glimpses of the brilliant culture of medieval Arabic Andalusia.

I caught my first glimpse of that lost world in Cordoba, 'the bride of Al-Andalus', when I stood beneath a statue of Ibn Rushd, known to Latin Europe as Averroës (1126–98). Averroës is generally held to be the greatest of all Islamic philosophers, renowned in the West for his interpretation of Aristotelian thought and his defence of rationalism against mysticism.

We also caught glimpses of the former splendours of Al-Andalus in Granada, particularly in the Alhambra, where Toots did a painting of the gardens of the magnificent Moorish palace that recaptures that lost world, reminding me of it even now as I look at her watercolour here in our library in Istanbul.

Other literary journeys took us around Anatolia, often crossing the track of our earlier travels. These were in connection with three books I had contracted to do for I.B.Tauris in London: *Storm on Horseback: The Seljuk Warriors of Turkey* (2008); *The Grand Turk: Sultan Mehmet II, Conqueror of Constantinople* (2008); and *Children of Achilles: The Greeks in Asia Minor from the Time of the Trojan War* (2009).

The book on the Seljuks took us all over central and eastern Anatolia, to their majestic fortresses, bridges, caravanserais, madrasas, hospitals and tombs, particularly the shrine of Mevlana at Konya, the last resting place of Jelaledin Rumi, the immortal Sufi mystic philosopher-poet. The ethereal music of the Mevlevi dervishes is played on tape in the *semahanes* (dancing halls) of the shrine, the haunting sound of the *ney* (Turkish flute) accompanying sung verses of the *Mesnevi*, Rumi's masterpiece of transcendental love. Gertrude Bell made a pilgrimage to the shrine on 13 May 1905, when the Whirling Dervishes were still in residence, and her description of what she saw and heard from the visitor's gallery of the *semahane* evokes that vanished scene:

Beyond the tomb are two great dancing halls with polished floors and the whole is enclosed in a peaceful garden, fountains and flowers set round with the monastic cells of the order. So he lies, Jelal ed din Rumi, and to my mind the whole quiet air was full of the music of his verses: 'Ah listen to the sound of the reed as it tells: Listen, ah, listen, to the plaint of the reed.' 'They reft me from the rushes of my home, my voice is sad with longing, sad and low.' (But the Persian is the very pipe, the plaintive pipe of the reeds, put into words and there is nothing so invades the soul.)

*The Grand Turk* took us to many of the places that Sultan Mehmet II had conquered in his meteoric career, but none more evocative than the walls of Constantinople itself. When we first came to Istanbul the ruined walls were just as they were when the city fell to Mehmet on 29 May 1453, and although they have been restored somewhat in recent years they still evoke an image of what happened on that fateful day.

Mehmet had given his soldiers permission to sack the city on condition that they did not destroy its public buildings, which now belonged to him. But from contemporary accounts it would appear that the Turkish forces did considerable damage to the city during their orgy of looting, enslavement, rape and massacre. Michael Critobulus writes of Mehmet's reaction to the death and destruction he saw when he first entered the city he had conquered.

> After this the Sultan entered the City and looked about to see its great size, its situation, its grandeur and beauty, its teeming population, its loveliness, and the costliness of its churches and public buildings. When he saw what a large number had been killed, and the wreckage of the buildings, and the wholesale ruin and desolation of the City, he was filled with compassion and repented not a little at the destruction and plundering. Tears fell from his eyes as he groaned deeply and passionately: 'What a city have we given over to plunder and destruction.'

*The Children of Achilles* took us back to the time and place
where our odyssey really began, that bright spring day in 1961,
when Toots and I and Andrea Dimitriades stood out the Hisarlık
mound and looked out over the 'blossoming meadow' of the
Trojan plain, identifying the tumulus of Achilles and Patroclus.
We found the site completely transformed and overrun, but the
windy plain of Troy was crimsoned with poppies, and the tumulus
where Andrea and I had shared a bottle of wine was clearly visible
near the promontory where the 'swift flowing' Hellespont enters
the Aegean. And so once again I read from Book 24 of the *Odyssey*, where the shades of the fallen heroes meet in the Underworld
and Agamemnon tells Achilles of the funerary monument that
the Achaeans had erected in memory of him and Patroclus, whose
cremated remains they buried together on the Trojan plain:

> For ten and seven days, alike in the day and the night time,
> we wailed for you, both mortal men and the immortals.
> On the eighteenth day we gave you to the fire, and around you
> slaughtered a great number of fat sheep and horn-curved cattle
> ...
> But after the flame of Hephaistos had consumed you utterly,
> then at dawn we gathered your white bones, Achilleus ...
> Around them then, we, the chosen host of the Argive
> spearmen, piled up a grave mound that was both great and
> perfect,
> on a jutting promontory there by the wide Hellespont,
> so that it can be seen afar from out on the water
> by men now alive and those to be born in the future.

Other literary journeys took us to France, Italy, Spain and
Greece, as well around Anatolia and into Istanbul itself, and on
virtually all of them we found ourselves re-crossing the tracks of
earlier travels.

One of these books was *John Freely's Istanbul*, published in
London by Skala Press in 2004. The writing of this took me back
to all my favourite places in Istanbul, some of which I hadn't seen
for many years, during which time they had changed profoundly.
The final paragraph of the book catches the feelings that I had

on returning to old haunts in the city, in this case Nazmi's café at Bebek on the Bosphorus, where I had stopped for a couple of beers shortly after we first arrived in Istanbul in 1960, and where I often sat and talked with an old salt named Riza Kaptan, one of the fishermen who moored their boats in the little cove across the shore road.

When I returned to Istanbul in 1993, after an absence of 17 years, I found that Nazmi's had closed and that Riza Kaptan had passed away. I sat on a park bench on the quay opposite the site of Nazmi's, now occupied by an apartment house, and from there I could see two old fishermen sitting in a shack they had built on a bit of strand beside a seaside mansion, all that now remained of the cove. After a while one of the fishermen joined me, having no idea who I was, although I recognized him as one of Riza Kaptan's younger cronies, his beard now as white as mine. He asked me who I was and I said that I was an American teaching at Bosphorus University, the old Robert College. He smiled at that, saying that he remembered an American teacher from the college who used to sit and talk with Riza Kaptan in Nazmi's – someone like me, he said – but with a reddish beard rather than a white one. Then I realized that he was talking about me, but I let it pass, so that he could think of me as I was, just as I chose to remember the Istanbul that I first knew, looking back on it from the twenty-first century.

We returned to the US briefly in 2005, when Toots' mother celebrated her 100th birthday surrounded by four generations of her family, all of whom she remembered well except me, probably because we had seldom seen one another in recent years. When I wished her happy birthday, she responded by saying, 'Do you have a wife?', and when I told her that I did she said, dismissively, 'Then go home to her!', which were the last words she ever spoke to me, for she passed away six months later.

I celebrated my 80th birthday on 26 June 2006, together with Toots, our extended family and a few close friends. I let my mind drift back to my sixth birthday, 26 June 1932, the earliest I can remember, fixed in a colour photograph in one of our family albums, showing me and my sister Dorothy and several of the

Sayers children, our arms full of wild flowers, seated on the huge rock above the rocky beach at Murphy's Landing, looking out across the ungovernable sea. And now here I was half a world away from the Dingle Peninsula at the opposite end of Europe.

A few months later the university honoured me at an event in the auditorium of Albert Long Hall, where several of my former students spoke of what it had been like to have me as a teacher. I was pleased that they seemed to have enjoyed my lectures and to have learned something, not only about the courses I had taught them but about everything else that I was interested in too.

Ayşe Soysal concluded the event by announcing that my old lecture hall in Albert Long Hall would thenceforth be known as the John Freely Seminar Room. I was deeply moved by this, particularly when I recalled that after my first lecture in that room the students had gone straight to Bob Hall, complaining that they hadn't understood a word I had said.

I was still teaching my course in the history of science at the university, but although my classes were very large, most of the other students had no idea who I was. This reminded me of what it was like to be absolutely nobody on the New York subway when, as a teenager, I was on my way to and from work in the condom factory. All of this came into comic perspective a couple of years later when an old friend of Maureen's from Harvard, Alkis Doxiadis, came to Istanbul to give a lecture in our social science department. Alkis had recently re-established contact with Maureen, who suggested that he see me while he was at the university. A young woman graduate assistant went to the airport to greet Alkis, who said he was hoping to meet me. She laughed and said, 'Oh, sir, John Freely is not a person, it's a room!' Alkis withheld his laughter until he told me the story the following day, when he finally met someone who knew that I was a person and not just a room.

During the summer of 2008 Toots and I travelled around Ireland with our friends Memo and Anna Marie Sağıroğlu. It had been a long time since I had visited the places where I had lived as a boy, and I wanted to see them again while there were still people I had known living there with whom I could share my memory of what was beginning to seem like another country in the lost world of my youth, along with Brooklyn and China.

Memo hired a car in Dublin and drove us across the width of Ireland to Ballyhaunis in County Mayo, where we stayed at a bed-and-breakfast motel outside of town. The only one left of our family was my cousin Eileen, my uncle Luke's daughter, who had married a local farmer named Kevin Lyons.

Eileen had been 18 when I last saw her, whereas now she was almost 60, her hair as white as mine, and so it took a moment before memory stripped away the years and we embraced one another. After exchanging introductions we sat around talking for half an hour while Eileen filled us in on the details of her life since we had last seen her.

She said that she had lived on the Freely farm until she married Kevin, who had inherited his family farm not far from Scragg. Eileen herself had inherited the Freely farm after Jim and Agnes passed away, but she and Kevin had been forced to let the cottage fall into ruins, as they were unable to maintain or sell it.

We then drove to the old Freely cottage, which was a heart-breaking sight. Only part of one wall was still standing, its ruins overgrown with brambles and weeds. The Freelys had lived there for five centuries, but now they had been scattered to the four winds, as Peg used to say, speaking of her own family, the Murphys, of whom there was not a single one left in Ireland, while only Eileen Lyons remained of my paternal line.

The following day we drove all the way down to the Dingle Peninsula, where we had booked rooms in a bed-and-breakfast place in Anascaul. We spent the evening there and the next day drove down to Inch, where we stretched our legs on the immense sand peninsula on which I had often strolled as a boy, wondering where my travels might one day take me. We drove to Foley's pub at the base of the peninsula, thinking we might have lunch there, but the owner, a young man whom I figured was one of Jerry Foley's sons, said that the restaurant was only open in the evening, and so we booked a table for about seven o'clock.

I knew from my correspondence, such as it was, that many of our old friends had passed away since we were there in 1967, including Larry and Peig O'Shea and Jerry Foley. I had exchanged a couple of letters with Lawrence O'Shea, Larry and Peig's son, whom we had met in 1967, and he had told me that after his parents died he took early retirement and moved back into the family cottage in Lach. He had asked me to contact him if I ever returned, and so after we left Foley's we drove to Lach to call on him.

As in the past, I counted four milestones in turn beyond Foley's before we came to Lach, where we passed what I recognized as the Murphy cottage and then stopped at the O'Sheas'. We had no sooner stepped out of the car than Lawrence came running out to greet us. I hardly recognized him at first, for he had become somewhat corpulent and his red hair and beard were now almost white, as well as long and unkempt, giving him the appearance of some of the monks I had seen on Mount Athos. But he was just as charming and funny as ever and kept us amused while he served us tea.

He said that the retired Irish-American and his wife who had bought the old Murphy house had renovated it, so that it now had electricity, running water and a toilet, as well an outside patio where they sometimes dined during the summer. Lawrence said that he himself had also installed modern conveniences, but the idea of outside dining struck him as a ludicrous American inno-vation, the kind of thing that had led him to get away from the modern world here on the Dingle Peninsula. He laughed and said to me, 'You know, Jackie, when we were lads we ate inside and shat outside, but now they do the opposite!'

Lawrence suggested that we pay a brief visit to the old Murphy cottage, for he knew we hadn't seen it during our last visit. We followed Lawrence as he led us next door, where his neighbour very cordially invited us in, apologizing for the mess, for his wife was in the States visiting relatives.

I held my breath as I entered the cottage, which I hadn't seen in 72 years, though the memory of what it had been like was engraved deep in my memory, sitting by the hearth with its turf fire glow-ing, listening to the flow of Irish as my grandfather Tomas talked to his old friends, translating the interesting bits into English for me. But everything had changed, for the hearth had now been replaced by an electric radiator and the talk was coming from a huge TV tuned to a quiz show. We departed as soon as we could do so politely, and as I left the cottage I realized that I was leaving behind the earliest of my childhood memories, yet another part of my lost world.

When we arrived at Foley's that evening we found that the only other guests, about a dozen of them, including several children, were sitting at a long table at the back of the restaurant, laughing and talking with great animation, though they quieted for a moment when we appeared, the older ones nodding to us in silent greeting, as the Irish do, and I did the same, wondering who they were.

We talked quietly during our meal, as I told Memo and Anna Marie about the pub's long history and of how my mother had worked here as a girl looking after Jerry Foley when he was a baby, adding the story of my own emotional evening here with Brendan when I first returned to Inch.

As we were having our after-dinner drinks, I noticed that the adults at the other table were all looking in our direction, listening to an older woman who seemed to be talking about us. At that moment a very attractive woman rose from the table and came over to speak to us, apologizing for the intrusion. She introduced herself as Máire Foley, and said that her mother-in-law Bridey wanted to know if I was Peg Murphy's son. I said that I was indeed, realizing that Bridey was the older woman who had been talking about us, so I waved to her and asked Máire if they would all join us.

The adults all came over, while the children, who had been amusing themselves, remained behind. I embraced Bridey, who looked wonderful, though she was approaching 90. I introduced her and the others to my party, and Máire did the same for theirs, as we all pulled up chairs and tables to sit together. Besides Bridey they were Máire and her husband Pat, his brother Shaun, who ran the pub along with his wife Colleen, and their old friends Dion and Maureen, who were visiting from Sligo.

Thus began a truly memorable gathering as our two parties

from the opposite edges of Europe traced the separate strands of our lives that had now brought us together here. Bridey had known my mother and my grandparents well, and she remembered stories of my great-grandfather Thomas Ashe, the Crimean War veteran, whose recuperation in Florence Nightingale's hospital 70 years before my birth had been the first strand in a knotted Ariadne's thread that had led me too all the way from the Dingle Peninsula to Constantinople and now back again to my Irish Ithaca, where in old age as in childhood I was still an exile.

Talk soon gave way to song, as it always does among the Irish. Bridey began with a beautiful old lament called 'The Kerry Dancing', one of Peg's favourites, reminding me of how she had missed the old ways of her youth, which had now been lost even in Ireland itself.

Pat Foley then sang 'The Boys of Barr na Straide', which I remember his father Jerry singing for us at our farewell party in Anascaul in 1967. This was another lament about the old ways that had been lost forever, in this case the hunting of the wren on St Stephen's Day, the oldest of all customs on the Dingle Peninsula, going back to prehistoric times.

The lost world of my youth was gone forever, but at least I was among my own people, who were preserving what was left of the old ways of our ancestors, here where we began at the outer edge of Europe.

Toots celebrated her 80th birthday in Istanbul on 30 July 2009, when Nina and Murat Köprülü gave a fabulous party for her at their *yalı* at Kanlıca on the Asian shore of the Bosphorus. My friend, the Byzantine architectural historian Bob Osterhaut, had fashioned an imperial Byzantine tiara for Toots to wear, though none of the empresses who ever sat on the throne of Byzantium could compare with her regal beauty as she appeared that evening, enthroned among her family and friends on the shore of the Bosphorus.

We spent the summer of 2010 in the UK, where we had the great pleasure of going to the weddings of two of our granddaughters. The first was Eileen and Tony Baker's daughter Ariadne, who married Jeff Bates in Bath in July. Then in August her cousin Emma, Maureen's daughter by her first husband Paul Spike, married Matthew Waghorn in London. Then on 19 December 2010 our grandson Matthew Spike's wife Özge gave birth to a girl, whom they named Mina Dolores, our first great-grandchild, whom we would see for the first time the following summer at the home of Özge's parents in Izmir.

Meanwhile, early in 2011 I began to show serious signs of heart failure, and on 22 March underwent an operation at the American Hospital in Istanbul to replace my aortic valve. The operation was a complete success and I was soon able to resume my normal activities, but in much better physical condition than I had been before. I had been given a new life and I was very grateful, for there was so much that Toots and I wanted to see and do before we ended our odyssey.

But less than a year later, while we were planning new journeys, our little world was changed forever, or so it would seem.

On the evening of 17 March 2012, on our way to a St Patrick's dinner, Toots took a bad fall that left her unconscious. It took me a while to find help and bring her to the American Hospital, where we learned that she had suffered a stroke.

By this time I had been joined by Brendan and our friends Emin Saatçi and Memo and Anna Marie Sağrıoğlu, and shortly afterwards by Eileen and Tony Baker and Maureen, who, along with Gülen Aktaş, have formed the support group that has kept me going ever since.

Toots had a second stroke a few days later and was kept in the intensive care unit for several weeks before she was moved to a regular ward. She remained in a coma, though, and after five months the doctors told us that there was little more they could do for her in the hospital. Our medical care plan would in any case no longer cover the hospital costs, which were far beyond our means.

We were advised to arrange for medical care at home, and so we hired a Turkish healthcare firm, who set up the bedroom of our apartment at the university as a hospital room, complete with a round-the-clock nurse as well as oxygen and other life-support facilities, while I set up a single bed in my office and library.

When all was ready, early in September 2012, Brendan went to the American Hospital to accompany Toots home in the ambulance. I watched from our balcony as the medics carried her in a stretcher up the garden path and into the house and our second-floor apartment, where they helped the nurse lift her into the hospital bed.

Then, while the nurse set up the oxygen and other life-support facilities, Brendan gave me some good news. He said that as Toots was being carried up the garden path, she opened her eyes and looked up at the trees that embowered our house, their dappled shade and the sunlight flickering through their leaves, apparently having made her feel that she was in familiar surroundings.

Then, after Brendan helped the nurse shift Toots to a more comfortable position in bed, we stood and looked at her for a while to make sure that she was breathing properly. As we did so she opened her eyes for a moment and smiled at us. We kissed her and welcomed her home, after which she went back to what seemed to be a sound sleep rather than a coma, as if she realized that she had in fact come home.

While Toots was still in the hospital, on 26 July, I learned that our granddaughter Ariadne had just given birth to a son, whom she and her husband Jeff Bates called Theo Daedalus. Theo was born just as the flame was lit to begin the 2012 London Summer Olympics, and his photograph appeared on CNN News, dressed in pink pyjamas and wearing an Olympic gold medal around his neck, with the caption 'Born to Win'. I wanted to show the photo to Toots in the hospital, but she was still in a coma and so I couldn't let her know that we now had a victorious great-grandson.

Some four months later, on 11 November, I was devastated to learn that Frank Longstreth had died suddenly of a massive stroke. Maureen had telephoned me from the hospital in Bath to tell me what had happened, and in the days that followed we called one another daily, as she told me how her children and friends had supported her through the bereavement. But, unfortunately, there was no way I could get to Bath to be with her.

The Turkish healthcare plan turned out to cost much more than I could afford, and so, once we knew how things operated, we rented the medical equipment ourselves and hired a nurse from Turkmenistan named Ayşe, who turned out to be a gift from heaven. Ayşe looked after Toots night and day six days a week, arranging for one or another of her female relatives, all qualified nurses, to fill in on her day off. She also helped us hire a house-keeper, first a Filipino woman and then a succession of young women from Turkmenistan, until we finally found someone suit-able.

At first we thought we saw signs that Toots was making prog-ress, but it proved to be wishful thinking, and a series of tests by neurologists showed that we could hope for no significant improvement. Otherwise, tests showed that her general health was good. She had a bit of movement in her fingers and feet, and she appeared to recognize us and show some response in her eyes when we spoke to her. We rigged up an iPad and earphones so that she could listen to opera in the evening, and that appeared to make her happy. She smiled every now and again, and then only fleetingly, but whenever she did I thought I couldn't ask for more.

Throughout our married life Toots had always taken care of all the practical details of the household, including finances, so that I wasn't even aware of such things as bank account numbers, and it took my son-in-law Tony Baker considerable time and effort to sort out our affairs. Anne Marie called daily concerning medical matters and Emin Saatçi was always on hand to look after the emergencies that regularly came up, including problems concern-ing our residence permits and Turkish social security. Gülen Aktaş, who was now dean of the School of Arts and Science, made all the facilities of the university available whenever I needed them, and ensured that my faculty status remained intact. The rector of the university, Kadri Özçaldıran, told me that I need no longer teach and that I would continue to receive my salary as a full professor of physics and free housing in our faculty apartment, an arrangement that was confirmed by the succeeding rector, Gülay Barbarosoğlu.

My university salary paid for only about half of our expenses, the remainder being covered by my US social security and Teach-er's Retirement Annuity Fund (TIAA), together with income from my books, so that our modest bank balance remained constant, which was more than a minor miracle, considering that just 20 years before we had been flat broke.

The change in our financial situation was principally due to the fact that in those 20 years I had written 32 new books, many of them published by I.B.Tauris, largely through the efforts of my editor Tatiana Wilde. I.B.Tauris also reprinted revised editions of some of my earlier books, most notably *Strolling Through Istanbul*, which was published in an updated version in 2009 and has sold very well ever since, even after being continuously in print for more than 40 years.

I had also written eight more books that I.B.Tauris will be publishing over the next few years, as well as one that came out in May 2014: *A Traveller's Guide to Homer: In the Wake of Odysseus in Turkey and the Mediterranean*. This contains a great deal of autobiographical information, including my crossing of the wake of Odysseus in mid-October 1945 on my way home from the war in China. The book had in fact been developing in a back room of my mind for many years, particularly when Toots and I visited Ithaca, recalling the elegiac lines from Cavafy, for they echoed the feeling I had as the goal of my quest came into view:

As you set out for Ithaka
Hope your road is a long one,
full of adventure, full of discovery ...
May there be many summer mornings when,
with what pleasure, what joy,
you enter harbours you're seeing for the first time ...
But don't hurry the journey at all,
Better if it lasts for many years.
So you're old when you reach the island ...
Ithaka gave you the marvelous journey.
Without her you wouldn't have set out.

The book on Homer is dedicated 'To Toots, my Penelope', since without her there would have been no odyssey. Had I not met her I might have returned from the war to a settled life, as soldiers had since the beginning of history, but the pact in blood we signed together had set us off on our journey.

When the book on Homer was finished I began working in earnest on the story of our own odyssey, *The Art of Exile*, particularly after I looked at a photograph of Toots taken on her 80th birthday, when the sight of her wearing a Byzantine tiara reminded me once again that she was in fact my queen, though I'd had no kingdom to offer her, just a lifelong journey.

Now I have become my own Homer, composing the story of a life perpetually on the move, always an exile, though I seem to have found my Ithaca here in Istanbul as I ponder the meaning of exile as an art that takes a lifetime to master.

Toots passed away peacefully on 18 July 2015, and three days later we buried her in the Christian cemetery in Istanbul, on our 64th wedding anniversary.

And so the odyssey continues, my Penelope still with me, though she is now in the Country of Dreams.